Beethoven
Studies

EDITORIAL COMMITTEE

Joseph Kerman
Lewis Lockwood
Alan Tyson

Beethoven
Studies

EDITED BY
Alan Tyson

W · W · NORTON & COMPANY · INC ·

NEW YORK

FIRST EDITION

Library of Congress Cataloging in Publication Data
Tyson, Alan.
    Beethoven studies.
    Includes bibliographical references.
    1. Beethoven, Ludwig van, 1770–1827.
I. Title.
ML410.B42T9   780'.92'4   73–4579
ISBN 0–393–02168–8

1 2 3 4 5 6 7 8 9 0

Contents

Plates   vii

Preface   ix

Abbreviations   xiii

Beethoven to the Countess Susanna Guicciardi: A New Letter
ALAN TYSON   1

Beethoven and Carl Heinrich Graun
RICHARD A. KRAMER   18

"Extra" Measures and Metrical Ambiguity in Beethoven
ANDREW IMBRIE   45

A Reconstruction of the Pastoral Symphony Sketchbook
(British Museum Add. MS. 31766)
ALAN TYSON   67

Beethoven's Sketches for *Sehnsucht* (WoO 146)
LEWIS LOCKWOOD   97

An die ferne Geliebte
JOSEPH KERMAN   123

The Authors of the Op. 104 String Quintet
ALAN TYSON   158

The Artaria Collection of Beethoven Manuscripts: A New Source
DOUGLAS JOHNSON   174

Index of Beethoven's Compositions, Sketches, and Letters   237

General Index   243

Plates

I–III   *Letter to the Countess Susanna Guicciardi, pages 1, 2, and 3.*   2, 4, 6

IV   *Watermark of the Pastoral Symphony Sketchbook, quadrant 1, the two molds (beta radiographs).*   77

V   *Watermark of the Pastoral Symphony Sketchbook, quadrant 2, the two molds (beta radiographs).*   78

VI   *Watermark of the Pastoral Symphony Sketchbook, quadrant 3, the two molds (beta radiographs).*   79

VII   *Watermark of the Pastoral Symphony Sketchbook, quadrant 4, the two molds (transmitted-light photographs).*   80

VIII   *"Scheide" Sketchbook (library of Mr. William Scheide, Princeton), page 60.*   106

IX   *"Scheide" Sketchbook (library of Mr. William Scheide, Princeton), page 61.*   108

X   *"Scheide" Sketchbook (library of Mr. William Scheide, Princeton), page 70.*   151

XI   *Grasnick 11 (StPK, Berlin), title page (folio 1^r).*   160

XII   *Grasnick 11 (StPK, Berlin), folio 1^v (measures 1–17 of the first movement of Op. 104).*   164

XIII   *Grasnick 11 (StPK, Berlin), folio 15^r (measures 65–72 of the second movement of Op. 104).*   165

XIV   *Grasnick 11 (StPK, Berlin), folio 4^r (measures 83–99 of the first movement of Op. 104).*   170

XV–XVII   *Autograph 47a (DStB, Berlin), pages 1, 3, and 7.*   181–83

XVIII   (*a*) *Cover of Landsberg 7* (*StPK, Berlin*)—*Noti-*
        rungsbuch F in the first Artaria classification.
        (*b*) *Cover of Artaria 201* (*StPK, Berlin*)—*Skizzen-*
        buch E in the second Artaria classification.   187

Preface

❋ THE ESSAYS brought together in the present volume, the first in what is hoped will be a continuing series, represent among them a number of growing interests in Beethoven studies. A word or two is needed to define their relation to other recent work in this field. It is, I think, becoming clear that the major achievements of nineteenth-century Beethoven scholarship—the definitive biography of Thayer, scrupulous in method and mature in judgment but unfortunately left uncompleted by him, the immensely fertile studies over the whole range of the sketches conducted by Gustav Nottebohm, and the twenty-five volumes of the old *Gesamtausgabe*—were not followed in the next half century by work of anything like the same comprehensiveness and acuity. It is possible to think of scholars who have been honorable exceptions, but they have been few; and it may even be the case that Thayer and Nottebohm, by their very impressiveness, came to exercise a somewhat inhibiting effect on their epigoni.

As a result, Beethoven studies have recently found themselves in a rather curious state. Much of the work of the last few decades has been sporadic and ill-organized. Even such impressive *monumenta* as the thematic catalogue of Kinsky and Emily Anderson's edition of the complete letters (in an English translation) have had a somewhat old-fashioned appearance; prepared over many years, by their nature they incorporated digests of scholarship of a much earlier age. Again, the main biographical study of the period, the updating of Thayer by Forbes, was firmly rooted in the nineteenth century. The most widely discussed analytic work on Beethoven today remains that of Schenker, Tovey, and Réti. These analysts still have much to teach us, certainly, just as Kinsky and Anderson remain basic tools for the location of source materials and Thayer-Forbes serves as a valuable compendium of twentieth-century biographical findings. But it is generally true that these bodies of work have not benefited from the infusion of modern techniques and attitudes which have been fruitfully applied in studies of many of the great composers.

Other ambitious projects are continuing at the present time, such as the East Berlin edition of the conversation books and the various series sponsored by the Beethovenhaus at Bonn. These have to be appraised with some degree of caution, if only because it is too early yet to see them clearly. Among the publishing programs of the Beethovenhaus are a new *Gesamtausgabe* of the music, a *Gesamtausgabe* of the letters, and a *Gesamtausgabe* of the sketchbooks, in transcription and (with later volumes) facsimile. In spite of the scale on which they have been planned, it seems that these editions will be restricted to the presentation of texts, with a minimum of commentary. This has its uses, but one can fairly expect a more comprehensive treatment at this stage of musicological development, and there are already signs that opportunities have been missed (e.g. of reassembling within a single publication sketches that were originally together but are now scattered). No volume of the letters has yet appeared, and the value of the new editions of the music —twelve volumes have come out since 1951—must remain an open question until the corresponding critical reports are published. In any case, the promotion of scholarly texts is only the beginning of the process of studying or restudying a composer of Beethoven's universality, not its end product. In the broad area of interpretation, whether historical, analytical, or critical, there has been little recent work that is penetrating and original.

The impression that the main lines of Beethoven scholarship are fixed and settled is a wholly misleading one. Even in so fundamental a matter as the chronological sequence of his major works (to take but one instance) there remains much to be determined or reappraised. The conclusions of Thayer and Nottebohm concerning the manuscript sources and their implications for biography and chronology have been assimilated and passed on in later editions of Thayer's *Life* and in Kinsky's catalogue, two works whose "definitive" nature has seemingly obviated the need for re-evaluation. But in fact both Thayer and Nottebohm were often suggestive rather than conclusive in their use of manuscript sources; neither was exhaustive in describing them; and certain techniques for scrutinizing those sources, such as studies of paper or handwriting, were either unknown to Thayer and Nottebohm or not systematically used by them. Much of their work needs to be reconsidered, elaborated, and completed by questioning possibly mistaken conclusions and by searching for further evidence that might be brought to the unsolved problems.

It is obvious that new studies of the manuscript sources for Beethoven's works are now called for; they are indeed a prerequisite to projects like the new *Gesamtausgaben*. Moreover, the possibility of opening up unexplored territory has never been better. To name one obvious area: not for a hundred and fifty years has the world of the sketches been more accessible. For the vast majority of the surviving sketchbooks and sketch leaves are now in public collections, their locations are in most cases easily ascertainable through Hans Schmidt's *Verzeichnis der Skizzen Beethovens* (1969), and modern techniques—the circulation of microfilms, and recent investigations of paper types and bibliographical make-up—make their scrutiny easier than ever before. In the sphere of biography, too, the way is wide open for evaluations of Beethoven's personality and relationships that can escape from the inevitable moral certitudes of nineteenth-century biographers, evaluations more in key with modern psychological and sociological insights. In any case, we now have access to many letters and documents of crucial biographical importance that were simply unknown to Thayer or his contemporaries.

New approaches of this kind will inevitably have a somewhat specialized appearance, especially to those coming to advanced work on Beethoven for the first time. The present essays are probably no exception, but their specialization covers a wide enough range, it is hoped, to engage readers with a corresponding range of musical interests. The first essay is essentially biographical, explicating a striking letter of 1802 which recently came to light. It is followed by an inquiry into one of Beethoven's early efforts at self-instruction, in the art of recitative, and by a close analytical study of his music from a standpoint that is now attracting special attention from musical analysts—rhythm. Physical aspects of the sketchbooks—their make-up, paper, watermarks, etc.—and the significance of these features in determining the original sequence of collections of sketch pages are discussed in relation to a proposed reconstruction of the famous Pastoral Symphony Sketchbook of 1808. Two essays are devoted to songs of 1816, *Sehnsucht* and the song-cycle *An die ferne Geliebte;* both of these deal closely with sketches in the "Scheide" Sketchbook at Princeton. In the former essay a complete series of Beethoven melodic sketches is analyzed exhaustively, we believe for the first time; in the latter, points of contact are explored between the song cycle and Beethoven's emotional life on the one hand and the broad course of his musical development on the other. Another study raises problems of authenticity and of textual analysis: it seeks to test the received view that Beethoven himself made the string quintet version of his early C-Minor Piano Trio, which was published as Op. 104. Finally, an account of the Artaria Collection of Beethoven manuscripts presents a somewhat alarming picture of the ways in which many of the sketchbooks and autographs were disrupted or rearranged—essential information for anyone who wishes to work with them today. It seems likely, in fact, that research into the vicissitudes of Beethoven's *Nachlass* will come to be recognized as a major clue to the present distribution and condition of the sketchbooks.

The essays, then, embrace biographical, textual, analytic, bibliographical, and critical approaches. Much of this material could not have been presented even five years ago. In many centers, we believe, there is now an awareness of new possibilities for Beethoven studies and an interest in new techniques for pursuing them.

ALAN TYSON

Abbreviations

Adler	Guido Adler, *Verzeichnis der musikalischen Autographe von Ludwig van Beethoven . . . im Besitz von A. Artaria in Wien* (Vienna, 1890).
Anderson	Emily Anderson, ed., *The Letters of Beethoven*, 3 vols. (London, 1961).
Artaria	August Artaria, *Verzeichnis von musikalischen Autographen . . . vornehmlich der reichen Bestände aus dem Nachlasse . . . Ludwig van Beethovens . . . im Besitze von August Artaria* (Vienna, 1893).
BM	British Museum, London.
DStB	Deutsche Staatsbibliothek, Berlin.
GA	*Beethovens Werke. Vollständige, kritisch durchgesehene Gesamtausgabe*, 25 vols. (Leipzig, 1866–68, 1890).
GdM	Gesellschaft der Musikfreunde, Vienna.
Hess	Willy Hess, *Verzeichnis der nicht in der Gesamtausgabe veröffentlichten Werke Ludwig van Beethovens* (Wiesbaden, 1957).
Kinsky-Halm	Georg Kinsky, *Das Werk Beethovens. Thematisch-bibliographisches Verzeichnis seiner sämtlichen vollendeten Kompositionen,* completed and ed. Hans Halm (Munich-Duisberg, 1955).
Nachlass	*Nachlass* auction catalogue.
N I	Gustav Nottebohm, *Beethoveniana* (Leipzig-Winterthur, 1872).
N II	Gustav Nottebohm, *Zweite Beethoveniana: nachgelassene Aufsätze* (Leipzig, 1887).
PrStB	Former Preussische Staatsbibliothek, Berlin.

Schindler (1840)   Anton Schindler, *Biographie von Ludwig van Beethoven*, 1st ed. (Münster, 1840); Eng. trans., *The Life of Beethoven*, ed. I. Moscheles, 2 vols. (London, 1841).

Schindler (1860)   Anton Schindler, *Biographie von Ludwig van Beethoven*, 3rd ed., 2 vols. (Münster, 1860); Eng. trans., *Beethoven As I Knew Him*, ed. Donald W. MacArdle (London, 1966).

SBH   Hans Schmidt, "Die Beethoven Handschriften des Beethovenhauses in Bonn," *Beethoven-Jahrbuch*, VII, Jahrgang 1969/70 (1971), vii–xxiv, 1–443.

StPK   Stiftung Preussischer Kulturbesitz, Berlin.

SV   Hans Schmidt, "Verzeichnis der Skizzen Beethovens," *Beethoven-Jahrbuch*, VI, Jahrgang 1965/68 (1969), 7–128.

Thayer I (1866)   Alexander Wheelock Thayer, *Ludwig van Beethovens Leben*, 3 vols. (Berlin).
II (1872)
III (1879)

Thayer-Deiters-   A. W. Thayer, *Ludwig van Beethovens Leben*, continued Hermann Deiters, completed Hugo Riemann, 5 vols. (Berlin-Leipzig, 1901–11). (Vol. I again revised 1917, remaining vols. reissued 1922–23.)
Riemann I–V

Thayer-Forbes   *Thayer's Life of Beethoven*, rev. and ed. Elliot Forbes, 2 vols. (Princeton, 1964).

Thayer, *Verzeichnis*   A. W. Thayer, *Chronologisches Verzeichnis der Werke Ludwig van Beethovens* (Berlin, 1865).

WoO   *Werk(e) ohne Opuszahl* [i.e., work(s) without an opus number], in the listing of Kinsky-Halm.

Beethoven
Studies

Beethoven to the
Countess Susanna Guicciardi:
A New Letter

Alan Tyson

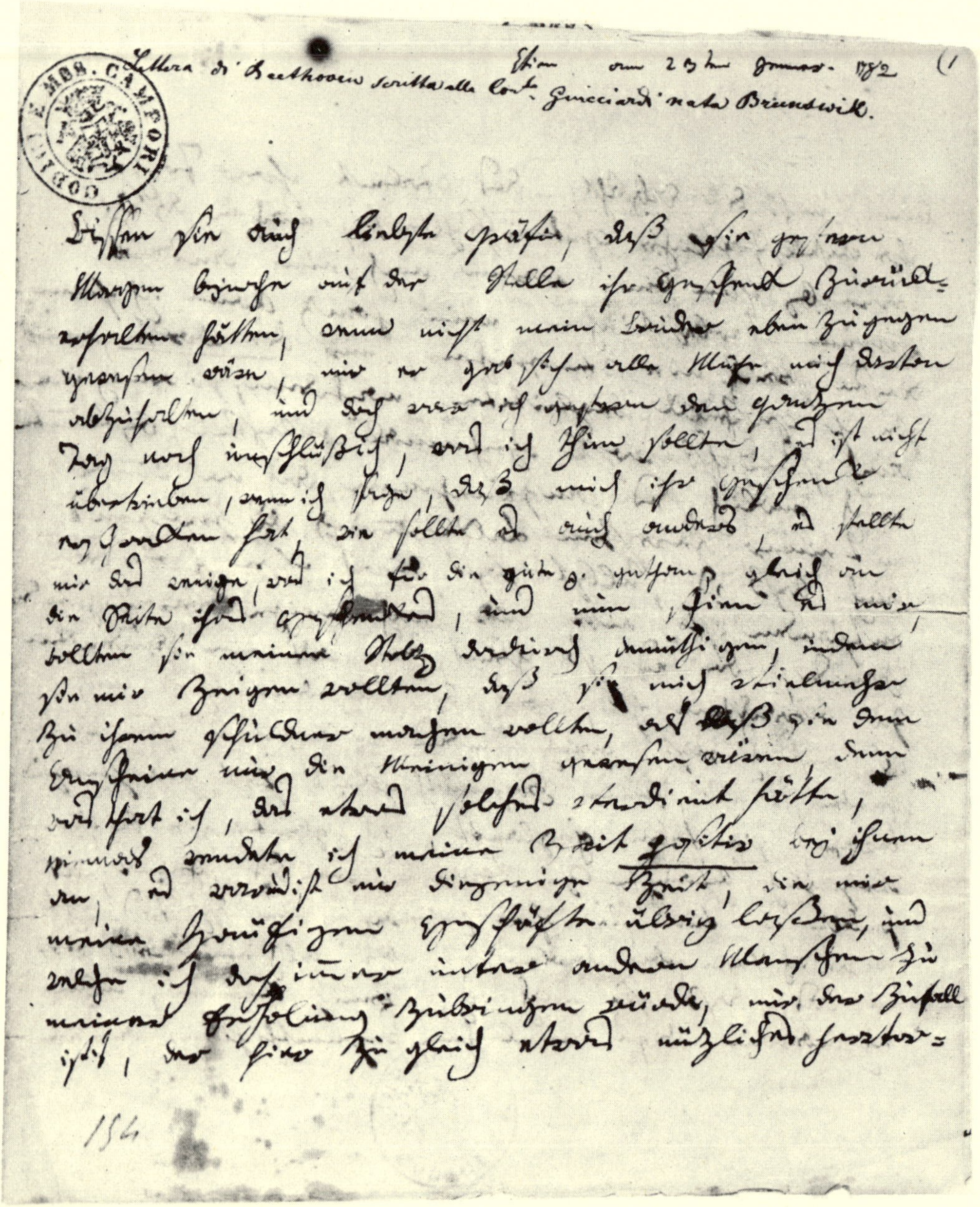
Lettera di Beethoven scritta alla Cont. Guicciardi nata Brunswik.
Wien am 23ten Januar 1782
CODICE E MSS. CAMPORI
154

Plate I ❦ *Letter to the Countess Susanna Guicciardi, page 1.*

Vien am 23 ten jenner - 1782

*Wissen sie auch liebste Gräfin, daß sie gestern
Morgen bejnahe auf der Stelle ihr Geschenk zurück=
erhalten hätten, wenn nicht mein Bruder eben zugegen
gewesen wäre, nur er gab sich alle Mühe mich davon
abzuhalten, und doch war ich gestern den ganzen
Tag noch unschlüßig, was ich thun sollte, es ist nicht
übertrieben, wenn ich sage, daß mich ihr Geschenk
erschrocken hat, wie sollte es auch anders, es stellte
mir das wenige, was ich für die gute J. gethan, gleich an
die Seite ihres Geschenkes, und nun schien es mir,
wollten sie meinen Stolz dadurch demüthigen, indem
sie mir zeigen wollten, daß sie mich vielmehr
zu ihrem schuldner machen wollten, als daß sie dem
Anscheine nur die Meinigen gewesen wären, denn
was that ich, das etwas solches verdient hätte,
Niemals wendete ich meine Zeit* positiv *bej ihnen
an, es war und ist mir diejenige Zeit, die mir
meine Haüfigen Geschäfte übrig laßen, und
welche ich doch im̄er unter andern Menschen zu
meiner Erholung zubringen würde, nur der Zufall
ist's, der hier zu gleich etwas nüzliches hervor=*

3

Plate II 🎜 *Letter to the Countess Susanna Guicciardi, page 2.*

bringt, nicht die Absicht;—das Talent ihrer Tochter,
ihre gesellschaftliche Gutmüthigkeit, machen daß ich
gerne bej ihnen bin, warum noch ein anderes
Warum herbej ziehen, nein ganz kann ich ihnen
diesen streich nie verzeihen, nur die Worte, womit
sie ihr Geschenk begleiteten, nachdem, so wenig ihrer
auch sind, ich sie wohl zehnmal gelesen, bestimten
mich endlich, es anzunehmen, doch noch imer
mit einer gewißen Beklemung des Herzens,
auch daß es selbst fast durch ihre Hände
entstanden ist, gibt mir noch einige beruhigende
Gründe, da es so gleichsam als ein Andenken
zu betrachten ist, aber bey alle dem ist es mir,
als müst ich jezt ganz anders in Ansehung ihrer werden,
gestehen sie nur, meine Frejmüthigkeit hat sie hierzu
bewogen, sie haben geglaubt, ich glaube sie bej ihnen
vorzüglich behaupten zu können, weil es scheint, als
handelte ich für sie ohne Interesse, und doch ist es nicht
so, wie ich ihnen oben bewiesen, aber welch ein Beweiß gibt
mir das, daß sie mich noch so wenig kennen, indem
ich überall diese nemliche Freymüthigkeit ausübe,

Plate III ❧ *Letter to the Countess Susanna Guicciardi, page 3.*

selbst da, wo ich nur handle, um Belohnung zu erhalten—
Nein—Nein, ganz verziehen wird's ihnen ewig nicht,
daß sie mich nun gänzlich des Vergnügens beraubt haben,
einmal dem Anscheine nach wenigstens ein uneigennüziger
Mensch zu scheinen, aber ich werde auf Rache sinnen,
diese soll darinn bestehn, daß ich auf nichts sinnen
werde, als wie ich sie mir so verbindlich machen
werde, ja in einem so hohen Grade, daß es ihnen
gewiß nicht einfallen soll, drauf zu denken, wie
es nur möglich wäre, mich wieder so abzumachen,
und eigentlich—mich—zu ihrem Schuldner
zu machen—Nein—Nein! Abscheulich ist's, mich
so, um meine Liebsten Gefühle zu bringen;—
ist das Freundschaft?—Freundschaft hat keinen
andern Lohn, als den, der schon selbst in ihr liegt—
ewig, ewig werd ich ihnen nicht mehr so herzens=
gut sejn, als vor diesem—aber nun zur
Warnung, dieses nehme ich an, aber laßen sie
sich je einfallen, nur auch auf die entfernteste Art
auf so was wieder zu denken, so schwöre ich bej allem, was
mir heilig ist, daß sie mich nie mehr in ihrem Hause
sehen werden—jezt leben sie wohl—ja Böß
bleibe ich nun einmal, wie soll ich mich jezt unterschreiben,
ihr Freund etwa?—das darf ich ja nicht mehr—so gerne ich's
mögte, dafür, und wie sie's verdienen—ihr höchstaufgebrachter

                                                                Beethoven

      vieleicht sehe ich sie heute noch—

[Page 4 is blank]

I think you should know, dearest countess, that you would have received your present back yesterday morning almost on the spot if my brother hadn't happened to be with me; he did his very best to stop me. Even so, I was still undecided the whole of yesterday about what I should do. I'm not exaggerating when I say that your present gave me a shock. What else could it have done? It immediately put the little I had done for dear J. on a par with your present, and it seemed to me that you wanted to humble my pride by wanting to show me that you wished far rather to put me in your debt than to have the appearance of being in mine. What, after all, did I do to deserve anything like this? None of the time I ever spent at your house was for gain*—it was and is the time that my many occupations leave free to me and that I would otherwise spend with others for my recreation. It is only by accident that I get something advantageous as well here—it is not through design on my part. The talent of your daughter and your social ease make me glad to be in your house; why drag in any other* whys? *No, I can't ever wholly forgive you for this trick; it was only* the words *accompanying the present which, after I had read them (few as they were) a good ten times, finally made me decide to accept it, though still with a certain anguish at heart; the fact, too, that it was almost created by your hands reassures me to some extent that I can see it in this way as a kind of memento. But despite all that, I have a feeling that I must now become quite different in your esteem. Please admit that my frankness has driven you to it; you thought I believed I could adopt this frankness very freely in your house since it appeared as though I worked for you disinterestedly; yet that is not the case, as I have shown you above. But what a proof this gives me of how little you still know me, seeing that I adopt the same frankness everywhere, even where* I only work for payment. *No, no! I can't ever completely forgive you for now robbing me entirely of the pleasure of ever giving at least the appearance of seeming an unselfish person. But I shall plan my revenge; this shall consist of my thinking of nothing else than of how to put you so much in my debt, to such an extent in fact that it won't even occur to you to reflect how it would even be possible to dispose of me again in this way— in other words, to make* me *indebted to* you. *No, no! It is terrible to cheat me in this way of my most treasured feelings—is that friendship?* Friendship has no other reward than that which lies within it. *I'll never, never again be so openhearted toward you as before this. But now for my warn-*

ing. I accept this present; but should it ever occur to you to let yourself think up anything even remotely similar, I swear by everything that I hold sacred that you will never see me again in your house. And now, farewell —I'm staying cross this time. Now how am I going to sign myself? As your friend, perhaps? I can't do that any more, much as I'd like to, so instead, and as you deserve,

Your greatly upset
Beethoven

Perhaps I'll still see you today—

❋ THIS REMARKABLE LETTER, the original text of which seems never to have been published,[1] is in the Autografoteca Campori in the Biblioteca Estense at Modena. Since it is by no means clear at first when it was written or to whom it was addressed, and since the circumstances that provoked it are also obscure, I shall limit myself here to an attempt at resolving some of these problems. It soon becomes plain, nevertheless, that they lead to issues that were central to Beethoven's emotional life.

The date. The letter is dated by Beethoven "Vien am 23 ten jenner." This is followed by a dot (or very short dash) and the year "1782." This year cannot, of course, be correct, for at that time Beethoven was living in Bonn and was only eleven years old. Can it have been written by Beethoven? The figure 7 is certainly unusual: it is small and narrow and gives the impression of having been inserted later. But all four figures are apparently in the same ink as the rest of the date, and I think we must conclude that, whatever the explanation behind the mistake, Beethoven himself dated the letter 1782 at the time that he wrote it. The general style of the handwriting furnishes only a very approximate guide to the true date; the most that can be said is that the letter belongs to Beethoven's earlier Viennese years.

The watermark of the paper is: J HONIG/&/ZOONEN under a "post-horn shield" (much the commonest device in Beethoven's letters) which

---

[1] An English translation and commentary appeared in *The Musical Times*, CXII (1971), 842–45; the present commentary is a somewhat revised and expanded version. The presence here of the original German text of the letter permits a freer translation to be offered. I wish to record my thanks to Angela Harris, Christa Landon, Albi Rosenthal, and John Thomas for a number of suggestions.

is surmounted by a crown. It corresponds fairly closely to number 220 in Schmidt-Görg's impressive list.[2] There are, however, small differences, precisely of the kinds that are significant in such cases; and they lead to the conclusion that the Modena watermark is distinct from any of those described or illustrated by Schmidt-Görg.[3]

It will become clear from what follows that I believe the most likely date of the letter to be January 23, 1802. Beethoven's date of 1782, which seems puzzling when we first encounter it, has to be understood as a writing error of a kind that is not uncommon in his dealings with numbers in letters and elsewhere. We shall return briefly to this point in a moment.

The person to whom it was addressed. The opening words of the letter, "Wissen sie auch liebste Gräfin . . . ," show that it was intended for a countess whom Beethoven could address, perhaps with an element of sarcasm, as "dearest," and with whom he had considered himself to be on terms of warm friendship. Clearly he had often been to her house, where he felt at ease with her and with her talented daughter. There are perhaps not so many titled ladies who meet all the above requirements, and it so happens that one of them is named on the present document; for the first page of the letter bears an inscription at the top in what is apparently a mid-nineteenth-century Italian hand: "Lettera di Beethoven scritta alla con.[ta] Guicciardi nata Brunswik." Although one's first reaction must be to treat anonymous and unsupported ascriptions of this type with great suspicion, a careful examination of the contents suggests that it is, in fact, correct. It may even be the case that the letter was originally accompanied by some form of cover or envelope that showed who was intended to receive it; none, however, is preserved in the Campori Collection today.

Susanna Guicciardi, née Brunsvik, was the fourth child of the first Count Anatol Brunsvik and a younger sister of the second Count Anatol.

---

[2] Joseph Schmidt-Görg, "Wasserzeichen in Beethoven-Briefen," *Beethoven-Jahrbuch,* V, Jahrgang 1961/64 (1965), 46 (with illustration on 41).

[3] In Schmidt-Görg's no. 220 the posthorn shield is described as suspending a bell which is marked with two circles (though these are not, curiously enough, depicted in the accompanying illustration), whereas in the Modena letter the watermark element below the shield is a letter A. There are further differences in the design of the crown: the Modena letter has a zigzag line not shown or described in Schmidt-Görg no. 220. Under this number Schmidt-Görg cites three letters of Beethoven, written at dates scattered as widely as 1787 (Anderson no. 1—his first surviving letter, written at Bonn when he was sixteen), 1797 (Anderson no. 23), and 1801 (Anderson no. 49). It seems unlikely that the watermarks of all three letters are, in fact, identical.

She was thus the aunt of four people with whom, in the years following 1799, Beethoven became extremely intimate: Therese Brunsvik, her brother Franz, and her sisters Josephine and Charlotte.[4] Therese has enjoyed a prominent place in biographical works on Beethoven from Thayer's time, since she was his candidate for being the intended recipient of the famous letter to "The Immortal Beloved" (though no one follows him in this view today); while the discovery as recently as 1949 of thirteen quite unknown letters of the years 1804–07 from Beethoven to the recently widowed Josephine Deym—a more recent, though also implausible, candidate for the role of being "The Immortal Beloved"—revealed that he was for a long time very much in love with her.[5] Rather less is known of the Guicciardis. The Countess Susanna's husband, whom she married in 1783, was Franz Joseph Count Guicciardi, an Austrian court councilor. In the 1790s the family had lived in Laibach (Ljubljana) and then Trieste, but in 1800 he was recalled from Trieste to Vienna, and the count and countess moved with their fifteen-year-old daughter to the capital.

This daughter, the Countess Julia (or Julie or Giulietta) Guicciardi, also figures at some length in the Beethoven literature; we owe this to Schindler, whose candidate she was for being Beethoven's "Immortal Beloved." Although Schindler's claims here are utterly discredited,[6] it seems to be the case that for some time around the years 1801 and 1802 Beethoven was in love with her. On November 16, 1801, he wrote a long letter (Anderson number 54) to his friend, Franz Gerhard Wegeler, which included the following much-quoted passage:

> I am now leading a somewhat more pleasant life, for I am mixing more with my fellow creatures. . . . The change has been brought about by a dear charming girl who loves me and whom I love. After two years I am again enjoying a few blissful moments; and for the first time I feel that—marriage might bring me happiness. Unfor-

---

[4] The literature on the Brunsvik family, which also touches on the Guicciardi branch, is now extensive. Cf. especially La Mara [Marie Lipsius], *Beethovens unsterbliche Geliebte. Das Geheimnis der Gräfin Brunsvik und ihre Memoiren* (Leipzig, 1909); idem, *Beethoven und die Brunsviks* (Leipzig, 1920); Marianne Czeke, *Brunszvik Teréz Grófnö Naplói és Feljegyzései*, I (Budapest, 1938—with useful genealogical tables); and see n. 5.

[5] Cf. Joseph Schmidt-Görg, "Neue Briefe und Schriftstücke aus der Familie Brunsvik," *Beethoven-Jahrbuch*, II, Jahrgang 1955/56 (1956), 11; idem, *Dreizehn unbekannte Briefe an Josephine Gräfin Deym geb. v. Brunsvik* (Bonn, 1957); idem, "Neue Schriftstücke zu Beethoven und Josephine Gräfin Deym," *Beethoven-Jahrbuch*, VI, Jahrgang 1965/68 (1969), 205.

[6] Modern scholarship has concluded that the love letter to "The Immortal Beloved" dates from 1812; it is that fact above all that disqualifies all three of the candidates mentioned here.

tunately she is not of my class—and at the moment—I certainly could not marry—I must still bustle about a good deal.

This has generally been taken as a reference to Julia Guicciardi, whose seventeenth birthday fell a week later. But hardly anything is known of the course of the relationship, although conjecture has made the most of the few facts available. From a highly prosaic interview that she gave to Otto Jahn half a century later, in 1852, we learn that Beethoven gave her piano lessons and was rather strict; [7] and some confusing entries in a conversation book of 1823 (they were written in French by Beethoven and subsequently tampered with by Schindler) [8] have been studied for the light that they may possibly throw on the relationships among Beethoven, Julia, and the man that she married on November 3, 1803—Count Wenzel Robert Gallenberg, a prolific composer of ballet music, who was only a year older than she. Did she ever really love Beethoven? *He* thought so. It seems likely that, in fact, she was flattered for a time by the attentions of a famous and much-admired composer, but not deeply involved with him; nothing, at any rate, of much significance is to be found in the gossipy letters that she wrote to and that passed between her cousins, apart from the information that at a certain date Franz Xaver Kleinheinz had replaced Beethoven as her teacher. [9] The references to Beethoven's music and to his playing are another matter: they are unfailingly warm. Sentimentalists have, of course, made much of the fact that it was to her that Beethoven dedicated his "Moonlight" Sonata, Op. 27, no. 2, which was published in March, 1802. They fail, however, to notice that (according to her own account to Otto Jahn) the sonata was

---

[7] See Thayer II (1872), 171–72; Thayer-Deiters-Riemann II (1910), 307.

[8] See Thayer II (1872), 170–71; Thayer-Deiters-Riemann II (1910), 309–10. A much more accurate text will be found in Georg Schünemann, ed., *Ludwig van Beethovens Konversationshefte*, II (Berlin, 1942), 363–64. For a facsimile of fols. 44ʳ–47ʳ of Heft 21 (Feb., 1823), see H. C. Robbins Landon, *Beethoven* (London, 1970), pp. 142–43; the facsimile of the same pages in Paul Bekker, *Beethoven* (Berlin-Leipzig, 1911), pls. 44–48, seems to have been made from a tracing and is inaccurate in many of the smaller details. Schindler's glosses are, fortunately, easy to recognize.

[9] La Mara, *Beethoven und die Brunsviks*, p. 22, says that Beethoven had recommended him. The letter from Josephine to Therese (quoted in La Mara) mentioning the change of teacher is undated; Kleinheinz's Piano Sonata, Op. 6, which he dedicated to "Mademoiselle Julie Comtesse de Guicciardi," was advertised in the *Wiener Zeitung* on Aug. 12, 1801. For details of this and other works by Kleinheinz see Adolf Sandberger, *Ausgewählte Aufsätze zur Musikgeschichte*, II (Munich, 1924), 226–47; and for evidence that he may not have been in Vienna but with Josephine's and Therese's and Julia's uncle Graf Joseph at Schloss Korompa in Hungary, see Schmidt-Görg, *Beethoven-Jahrbuch*, II, 18.

a replacement for another piece—the Rondo in G, Op. 51, no. 2—that he had given to her and was then obliged to retrieve when he needed something to dedicate to Countess Lichnowsky. It may be that his disappointment with Julia as well as his deafness contributed to the mood of profound depression in which he composed the "Heiligenstadt Testament" in October, 1802.

Beethoven appears to have continued his visits to the Guicciardi household in the summer of 1803, and in a letter of Julia to her cousin Therese of August 2,[10] there is no hint of any breach with him. After the wedding in November the Gallenbergs went to live in Italy for some years. From then on we hear little of the Guicciardi branch; but the Countess Susanna makes a brief appearance (as "Tante Gui" or "Tante Gu") in a love letter from Beethoven to Josephine Deym of the spring of 1805 (Anderson number 110). The letter tries to allay Josephine's anxiety over the gossip in the Brunsvik circles concerning the developing relationship between them; it sounds rather as if Tante Gui was among those who were dismayed. The Countess Susanna died in Vienna in 1813.

The circumstances that provoked the letter. If this letter is, as has already been suggested, addressed to the Countess Susanna Guicciardi, there can be no doubt who is meant by "dear J."; and it is on the assumption that Beethoven's feelings for Julia are part of the background of the letter that I have tried to summarize such clues as there are to the chronology of their relationship.

My own impression is that the letter was written when his feelings for her were still very warm, and when he was paying frequent visits to the Guicciardi house. Since Julia only reached Vienna from Trieste with her parents in the summer of 1800 [11] and left it with her husband in November 1803, the only possible dates for the letter are January 23 of 1801, 1802, and 1803. But the first of these is surely too *early*. In 1801 Beethoven wrote two long and intensely personal letters to Franz Wegeler, only the second of which has been quoted. The earlier letter, written on June 29, 1801 (Anderson number 51), contains the first discussion of the onset of his deafness and of the misery that it had caused him; the letter of November 16 announces a *recent* change for the better, a "somewhat more pleasant life" after two years of "an empty, sad life." Thus it looks as though the enrichment brought about by the "dear charming girl" had come about in the two or three preceding months, and

---

10 Quoted in La Mara, *Beethoven und die Brunsviks*, pp. 28–29, and Czeke, c–ci.
11 She was still in Trieste on June 16, 1800—see her letter of that date, quoted in La Mara, *Beethoven und die Brunsviks*, pp. 11–13.

had certainly developed after the first letter to Wegeler. On the other hand, the possible date January 23, 1803, seems to be too *late*. By that time the relationship had surely passed its greatest intensity, and Julia must have been spending much of her time with young Gallenberg.[12] January 23, 1802, fits in best with the date of the second letter to Wegeler and with the other available clues.[13]

The letter is, of course, a reaction, or overreaction, to a present from the countess, which Beethoven is very reluctant to accept (although he ends by accepting it). There may have been two reasons for Beethoven's intense embarrassment, probably not clearly distinguished in his mind. The first reason why the present had shocked him was that (in his own words) "it immediately put the little I had done for dear J. on a par with your present." Veiled as it is, this must mean that a specific price or valuation had been placed on the services that Beethoven had rendered to Julia—presumably the attention that he had paid, whether in formal lessons or in less formal encouragement and interest, to the development of her musical abilities. It is only natural that it would be this side of his "attentiveness" to Julia that Beethoven would stress in a letter to her mother. "The talent of your daughter" is a mild enough piece of dissembling; but doubtless it was infuriating to have it taken at its face value and to be offered anything that recalled the sort of remuneration that professional musicians normally received from the mothers of talented daughters.

The second part of the letter seems to allude, with rather greater ob-

---

[12] She had met him soon after her arrival in Vienna: a letter of Josephine dating from January, 1801, refers to Julia and adds: "she is intimate with the Gallenbergs." See La Mara, *Beethoven und die Brunsviks*, p. 14.

[13] Beethoven's dating of the letter 1782 must, then, have been an error. And there is a striking parallel: the autograph of the Op. 33 bagatelles, written out in 1802, is inscribed by Beethoven on the first page: "Des Bagatelles par louis van Beethoven/1782." (See Max Unger, *Eine Schweizer Beethovensammlung* [Zurich, 1939], pl. VIII.) This singular dating has sometimes been explained as an attempt by Beethoven to indicate that some of the material of the bagatelles dated from his boyhood—a notion for which there is absolutely no evidence. What seems most likely is that in the case both of these bagatelles and of the letter Beethoven became confused over the correct way to write the year (the 7 on the bagatelles even appears to have been written over another figure, possibly 8 or 0). Simpler slips over dates and figures are notoriously common with Beethoven: cf., for instance, Anderson no. 143 (1806 for 1807), no. 178 (1088 for 1808), and no. 764 (1816 for 1817), or the error of IV for VI in the autograph of Op. 98 (below, p. 123, n. 2). Beethoven apparently wrote 41 for 14 in giving his age on the autograph of the very early trio for flute, bassoon, and pianoforte, WoO 37.

Beethoven
and
Carl Heinrich Graun*

Richard A. Kramer

I

❋ Of the workshop papers sold at the auction of Beethoven's musical effects, the five packets of contrapuntal studies encouraged some of the heaviest bidding, as we read in a first-hand report which appeared some months later in the *Allgemeine Musikalische Zeitung*.[1] The Viennese publisher Tobias Haslinger was forced to a very high price in his zeal to acquire the studies.[2] Haslinger, of course, saw profit in their future publication. The task was assigned to Ignaz Seyfried, whose distorted edition of their content, published in 1832, was early and thoroughly discredited —first by Franz Derckum in the *Rheinische Musik-Zeitung* of 1852, and later by Gustav Nottebohm in several contributions to the *Allgemeine Musikalische Zeitung* of 1863 and 1864 (later synthesized in the well-known final essay in his *Beethoveniana*).[3] Derckum, writing from Cologne, evidently had no access to the Beethoven papers, and his was simply a brief and initial attempt to identify obvious theoretical sources

---

* Presented, in a somewhat different version, at the annual meeting of the American Musicological Society at Durham, N.C., Nov., 1971. Thanks are due to Dr. Hans Schmidt for granting me access to manuscripts and photocopies at the Beethovenhaus, Bonn.

[1] *Allgemeine Musikalische Zeitung*, XXX (1828), 29.

[2] See Georg Kinsky, "Zur Versteigerung von Beethovens musikalischem Nachlass," *Neues Beethoven-Jahrbuch*, VI (1935), 66–86 (in particular p. 75).

[3] Ignaz Ritter von Seyfried, *Ludwig van Beethovens Studien im Generalbasse, Contrapuncte und in der Compositions-Lehre* (Vienna, 1832); N I, pp. 154–203. Derckum's report was publicized by Anton Schindler in the third edition of his Beethoven biography. See Schindler (1860), II, 308–23; Eng. trans., pp. 464–74.

for the material that Seyfried, through implication, had given as Beethoven's own. Nottebohm could go deeper, and he was able to demonstrate that the papers that Haslinger had purchased dated, in fact, from two distinct points in Beethoven's career. Certain leaves record his early Viennese studies with Haydn, Schenk, and Albrechtsberger. Others date from around 1809, when it is believed that Beethoven was putting together notes for a formal course in thoroughbass and counterpoint for Archduke Rudolph.[4]

The final pages in Seyfried's book are particularly concerned with recitative. These pages have drawn no notice since Derckum and then Nottebohm pointed out that their source was the pertinent article in Johann Georg Sulzer's *Allgemeine Theorie der schönen Künste,* whose second volume—that containing the article on recitative—was first published in 1774.[5] But Nottebohm observed that the immediate source for what Seyfried had given here was no longer to be found among the papers then in Haslinger's possession. Nor could he locate the source for some notes in the same chapter on the physical properties of the voice and its relationship to range. And Nottebohm had hardly enough confidence in the authenticity of Seyfried's book to say positively that these leaves had ever existed.[6]

In fact, they do. A single leaf now in the Vienna Stadtbibliothek [7] preserves the material on voice range—memoranda which, to judge from the handwriting, were made considerably later than 1809. An inscription at the bottom of one side tells us that Carl Haslinger parted with it in 1861, not long before Nottebohm was to search through the corpus to which it had belonged.

Of greater substantive worth is a double leaf or bifolium which H. C. Bodmer acquired at auction in 1950, and which now belongs to

---

[4] For the date of 1809, see N I, pp. 160–62, 200–02. Nottebohm subsequently published a study of the earlier papers, those prepared for Haydn and Albrechtsberger, in *Beethovens Studien* (Leipzig-Winterthur, 1873); this includes an ingenious preliminary chapter entitled "Die Bonner Studien: eine hypothetische Untersuchung" and a closing chapter that takes up the papers prepared for Antonio Salieri (see below). Alfred Mann reassessed one segment of the early papers in a recent essay, "Beethoven's Contrapuntal Studies with Haydn," *The Musical Quarterly,* LVI (1970), 711–26.

[5] For the complex publication history of the encyclopedia, see Peter Schnaus, "Sulzer, Johann Georg," in *Die Musik in Geschichte und Gegenwart,* XII (Kassel, 1965), cols. 1733–35. The recent reprint of Sulzer's encyclopedia (Hildesheim, 1967) uses the "neue vermehrte zweyte Auflage" (Leipzig, 1794; four volumes plus index), where the article "Recitativ" is located in IV, 4–19.

[6] N I, p. 196.

[7] Shelf no. R/IN 5784.

the Bodmer Collection at the Beethovenhaus in Bonn.[8] The leaf permits us finally to verify that Seyfried did, indeed, base his recitative chapter upon a Beethoven autograph; and while Beethoven's notes are telegraphic and not thoroughly comprehensible taken alone, we also now know that Seyfried's garbled account is an inaccurate view of the document, an imaginative attempt to reconstruct a sensible discourse made by someone who lacked the control of Beethoven's original source. More important, the leaf affords some evidence for gauging its chronological position— handwriting, watermark, and staff-liner characteristics are useful here— which, in turn, allows us to assess the function of these studies in the larger thrust of Beethoven's creative output.

The Bodmer bifolium is the lower half of a sheet. Its watermark reads (left) GFA and (right) three crescent moons (their lower portions). On a complete sheet these letters very frequently appear beneath the figure of an eagle with crown; but the upper half of the present sheet—a bifolium whose watermark presumably reads (left) a crowned eagle and (right) the top parts of the three moons—has not been traced. Both the letters GFA and the eagle are found among Beethoven manuscripts in a number of slightly different forms. So far as I can judge, the GFA in the Bodmer bifolium agrees most closely with the following sources (for abbreviations, see pages xiii–xiv):

1. (? 1800) DStB, Artaria 166: exercises for Salieri, pages 13–14 (Hess 213) and pages 43–46, a bifolium (Hess 211, 220, sketches for Hess 231, 232). Only the upper quadrants of the sheet.
2. (1801) SBH 526: autograph of Op. 27, no. 2, folios 6–16 (finale).
3. (spring, 1802) SBH 528: autograph of Op. 30, no. 2, folios 1–17 (excluding the single leaf stitched to folio 9ʳ).
4. (spring, 1802) BM, Add. 37767: autograph of Op. 30, no. 3, folios 1–8.
5. (before the end of 1802) DStB, Grasnick 14: gathered sheet (two bifolia) containing a quintet score in Beethoven's hand of the Fugue in B♭ Minor from Bach's *Well-Tempered Clavier*, Book I, and sketches for Op. 33, nos. 5 and 7.[9]

---

[8] SV 164 and (for a more accurate description) SBH 706.

[9] For a facsimile and discussion of the Bach arrangement, see Willy Hess, "Eine Bach-Bearbeitung Beethovens," *Schweizerische Musikzeitung*, XCIII (1953), 402–05. Sketches for Op. 33, no. 5, may put the date for this sheet at late 1801, for there are other sketches for this piece on a leaf now in Cambridge (Fitzwilliam Museum) which evidently belonged to a sketchbook (now dismembered) with ideas for the piano sonatas, Op. 27, no. 2, and Op. 28, and the String Quintet, Op. 29. The existence of such a book was first inferred by Wilhelm Virn-

6. (? winter, 1802–03) SBH 733: copyist's score of Op. 116, *Tremate, empi, tremate*, with autograph corrections, folios 1–20.

7. (winter, 1802–03) Stanford, Memorial Library of Music: three leaves (two sides blank), a rudimentary autograph score-fragment of WoO 93 (*Nei giorni tuoi felici*).[10]

8. (April–May, 1803) SBH 534: autograph (fragment—exposition of first movement only) of Op. 47, folios 1–6 (all extant).

9. (? 1802–04) GdM, A 75: a bifolium plus a single leaf, in a folder recently marked "IV. Abschriften/Bach u. Händel/11 Bl.," a copy in Beethoven's hand of Handel's overture to the oratorio *Esther*.[11]

10. (spring, 1804) StPK, Artaria 179: score (partly autograph) of Op. 85, *Christus am Oelberge*, folios 99–102, 118–21.[12]

11. (1805) DStB, aut. 5: copyist's score of *Leonore* (1805), Introduction to act 3. The eagle is of a significantly different mold.[13]

Except for SBH 733 (twelve staffs to the page), all these papers show one and the same pattern of staff-liner imperfections—a sixteen-staff ruling whose left edges form a distinct and repeatable profile. It is easily

---

eisel, "Aus Beethovens Skizzenbuch zum Streichquintett op. 29," *Zeitschrift für Musik*, CXIII (1952), 142–46; about fifteen additional leaves have been identified with that book since Virneisel's initial description.

[10] SV 371 (but not identified there). The document itself is too reticent to allow the conclusion that it was withdrawn from a preliminary score. More likely, Beethoven merely sought to draft only this brief, though very troublesome, passage—just before and after the meter change at m. 68—into a full score.

[11] Seyfried (*op. cit.*, pp. 348–52) published the Handel overture, unidentified as such, directly after the recitative studies, without any suggestion of a break between the two topics. He must have found A 75 and the sheet of recitative studies together and have felt some compulsion to preserve that sequence. Whether or not this continuity reflects an original and authentic continuity is now impossible to say.

[12] On problems attending the dating of this score, see Alan Tyson, "The 1803

Version of Beethoven's 'Christus am Oelberge,'" *The Musical Quarterly*, LVI (1970), 551–84.

[13] To these should be added several other fragments. Their content puts them rather later than the main body of sources that show this watermark, but it is entirely possible that the Graun entries are similarly posterior to the date that the watermark suggests.

StPK, Landsberg 10, pp. 47–48, 67–72 (a sheet): sketches for Op. 67, Op. 69. Ten staffs to the page.

GdM, A 59: a bifolium (among three others of different paper) with sketches for Op. 67, Op. 138. Eight staffs to the page.

Finally, a close approximation of the same watermark turns up in some leaves which appear to date from 1796–97:

BM, Add. 29801 ("Kafka" Miscellany), fols. 63, 66–67: sketches for Op. 9, Op. 13, Op. 49, no. 1. Sixteen staffs to the page.

StPK, aut. 28, fols. 44–45 (bifolium): sketches for Op. 10, no. 3. Sixteen staffs to the page.

the most common type during these years, and seems to have had a life extending roughly from 1800 to 1806.[14]

Handwriting is a more difficult criterion here, for it is well known that the archetypes of Beethoven's notational mannerisms were clearly formed by 1800.[15] But it is a simple matter to distinguish the hand of, say, 1810 from that of 1803 on the basis of more general properties, not easily categorized—and on these grounds, too, the years 1802–04 seem very appropriate to the Bodmer leaf. This is an important point, for it dislodges these studies from the two cycles that compose the bulk of the Haslinger-Seyfried papers. It seems reasonably certain that the recitative papers date neither from the years of formal study during the 1790s, nor from the compilation of materials for Beethoven's own course of instruction around 1809, but from the years in between. These were precisely the years during which Beethoven faced critical problems in this genre for the first time on a large scale.

It is becoming clear that the corpus of exercises which Beethoven prepared for Salieri [16] need, as a whole, to be reassessed according to new criteria. Willy Hess, who has recently given us a fine publication of their content, has in fact revived Nottebohm's chronology for them.[17] Nottebohm argued that the Salieri papers stretch across ten years, beginning with Beethoven's arrival in Vienna in 1792. But a comparison with other datable Beethoven autographs will disclose that the entire portfolio can be dated roughly 1798–1801. Without arguing this in laborious detail, it may do here to offer two bits of negative reasoning which support this evidence. First, it would have made very little sense for Beethoven to have submitted these very modest exercises—simple homophonic settings for two, three, and four voices—at the rate of one or two each year for nearly a decade. This would have been an insult to Salieri's stature in Viennese musical life and hardly consonant with the rigorous standard of self-criticism so characteristic of Beethoven's lifelong odyssey. Second,

---

[14] This particular staff-liner pattern was mentioned briefly by Tyson, *ibid.*, 572, n. 22.

[15] Max Unger, *Beethovens Handschrift*, vol. IV of *Veröffentlichungen des Beethovenhauses in Bonn* (Bonn, 1926) —a pilot study, still unique, whose understated hypotheses have proved very sturdy.

[16] DStB, Artaria 166; GdM, A 69, 73, 79, and 75 (a bifolium now kept apart from the larger collection of counterpoint exercises under that signature). A 79

consists of only three quadrants of a sheet; the leaf that formed the fourth quadrant is now the final leaf in the sketchbook Grasnick 2 (SV 46) and appears to have been placed there by Aloys Fuchs.

[17] Willy Hess, ed., *Beethoven: Supplemente zur Gesamtausgabe,* I (Wiesbaden, 1959), 29–35 (*Revisionsbericht*). For further discussion of the manuscript sources and of other matters concerning these exercises, see Hess, *Verzeichnis . . . ,* pp. 55–64.

among the Salieri papers in Berlin are copies, in Beethoven's hand, of
works by two of Salieri's pupils—twelve pages of not very appetizing
music by Carl Doblhoff-Dier and Alexander Cornet—on paper that must
date from about 1800 and showing the idiosyncrasies of Beethoven's handwriting that began to emerge at just about that time.[18] It would seem very
odd for Beethoven to have copied these pieces after having worked with
Salieri for some eight years. All they could have given him was an outline
of the most elementary rules of prosody and perhaps some idea of the
type of piece Salieri expected of his pupils.

If the Salieri papers are assigned a later date, Beethoven's early development moves in a more logical sequence of intensive disciplines. The
1790s was a decade of great pianistic accomplishment for Beethoven,
to which attest the checkered prehistory of the two early concertos and
fragments of other, unrecovered or incomplete concertos as well as numerous entries for cadenzas and possibly for other improvisational memory
aids on workshop papers from those years.[19] We also know of Beethoven's
concentrated involvement with the rigors of Fuxian counterpoint and
advanced studies in *freie Satz* with Albrechtsberger.[20] Toward the end of
the decade, then, Beethoven began to inform himself in preparation for
dramatic vocal composition and for works directed to the theater. Apart
from the Salieri exercises, Beethoven's projects here went something like
the following:

1800–early 1801: the ballet *Die Geschöpfe des Prometheus*—not a
vocal work, but one which obliged Beethoven to coordinate musical
events with stage action, as is documented by entries in the pertinent
sketchbook, Landsberg 7 (SV 61).

1801–02: The major source here is the so-called "Kessler" Sketchbook
(SV 263), which occupied Beethoven from roughly the autumn of 1801
till his departure for Heiligenstadt in April, 1802. The book is best known
for the instrumental works that Beethoven composed during this period:
the Second Symphony, the three violin sonatas Op. 30, the piano sonatas
Op. 31, nos. 1 and 2, and the piano variations Op. 34 and Op. 35. But little
has been made of the rather extensive studies for works with Italian texts:
no less than fifteen pages of sketches for the *scena No, non turbarti*—
sketches which have some bearing on the recitative studies from Sulzer—
and twenty-six pages of intensive work on the terzetto *Tremate, empi,
tremate,* an impressive ensemble study which Beethoven was to revive for

---

[18] DStB, Artaria 166, pp. 15–26.

[19] The most substantial body of evidence is in Joseph Kerman, ed., *Beethoven: Autograph Miscellany from circa*
1786–1799. British Museum Additional
Manuscript 29801, ff. 39–162 (the 'Kafka
Sketchbook'), 2 vols. (London, 1970).

[20] See Mann, *op. cit.*

performance in 1814. Somewhat later in "Kessler" there also appear three drafts for an arietta with keyboard accompaniment on the text "Grazie al' inganni . . ." from Metastasio's cantata *La Libertà*—a very modest piece, hardly distinguishable on internal grounds from the earliest Salieri studies.

1802–03: Work in these years is recorded in the so-called "Wielhorsky" Sketchbook (SV 343). Very early on, Beethoven tackled an ambitious duet with orchestral accompaniment to the text "Nei giorni tuoi felici" from Metastasio's *L'Olimpiade,* act 1, scene 10. From about the middle of the book to its end are entries for *Christus am Oelberge,* first performed on April 5, 1803. Beethoven himself claimed that the piece was composed in the space of several weeks before the first performance, but he could scarcely have galvanized those sketches into a work of this magnitude in so little time. It is, after all, an ambitious work in a genre that he had not approached since the two early occasional cantatas of 1790.[21]

Finally, opera. Beethoven was interested in Schikaneder's libretto *Vestas Feuer* as early as November, 1803. Parts of it had been sketched in the "Eroica" Sketchbook, Landsberg 6 (SV 60), and put into score before Beethoven abandoned the project by January, 1804,[22] at which point he reports (in a letter to Johann Friedrich Rochlitz)[23] to have had an old French libretto adapted: Bouilly's *Léonore ou l'Amour conjugal.* The sequence in the "Eroica" Sketchbook implies that he set to work nearly at once after having abandoned *Vestas Feuer.*

This brief survey suggests, I think, the intensity with which Beethoven pursued the problems of theater music. It is in this light that we must view the studies in recitative for which Beethoven consulted Sulzer's encyclopedia.

II

The authorship of the article on recitative in the encyclopedia is something of a puzzle. It is known that Sulzer himself was responsible for its first section, a broad historical and critical study of declamation, viewed in relation to a variety of sister disciplines. But the more significant, musical portion seems to have been written exclusively by Johann Abraham Peter Schulz, under the editorial eye of his mentor, Johann

---

[21] Cf. Tyson, *op. cit.,* 558, n. 10.

[22] The autograph score fragment is in in Vienna (GdM, A 6), and was published by Willy Hess in *Beethoven: Sup-* *plemente zur Gesamtausgabe,* XIII (Wiesbaden, 1970).

[23] Anderson, no. 87a.

Kirnberger. In the 1800 *Allgemeine Musikalische Zeitung*,[24] Schulz himself illuminated the division of labor with respect to the musical articles in the encyclopedia, in reply to an attack on one of those articles by Carl Ditters von Dittersdorf. Schulz also expressed, somewhat forlornly, his dissatisfaction with the bulk of the articles that had been his exclusive responsibility—a dissatisfaction that, I think, stemmed partly from what must have seemed to Schulz a narrow view of contemporary music in light of his subsequent experience after leaving Berlin around 1780.

But the recitative article, a unique contribution to eighteenth-century music criticism, may in some sense even have gained from this narrow view. For it would have been very difficult for Schulz to have focused so sharply upon a restricted body of works—those which he knew to embody the best principles of recitative—and to have examined it with equal thoroughness had he attempted this as late as 1800. Nor is it likely that he could have summoned equal fervor. In 1773–74 Schulz was writing with the partisan passion of a man in his early twenties, and his achievement here deserves to be recognized as one of the important contributions to eighteenth-century critical writing.

The essay is no mere prescriptive lesson in technical convention, but rather a true inquiry into the properties of recitative, with insight into the relationship of text to harmonic motion and rhythmic articulation. Part of Schulz's success here lies, I think, in the balance he strikes between enumerative pedagogy—he outlines no less than fifteen points essential to good recitative—and a rather more subjective criticism of music examples chosen to illuminate those fifteen points. The bulk of these examples were reproduced on plates separate from the text, a distinction unique to this of all the musical essays in the encyclopedia.

As the two Bodmer leaves inform us, Beethoven made careful copies of nearly all those examples that Schulz had chosen in order to illustrate qualities proper to good recitative. For the most part they had been culled from a cross section of works by Carl Heinrich Graun. And Beethoven pursued this with admirable thoroughness from the beginning of

---

24 *Allgemeine Musikalische Zeitung*, II (1800), 278: "Von dem Artikel Preludiren bis zu dem Buchstaben S hat Sulzer ausser dem Artikel System, der schon fertig war, und der ersten Hälfte des Artikels Recitativ, nur noch weniger Antheil an den musikalischen Artikeln. Aber auch Kirnberger, der wohl wusste, dass ich aus seiner Seele schrieb, überliess mir, von dem Buchstaben S an, die alleinige Beendigung des Werks." Kirnberger, then, may have had something to say about the material that Schulz had assembled for the recitative essay. In a footnote on that same page, Schulz wrote of Sulzer's own dependence upon Kirnberger's theoretical teaching, and how Sulzer was himself indirectly responsible for the formulation of those theories into *Die Kunst des reinen Satzes*.

the essay to its end, leafing back to relevant pages to find the proper gloss for each example. The Bodmer bifolium, incidentally, records only the central portion of Schulz's essay; we can assume that it was originally the inner bifolium of a gathering whose outer leaves are missing (although they were present when Seyfried had the papers). If Beethoven could respond only minimally to some of these music examples, certain others seem to have impressed themselves upon his thought, though not entirely for the reasons that had prompted Schulz to publish them.

Schulz chose the beginning of Graun's unpublished cantata *Disperata Porcia* to demonstrate two principles: that an irregular melodic rhythm assumes its shape through the simple observance of caesura and periodicity of text; and that rests should be avoided except where the text shows grammatical completion. Having cited several examples where rests are improperly placed and leading tones prematurely resolved, Schulz remarks—I paraphrase him here—that neither leading tone nor dissonance should resolve before the sense of the text has been completed. If the sentence is rather long, or if the expression of the text requires that the harmony modulate often, then each resolution of leading tone or dissonance must immediately be replaced by another leading tone or a new dissonance, so that the sense of expectation ("Erwartung") shall be sustained in the harmony, as in the Graun example. Here, all chords are intertwined ("in einander geschlungen") by means of leading tones and dissonance, except at the word "dolor," where, however, the motion is not articulated by a rest, but rather extended till the full close at the end. And (Schulz continues) such "Veränderungen" in the harmony in the midst of a sentence must always fall upon a "Hauptwort," never upon a "Nebenwort."

But the example embodies certain other properties that recur in most of the other passages by Graun which Schulz has chosen. For one thing, the bass moves almost exclusively by step till the final cadence. Chords in $\frac{4}{2}$ inversion (seventh in the bass) are conspicuous here—more prevalent, in fact, than those in root position—generating the voice-leading inherent in this kind of harmonic continuity. Similarly, leading tones in the bass are frequently made to descend directly by step, sometimes to sevenths. This is a basic kind of "Veränderung," one that Kirnberger, in *Die Kunst des reinen Satzes*, was to identify in his discussion of sevenths which, in free style, may appear without the usual preparation.[25]

The very expressive vocal cadence (". . . con tui accenti") will be found again in *Christus* at the end of the first recitative, at ". . . erbarm

---

[25] Johann Philip Kirnberger, *Die* . . . , 2 vols. (Berlin and Königsberg, *Kunst des reinen Satzes in der Musik* 1771–79), I, 89–90.

Ex. 1 Graun, from the cantata *Disperata Porcia,* in
Johann Georg Sulzer, ed., "Recitativ," in *Allgemeine
Theorie der schönen Künste,* IV (rev. ed., 1794), ex. 3.
Schulz's example disagrees in some details with a
contemporary manuscript copy—Berlin, StPK, Mus. MS.
Graun 8240.

dich mein," with a similar prolongation of the dominant through neighbor
motion in the bass (example 2).

Ex. 2 Beethoven, *Christus am Oelberge* (Op. 85), end of
recitative *Jehovah, du mein Vater!*

Significantly, entries in the "Wielhorsky" Sketchbook show considerable
labor over this point.[26] The final form did not spring from a direct (conscious or semiconscious) imitation, but more likely appeared as a gesture
recollected only gradually—if recollection is the proper term here.

---

[26] The phrase is sketched at the following locations (page and staff): 91/2,
91/15–16, 92/16, 104/10–11, 105/13,
108/7. Only the final entry shows the
ultimate form, the others lacking even
remote resemblance to it.

Schulz goes on to an exemplary discussion of the proper setting of short, exclamatory phrases, and of the misuse of melismatic elaboration—he even cautions against spreading two tones across a syllable except in rare cases warranted by an expressive text, for he finds only a single example in the whole of Graun's *Tod Jesu*. There is intelligent discussion, too, of the observance of grammatical accent, and of written convention and performance practice, with pointed criticism of Johann Adolf Scheibe's *Tragische Cantaten nebst einem Sendschreiben vom Recitative* (1765), a work on which Schulz drew heavily for counterexamples to some basic principles of declamation and harmonic syntax.

But the crux of Schulz's essay lies in his effort to align harmonic motion and melodic direction with fluctuation in the quality he calls "Empfindung." As he puts it: "The rise and fall of the voice must regulate itself according to the waxing and waning of 'Empfindung,' across single syllables as well as across a series of them." The precept (which is, after all, inexhaustible) is elaborated in a number of directions, beginning with an excerpt from Graun's cantata *Apollo amante di Dafne* (example 3). Schulz remarks: "An exceptionally beautiful example by Graun illustrates this precept. Apollo calls out as he witnesses Dafne's transformation. His confusion is expressed in the upper register, whereupon the voice drops,

Ex. 3 Graun, from the cantata *Apollo amante di Dafne*, in Sulzer, ex. 14.

rising gradually by step till the final exclamation 'O dispietata!' In such cases [i.e. where feeling intensifies], the 'Transpositionen' in example 4 are of uncommonly good effect—a harmonic sequence which Graun frequently calls upon, chiefly for the expression of surprise and growing delight." And here Schulz cites a brief illustration from Graun's opera *Rodelinda,* showing precisely that harmonic sequence.

Ex. 4 Sulzer, p. 13.

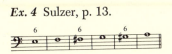

To this archetype, Schulz adds two more groups of "Transpositionen":

Ex. 5 Sulzer, ex. 16.

Ex. 6 Sulzer, ex. 19.

Of the first group, he writes: ". . . these, in passages of growing emotional intensity, are sad and plaintive, though the first and last are more passionate than the second." He then gives a passage from Graun's *Tod Jesu* and another from his opera *Demofoonte,* both showing the second formula in example 5. It is less passionate, evidently, because of the weak fifths in the bass at each dominant.

Of those in example 6, he writes: ". . . these are contrary to the previous examples, for they are appropriate to passages of sinking, mournful emotion ['sinkende und traurige Affekten'], the second of the two more melancholy than the first." And it is likely that Schulz had in mind Graun's *Disperata Porcia,* the passage given in example 1, where that paradigm is treated with some liberty.

These distinctions deserve some discussion. Of the three general types of bass given in examples 4, 5, and 6, Schulz distinguishes between those that express situations of rising emotional intensity (examples 4 and 5) and those that show an emotional recession: the former through ascending step motion in the bass, either directly through semitones or inflected by sevenths above each tone; the latter through descent by step, either directly through semitones (again, sevenths in the bass are crucial here) or inflected by leading tones from below. But beyond this, the sequence in example 4 shows leading tones in the bass resolving to major triads, and here it differs essentially from the first sequence in example 5, where the resolution to minor triads is appropriate to the expression of melancholy. Two separate qualities, then, inform Schulz's critical apparatus: the direction of the bass and the modal complexion of the harmony.

It would be unfair to accuse Schulz here of an inflexible critical response to these passages, for he points to the following music (example 7) from the opera *Rodelinda* to demonstrate Graun's control over internal contrast. As Schulz puts it: "In the second measure, one expects an E♭-minor chord after the D in the bass. In its place one hears the raw dominant of C, and the shock is reinforced when, at 'Grimoaldo crudel,' Rodelinda raises her voice to its upper register, following upon the deeper tones of her sighing."

Ex. 7 Graun, from the opera *Rodelinda* (act 1, scene 9), in Sulzer, ex. 22. Two contemporary manuscript copies—Berlin, StPK, Mus. MS. Graun 8204; Paris, Bibliothèque Nationale, fonds du cons. MS. D 5009—agree upon the first note as given in brackets.

III

The slight differences that I have indicated so far between the readings found in Schulz and those of the best Graun sources may only reflect typographical error; but the very next example precipitates a source conflict on a much grander scale. Citing example 8, allegedly from Graun's *Demofoonte*, Schulz gives an epitome of the drama here: "Timante happily believes that his father (who wants him to marry) is speaking of Dircea, to whom Timante is in fact secretly married; hearing a totally strange name at the end of the conversation, Timante replies as in example 8." It needs to be added that Timante had resolved to disclose the secret (necessary, by a complex of circumstances, to save Dircea's life), but in this new confusion to the situation he can only stammer the beginnings of a confession.

Ex. 8 Graun (attrib.), from the opera *Demofoonte*
(act 1, scene 3), in Sulzer, ex. 23.

And Schulz continues: "Nothing can be more peaceful than this sequence of tones, and yet it rests upon a simple progression of fifths [example 9] normally reserved for the expression of indifferent states of emotion. Here, then, is ample demonstration that paragraphs broken by short, contrasting phrases are more effectively supported by smooth harmonic sequence than by remote and involved relationships." Schulz might have drawn some relationship here to the basses in example 6, for here, also, roots descend through the circle of fifths. But it was crucial to Kirnberger's teaching that chord inversion affects expression; and while the disposition of root and bass in example 8 has evidently caught Schulz's ear, it is somewhat odd that he has not thought to observe its harmonic similarity to the sequence in example 6. A point of distinction here might have been critically illuminating.

Ex. 9 Sulzer, p. 13.

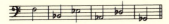

When Johann Friedrich Reichardt wrote his penetrating comparison of Hasse and Graun, published in 1774 as the first letter of *Briefe eines aufmerksamen Reisenden*,[27] he based most of his remarks on each composer's setting of Metastasio's *Demofoonte*—Graun's was first performed in 1746, Hasse's in 1748. It is clear from Reichardt's description that Johann Friedrich Agricola, who had succeeded Graun as Kapellmeister at the court of Frederick the Great, was responsible for certain revisions to

[27] Given in translation, with critical notes, by Oliver Strunk, in *Source Read-* ings in Music History (New York, 1950), pp. 699–710.

Graun's score in the performance that he directed in 1774, and Reichardt tells us that for this revival an affecting aria had been borrowed from Hasse's setting of the same libretto.[28] Schulz's essay was published in that same year, and it may well be that these circumstances hold the key to a very curious puzzle. Three manuscript scores in Berlin (one of them from the library of Princess Amalia and, therefore, accessible to Kirnberger if, indeed, he had not some responsibility in its making) as well as two other eighteenth-century manuscript scores, one of which now in Wolfenbüttel may record a performance in Braunschweig, show the Graun recitative as it appears in example 10.

Ex. 10 Graun, from the opera *Demofoonte* (act 1, scene 3), a conflation of the following sources: Berlin, StPK, Mus. MS. Graun 8216/1 ("wahrscheinlich autogr" penciled in the score, but this is unlikely, measured against other autographs in Berlin, notably some sketch leaves shelved with Mus. MS. autogr. Graun, K. H. 8); Berlin, StPK, Mus. MS. Graun 8216 (in the hand of several copyists); Berlin, DStB, MS. Amalia 194; Darmstadt, Hessische Landes- und Hochschulbibliothek, Mus. MS. 380; Rostock, Universitätsbibliothek (eighteenth-century manuscript copy); Wolfenbüttel, Herzog August Bibliothek, MS. [Vogel] 86.

---

28 *Ibid.*, p. 704. See also Johann Friedrich Reichardt, *Musikalische Kunstmagazin*, II (Berlin, 1791), 66n, where we learn that the aria was "Misero pargoletto" (act 3, scene 5); the substitution was evidently prompted by Frederick the Great's aversion to works that disturbed his refined palette of emotional

It is difficult to read expressive meaning here, for the whole point seems to have been to set up the augmented sixth toward the close of Timante's convulsive reply. But there is a very striking similarity between the passage that Schulz attributed to Graun and Hasse's setting of this scene (example 11)—though I tend to hear a higher level of sophistication in Hasse's setting, for the initial repose of Timante's reply (with its sequence of fifths similar to that in the Schulz example) breaks down at the deflection around D at "o padre," where the ascending bass expresses Timante's genuine distraction.

Ex. 11 Hasse, from the opera *Demofoonte* (act 1, scene 3)—Paris, Bibliothèque Nationale, fonds du cons. (eighteenth-century manuscript copy).

*The part of Timante was originally written in the soprano clef.

Graun must have known Hasse's *Demofoonte,* but if he himself revised this passage for a later performance, Schulz's essay would be the single evidence for that revision. It would be helpful if we could consult Agricola's performance score for the 1774 revival (by that date, Graun had been dead some fifteen years), for it seems likely that Schulz based his reading upon that source. It may well be that he unwittingly attrib-

response, although Reichardt was clearly aware of some contradiction here to his own critical estimate of the two composers. It is well known that Frederick himself composed three substitute arias for Graun's *Demofoonte* (these are bound into the Wolfenbüttel score), but they can have had no bearing on Schulz's source for the recitative example.

uted to Graun a passage that had been composed by Agricola in imitation of Hasse.

IV

The *scena No, non turbarti,* composed in 1801–02, appears to have been Beethoven's final exercise for Salieri. One wants to know if Beethoven consulted Schulz *before* setting to work—for this was evidently the single attempt at recitative to be submitted to Salieri—or only *after* its composition had exposed certain inadequacies. Beethoven certainly worked seriously on the project. The "Kessler" Sketchbook records an early draft for the vocal line of the recitative, with its corollary revisions, followed overleaf by a fascinating if cryptic complex of ideas exclusively for emendations to the harmonic plan of the recitative. After some eight pages of entries for the aria, Beethoven redrafted the recitative complete on two staffs (though the bass is rarely indicated) showing some interesting deviations from readings in the final version.

Salieri's corrections have been adequately dealt with by Nottebohm,[29] and Willy Hess published them as part of his first edition of the piece in 1949.[30] Salieri's corrections bear largely on matters of prosody and accent, but there is more to be said both about the larger concept of the recitative and about the localized choice of pitch. In the schematic reduction of the entire recitative in its final form (example 12), it is difficult to find a sustained sense of harmonic direction. Indeed, its harmonic periodicity, characterized by groups of two or three chords which stand in dominant-tonic relationship, is contrary to all the longer examples in Schulz's essay. Root position is very common, and there are no examples at all of deflected leading tones in the bass nor of $\frac{4}{2}$ inversions used to generate motion away from a tonic (as in the very first measure of *Disperata Porcia*). At the same time, it is difficult to apprehend any logic in the placement of the intermediate tonal centers. For all the licence that recitative affords in this respect, it is curious that Beethoven has allowed himself to fall into obvious redundancies: D minor at measure 13 and measure 27; C major at the outset, again at measure 18, and a third time at measure 35, where it is evidently to function as a large structural return; the subsequent move to the subdominant side, however, overpowers the final cadence, causing an unusual rhythmic ellipsis.

---

[29] Nottebohm, *Beethovens Studien,* pp. 221–26.

[30] Hess corrected several trivial errors when he republished the piece in *Beet-* *hoven: Supplemente zur Gesamtausgabe,* II (Wiesbaden, 1960), although regrettably he neglected to reprint Salieri's corrections.

Ex. 12 Beethoven, *No, non turbarti* (WoO 92a), reduction of the recitative.

The sketches betray considerable compositional agony at measure 35. This is perhaps due to a problem of interpretation posed by Metastasio's punctuation here—the dots which suspend time between "Nice, io pre-veggo . . ." and "Ah, non tel dissi?" From the first sketch, Beethoven articulated the phrase "Nice, io preveggo . . ." cadentially, in fact as the single intermediate full cadence, where it was to have established G minor (example 13a). The harmonic drafts on the following page, although they are not entirely certain in details of transcription, focus upon this very cadence, but now as a point of rupture. The dominant is answered not by its tonic, but by a first-inversion seventh chord whose bass lies a semitone above the dominant (recalling, by the way, one of the substitutes listed by Schulz as particularly suited to the intensification of feeling, in a catalogue of such alternative cadences). Two of Beethoven's entries here are shown as examples 13b and 13c. If the explicit relationship of these drafts to the recitative is not always ascertainable, it seems to me significant that these do demonstrate a preoccupation with the conduct of the bass, a point not evident in the final version. In the latest "Kessler" draft, the cadence at "Nice, io preveggo . . ." is obscured by a patchwork of alternate readings for the new instrumental interlude here, but the original layer is clear enough (example 13d). The cadential rupture recorded in earlier sketches is replaced by its converse; now Metastasio's temporal dots are reinterpreted as dissonance unresolved, and C major is put off till the final cadence. But the fortuitous nature of that final cadence is further underscored by an alternate final cadence in G which seems not to have been suggested by large-scale preparatory revision.

In the version submitted to Salieri, Beethoven reverted to that earlier tonal hiatus at "Nice, io preveggo . . . ," though, indeed, in a different key. But the autograph score, with its penciled corrections allegedly in

Ex. 13 Beethoven, *No, non turbarti* sketches for the recitative—Vienna, GdM A 34 ("Kessler" Sketchbook). Corruptions to the text have not been rectified.

Salieri's hand, reveals a mystifying coincidence touching upon the latest of the Kessler entries, for we see that Salieri's revision here (example 14b)—the single emendation to affect harmonic shape—reverts almost literally to that final draft in the sketchbook. We ought to consider, at any rate, that Beethoven may have had a hand in this particular revision, though the scale in sixteenth notes leading to the high D♯ was drawn too quickly for the handwriting to be recognizable beyond all doubt either as Beethoven's or as Salieri's.

Ex. 14 Beethoven, *No, non turbarti,* autograph score—
Berlin, DStB, Artaria 165, mm. 33–40.

(a) Beethoven's final inked version.

(b) Penciled emendations, allegedly in Salieri's hand.

[] = unchanged by Salieri

It may in some sense be unfair to expect *No, non turbarti* to reflect qualities that Schulz had located in works by Graun, for the piece rightfully belongs to another eighteenth-century tradition: the neoclassic operatic *scena*—to which Beethoven's *Ah! perfido* also belongs. This is a genre that affords little opportunity for the intimate expression characteristic of chamber cantata, still less the interactions basic to true opera. The rhetorical vocabulary of the grandiose *scena* is rather less personal. But it is largely the inexpressive, overarticulated harmonic frame of *No, non turbarti* that leads to the suspicion that Beethoven turned to Sulzer's encyclopedia sometime after its completion, when he faced recitative in works destined for public performance.

The oratorio *Christus am Oelberge* provided a first opportunity. If there is a single work to which Beethoven could have turned for reference,

Graun's *Tod Jesu* comes closest in technical matters of characterization: the personification of Christ is a case in point, one which, by the way, came under attack in Sulzer's contribution to the recitative article. Sulzer blamed the poet Ramler for having Christ's most expressive complaints sung in the first person by the narrator; conceivably Beethoven and his librettist Huber profited from Sulzer's criticism as they worked out the mechanics of the text. While it is not clear from Carl Czerny's account of Beethoven's first contact with Graun's *Tod Jesu* whether this took place before or after the completion of *Christus*,[31] we ought at least to consider that Beethoven learned something of that work from the recitative essay. Both Sulzer and Schulz drew heavily upon it for illustration, and unlike most of the other of Graun's vocal works *Der Tod Jesu* was easily accessible in several printed editions.

As was suggested above, the cadence ". . . erbarm dich mein" at the close of the first recitative in *Christus* may well have been a recollection of a similar cadence at the end of the first recitative in Graun's *Disperata Porcia*. And I think there is additional internal evidence that recitative in *Christus* owes something to Schulz's essay. In particular, the Seraph's recitative to the second number in *Christus* (example 15) shows precisely the kind of harmonic continuity characteristic of the Graun illustrations. Successive sevenths resolve unconventionally, and the $\frac{4}{2}$ inversion is used with a degree of confidence and imagination lacking in the earlier *scena*.[32] There is obvious congruence here between step direction in the bass and descriptive textual content: Christ, abandoned by His Father, His face pressed to the ground, prepared for martyrdom and resurrection. Furthermore, the extended step progression which regulates the voice from A–G♯ in the opening phrase through its gradual ascent to D at ". . . ewig leben" may owe something to a nearly analogous recitative from *Der Tod Jesu*, "Ach, mein Immanuel! da liegt er, tief gebückt im Staube. . . ." Schulz drew two examples from this recitative, the second of which shows a brightening from F♯ minor to D major, first inversion, very much like what Beethoven has at ". . . zu sterben, damit die Menschen. . . ."

---

[31] Czerny recounted to Otto Jahn (in 1852) that Czerny's father brought a copy of Graun's *Tod Jesu* to Beethoven, who, upon reading through the score at sight, could find nothing worthy of praise. See Thayer-Deiters-Riemann II (1910), 559; Thayer-Forbes, I, 367.

[32] I have not indicated the orchestral interruptions here, since they do not alter the harmonic plan. The Berlin score (Artaria 179) shows that the 1803 version of the recitative lacked one of these orchestral elaborations, a point dealt with by Tyson, *op cit.*, 560–66; the final measures of the recitative, in a copyist's hand with Beethoven's memoranda for the addition of that orchestral interpolation, are given in facsimile (565).

Ex. 15 Beethoven, *Christus am Oelberge,* second recitative.

Ex. 16 Sulzer, from ex. 26.

It is a simple matter to locate other examples of similar harmonic usage in *Christus,* but in the remaining space I prefer to take up two recitatives composed the following year for the 1805 version of *Leonore.* The first is Leonore's apostrophe before the aria *Komm, Hoffnung: Ach, brich noch nicht du mattes Herz* (replaced in 1814 by the well-known *Abscheulicher, wo eilst du hin?*).

The numbers from the 1805 and 1806 versions of *Leonore* that were subsequently revised or replaced in 1814 are now available in Willy Hess's

critical edition.[33] A reduction of *Ach, brich noch nicht . . .* (example
17) shows something of its step progression. Schulz might well have

Ex. 17 Beethoven, *Leonore* (1805), recitative *Ach, brich
noch nicht, du mattes Herz.*

chosen this to demonstrate "traurige, sinkende Affekte," and the same
may be said of the next examples, the 1805 and 1806 versions of *Gott,
welch' Dunkel hier.* But a point of distinction ought to be drawn between
these (and other Beethoven examples from the same period) and the
examples cited by Schulz. While it is true that nearly all the recitatives in
Christus and *Leonore* express some degree of emotional distress, I think
there may have been a good musical reason for the prevalence of descending bass lines, over and above considerations stemming from the
mood of the text. Schulz was able to demonstrate that an ascending
bass may also express a plaintive text and may, indeed, be more appropriate to growing angst. But ascending semitones in the bass tend to
generate sequences in the upper parts, and if this was stylistically acceptable to Graun, Beethoven's workshop papers even before 1803 show an
uneasiness toward sequence—normally an early target in the revision
process.

---

[33] Hess, *Beethoven: Supplemente zur Gesamtausgabe*, XI–XIII (Wiesbaden,
1967–70).

In his study of the three versions of *Fidelio*, Willy Hess had some harsh words for the 1806 revision of *Gott, welch' Dunkel hier*.[34] It was incomprehensible to him that Beethoven should have replaced the exquisite E-major passage at "Doch gerecht ist Gottes Wille" (restored, with some revision, in 1814) with the conventional G-major passage which took its place in 1806. I shall not attempt to defend either view here, but there does seem to be some justification for Beethoven's revision of the first half of the recitative, through "o schwere Prüfung." The compass of the larger step-motion in the voice is restricted to a minor third, the initial impulse Db–C ("Gott . . . stille") is reversed at the crux of the phrase to C♯–D over an augmented sixth, and the entire phrase is supported by a classic example of chromatic descent in the bass.

Ex. 18 (a) Beethoven, *Leonore* (1805), recitative *Gott, welch' Dunkel hier!*

It must have been difficult for Beethoven to have discarded the ravishing phrase at "o schwere Prüfung," in some sense the measure of difference between the two versions, for it seems to have been his purpose in 1806 to reinterpret the nature of Florestan's introspection, from a kind of melancholy *Sehnsucht* remote from the real darkness of his plight, to a rather more realistic pessimism—reinforced by the linear diminished fifth at the augmented-sixth cadence. It bespeaks of Beethoven's growth between 1806 and 1814 that the final version, while it presents "o schwere Prüfung" very nearly as it had appeared in 1805, establishes a preparation for the F♯ through the Gb Neapolitan at "Oed ist es

---

[34] Willy Hess, *Beethovens Oper Fidelio und ihre drei Fassungen* (Zurich, 1953), pp. 100–03.

um mich her," raising the whole harmonic significance of the passage
far beyond the realm of simple associative interpretation.

(b) Beethoven, *Leonore* (1806), recitative *Gott, welch'*
Dunkel hier!

What, finally, can we say of the impact that Schulz's essay may have
had upon Beethoven's music? I have suggested that on the simplest level
Beethoven responded especially to those examples by Graun which show
step progression and root direction across a considerable expanse of text
—qualities missing in *No, non turbarti*. And while Beethoven must have
responded equally to Schulz's codification of affective text setting, it seems
to me more succinctly put that the general notion of a bass that moves
by step was largely what Beethoven needed here. From that premise his
own harmonic vocabulary would lead to solutions only vaguely reminis-
cent of eighteenth-century recitative. The *Leonore* examples are clear
enough in this respect: the protracted diminished chords which penetrate
the opening of *Gott, welch' Dunkel hier* show a control of harmonic
diffusion well beyond the sphere of Graun's usage.

I have dealt with Beethoven's sketches for *No, non turbarti* not to develop an argument which excludes that work from Schulz's influence, for
these sketches do show an effort at long-range harmonic design; in this
sense, the sketches only reinforce what we infer from the Bodmer leaves.
But those harmonic skeletons in Kessler show curious nonalignment with
text, and it is arguable that Beethoven had to abandon them when he
sought to put the text in an immediate setting. It is not clear how harmonic direction in those drafts was in any sense determined by expressive
event, though in purely musical terms their logic may have been convincing. Schulz may have taught Beethoven something here. If the har-

monic labyrinths which pass from F minor to the A♭ at the beginning of
Florestan's aria are in neither version quite convincing as extensions of
the instrumental music from which they grow, the text illuminates the
source of that ambiguity, makes it expressive, and finds a measure of interpretation there—a useful tautology in seeking to define the elusive
bond between text and music.

This is not to say that *Leonore* would have evolved much differently
had Beethoven not studied Schulz. What is significant is that Beethoven
saw himself able to profit from historical inquiry; and it is precisely this
conscious endeavor to absorb the past which informs his quest to the
very end.

APPENDIX

Contents of the Bodmer Leaf

(All poetic texts have been normalized to agree with their accepted readings.)

1ʳ. top of page: remark "Steigen und fallen der ~~Sylben~~ Stimmen sich nach der
zu oder abnehmende/Empfindung richten—" (Sulzer, page 8).

staff 1, right: remark "in steigende transpositionen/gut in der j[nstru-
mente?] Füllen(?)" (Beethoven's own gloss to the following example).

staffs 2–9, in left margin, opposite staffs 2–3: identification "apollo/amante/
di dafne" (Sulzer, page 13); text incipit "Ma o cielo! che veggo mai?"
(Sulzer, example 14, from Graun's cantata *Apollo amante di Dafne*).

staffs 10–13, in left margin, opposite staff 10: remark "das Erstaunens/und
der Freude" (Sulzer, page 13, a remark to the following example); text
incipit "Caro Unulfo, guida mi a lei" (Sulzer, example 15, from Graun's
opera *Rodelinda*, act 1, scene 7).

staff 12: remark "traurige klagende affecten" (from Sulzer, page 13, a
remark to the following example).

staffs 13–14: (Sulzer, example 16—see example 5 above).

staffs 15–16, in left margin: remark "dass die singstimme/zugleich mit der/
Harmonie steige/und falle" (Sulzer, page 13, to the following example);
text incipit "Ach mein Immanuel! Da liegt er . . ." (Sulzer, example
17, from Graun's *Tod Jesu*).

1ᵛ. staffs 1–2: continuation of example from bottom of folio 1ʳ.

staffs 3–8: text incipit "Voi, che inspiraste i casti affetti . . ." (Sulzer,
example 18, from Graun's *Demofoonte*, act 1, scene 4).

staffs 8–9, right: remark "die folgenden transpositionen, sen [35]/das gegen-

---

[35] Apparently a false start at "senkenden," not canceled.

theil von den vorigen/sind gut zu senkenden und traurigen/affecten"
(from Sulzer, page 13, to the following example).

staff 10: (Sulzer, example 19—see example 6 above).

staffs 12–15; text incipit "Klauen des Ungeheurs entriss!" (Sulzer, example
20, from Scheibe's cantata *Ariadne auf Naxos,* in *Zwei tragischen Cantaten* . . .).

2ʳ. top of page, left: remark "bessere ~~gute~~ solche Contraste. von Graun" (Sulzer, page 13, to the following example).

staffs 1–4: text incipit "Sposo, figlio, meta de miei sospiri . . ." (Sulzer,
example 22, from Graun's *Rodelinda,* act 1, scene 9).

staffs 4–10: text incipit "Confessarti—(che so?) . . ." (Sulzer, example 23,
from [attributed to] Graun's *Demofoonte,* act 1, scene 3).

staffs 12–13: remarks "ganze Cadenzen" and "wird förmlich/geschlossen/
auf die folgende/Bass Cadenz:" to examples of final cadences from
Sulzer, page 14.

staffs 14–16: text incipit "Lass dein Bruder dich umarmen" (Sulzer, example 24, the second line of examples there), followed by the remark "Nb:
hiedurch berückt man den Schlussfall der/Periode, und zugleich die
bewertung einer folge[nden]" (Sulzer, page 14).

2ᵛ. top of page: remark "Ausserdem begnügt man sich an der blossen Cadenz
der recitativstimme,/und einer darauf folgende Pause." (Sulzer, page
14—a remark which occurs earlier in the paragraph which contains the
remark at the bottom of folio 2ʳ).

staff 2: remark "Zu den Schlusscadenz ergänz(?)" (Sulzer, page 14, to the
following example).

staffs 3–11: text incipit "Du nimmst ihn nicht? Wohlan!" (Sulzer, example
26, from Graun's *Tod Jesu*).

staffs 12–15: substitute cadences, written in figured bass. Before the conventional final cadences, the remark "statt"; before the alternatives, the
remark "so auch" (Sulzer, example 27, and text examples on page 15).

staffs 15–16: two examples from the above, singled out from example 27
and reprinted in the text (page 15):

15   16 "gut zu steigenden Emfindungen [*sic*]"

15   16 "in sinkenden Leidenschaften"

"Extra" Measures
and Metrical Ambiguity
in Beethoven

Andrew Imbrie

�֎ THE EXISTENCE OF "strong" and "weak" measures in Beethoven's music has long aroused the curiosity of theorists and performers. Beethoven himself explicitly pointed the way to our investigation of still higher units of metrical organization through his famous indications "ritmo di tre battute" and "ritmo di quattro battute." A certain amount of ink has been spilled over the "correct" metrical interpretation of various passages; yet the proper study of these matters has often been hampered by a persistent confusion, not only over appropriate criteria, but over the nature of rhythm and meter. The problem is further complicated by an apparent reluctance on the part of theorists to think in terms of the formal and expressive possibilities inherent in metrical ambiguity itself.[1]

In the present essay I shall attempt to explore these issues through two examples from Beethoven's work. In each of these, there is an "extra" measure that does not fit into an otherwise tidy metrical scheme. In each case, a theorist has taken note of the problem.

I

The first example comes from the first movement of the Sonata in D Major, Op. 10, no. 3. Sir Donald Tovey, in his discussion of the first group of the exposition,[2] subdivides it into phrases, calling them the "four-bar unison theme" and three "six-bar phrases."

---

[1] A notable exception is the discussion of the performer's options by Edward T. Cone, *Musical Form and Musical Performance* (New York, 1968); particularly pp. 45 ff.

[2] Donald Francis Tovey, *A Companion to Beethoven's Pianoforte Sonatas* (London, 1947), pp. 60 ff.

Tovey quite rightly distinguishes this phrase structure from the metric structure that determines which points are strong or weak. His judgment of the metric structure is expressed by the statement: "The rhythm dates its main accent from bar 2." Although he gives no supporting arguments, we might supply two reasons for the plausibility of this interpretation. First, it places all four phrase endings, both fermate and both sforzandi at metrically accented points. Second, it presupposes a two-measure module, which can easily be heard as governing the harmonic flow. We can, without undue strain, perceive the first group as consisting of a dominant preparation (extending through measure 1) followed by two measures of I, six of V, two of I, four of V, and six of I— each harmonic change taking place at the beginning of an even-numbered measure.

Ex. 1

Example 1 illustrates this interpretation by means of metric reduction. Each quarter note of the diagram represents a full measure of music; the bar lines represent the division into two-measure units, each beginning with a metric accent on the first beat of an even-numbered measure. The heavy bar lines represent a higher grouping by multiples of these two-measure units, according to the perceived harmonic changes. A primary metric accent occurs after each heavy bar line. There is one such downbeat for each phrase, with the exception of the third, which has two. Each phrase ends with such a downbeat accent, and is, therefore, perceived as being masculine.

The first irregularity takes place at measure 22; for as Tovey states, in his analysis of the subsequent transition, "the accentuation of the whole paragraph must be dated from bar 23. To shift the accent elsewhere leads only to confusion." Measure 22, then, must be perceived as an isolated "extra" measure intruding upon the even flow of the two-measure units or their multiples. Here we may choose to regard the span of time between accents as having been foreshortened—an effect somewhat mitigated by the presence of the fermata, which lengthens the measure to a size comparable, if not equal, to that of the two-measure module already established. Or we may choose to hear the fermata as "standing for" a full two measures, but as specifying a relaxation in the rigidity of the metronomic count. Whichever way we hear it, however, the fermata must presumably be perceived, and hence performed, differently from the fermata at measure 4, which occurs without any accompanying change in the prevailing module.

Tovey's interpretation gives rise to another discrepancy between two similar events—this time thematic events. The sforzando at measure 4, when treated not only as a dynamic but also as a metric accent, creates a sense of decisive shift from the tonic to the dominant, which then prevails (as we have seen) for six measures. In a similar manner, the tonic chord at measure 10, when perceived as a strong masculine cadence, shifts the prevailing harmony back to I, which lasts until challenged by the entrance of the A in the bass just before measure 12. But although measures 5 and 11 are thematically parallel, the first is dominant in effect and the second tonic, as a result of the influence of the accents that precede them. This discrepancy, in turn, tends retroactively to weaken the effect of the masculine cadence at measure 10 and to raise the question of whether, indeed, it should have been perceived as a primary metric accent. Our suspicions are increased by the sudden forte at the upbeat to measure 11.

Finally, Tovey himself acknowledges what seems to be a serious difficulty in his own analysis, without resolving it. At the end of the exposition, he remarks, "the rhythm has changed step; nobody knows when." He is apparently referring to the fact that, starting with measure 113, a series of low A's in the bass has confirmed the meter beyond doubt by placing the accents at the beginnings of odd-numbered measures. When the repeat is taken, the continuation of this clear meter brings the music out with an accent, not at measure 2 but at measure 1.

Is Tovey's analysis simply erroneous? Before taking up this question, let us consider the alternative. Suppose that the end of the exposition, instead of failing to connect with the repeat, serves rather to clarify it. This hypothesis entails a radical revision of our analysis of the first group,

turn a succession of suspiciously pat and formalistic statements into a series of incomplete gestures, building one upon another to a point of crisis, but it provides, through this accumulation, sufficient and appropriate energy for the modulatory process that follows. The first coincidence of cadential accent with structural downbeat is deferred to measure 53, the point at which such a coincidence can be most effective.

Yet this second reading raises some questions too. First, there is the objection that the listener can have no foreknowledge of future subtleties and must, therefore, accept at face value the simplest interpretation of events as they occur. This familiar argument, if carried to its logical extreme, leads to an atomistic theory of musical perception, according to which music is assimilated as a stream of raw data by a simple cumulative process; such a theory leaves out of account the listener's ability both to anticipate probabilities and to revise former impressions. However, the question still remains, as a practical matter, whether in the present instance the listener is given sufficient opportunity to perceive the music at all according to the second, more "precarious" interpretation. Of course, the performer can do much to encourage such an interpretation, by stressing, in a number of possible ways, the suspenseful character of the fermate, by boldly attacking each new phrase, and by underplaying the cadential formulas. Yet the fact remains that these formulas *do* sound like cadences; the arrivals of tonic harmony *are* strongly marked; the pauses between phrases *do* separate those phrases. It may be observed, in addition, that the sense of closure at the tonic cadences is enhanced by the thematic structure: the second phrase has all the earmarks of the classical "consequent" phrase, completing and balancing the first, "antecedent," phrase. The third is a varied repetition or confirmation.

Tovey could have brought still another argument in favor of his interpretation. Although he could not ignore the difficulty of relating the end of the exposition to the repeat of the beginning, he could have supported his case by pointing to the recapitulation.

The dominant preparation for the recapitulation begins at measure 167, and establishes a clear meter at the four-measure level, with downbeats at the beginnings of measures 167, 171, 175, 179, and 183. Assuming that the fermata here does not upset this basic meter, the next downbeat —by continuation—comes at the first beat of measure 187, which corresponds to measure 4 of the exposition! The cadence of the six-measure consequent phrase comes on the next downbeat (measure 193, corresponding to measure 10), and when the new transition arrives, there is no longer any extra measure: we come out effortlessly in six measures on the downbeat of measure 205, corresponding to measure 23. Even the sudden forte that disturbed our serene acceptance of the importance of the first beat of measure 10 has been replaced at measure 193 by a mere crescendo.

Although these facts do not invalidate the second interpretation, they make it impossible to dismiss the first—at least as far as the recapitulation is concerned. It would appear that we are to hear the exposition in one way and the recapitulation in another. Or, to put it more exactly, the ambiguity exists from the start. Our initial predilection to hear the music Tovey's way is somewhat compromised at the outset by the metrical imbalance at measure 22, and still more by the eccentricity of phrase divisions that appear to be overarticulated in a context of almost explosive forward thrust. But we probably cannot supply, in retrospect, any viable alternative until the metrical situation is clarified for us by the end of the exposition and its connection with the repeat. At the recapitulation, on the other hand, the need for tonic harmony is greater, while the need for explosive forward thrust is much less—such thrust having largely spent itself by now. The time is ripe for resolution and reminiscence in measured phrases. And because of our original predilection, the simple structure of the recapitulation strikes us, paradoxically, not as a new interpretation, but as the return of an old one.

II

I have chosen to open with this example because it seems to offer a preliminary demonstration of Beethoven's technique of metrical ambiguity. In Op. 10, no. 3, the ambiguity appears not merely as a characteristic detail but as a creative force, and the strategy of its deployment affects the psychological impact of the whole movement. I am suggesting that we accept the following notions: that two contradictory metrical interpretations of the same event can be simultaneously entertained in the mind of the performer and listener; that the subjective "color" of that event is partly attributable to this contradiction; and that the composer can, wherever the event recurs, favor one or the other side of the contradiction, thereby helping to satisfy the dramatic or formal requirements of the music.

Since the appreciation of metrical ambiguity presupposes a clear definition of accent and its relation to meter, it may be well at this point to set forth a few of the guiding principles that underlie the present discussion of Beethoven's music. These principles are, I believe, close to those tacitly assumed by Tovey and Schenker, theorists whose work provides the stepping-off points for the analyses in sections I and III of this essay. These analyses are predicated on the concept of accent as a concrete meter-defining agent rather than as an abstract element on a vague prosodic model—an alternative concept that has come to the fore in certain recent writings on rhythmic theory, notably those of Cooper and

Meyer.[4] Among other difficulties that many have felt with the Cooper-Meyer theory is its difficulty of application to actual musical performance. The present analyses are predicated on a return to a more traditional method of inquiry; I hope they may serve to reaffirm for the theorist a concept whose practical usefulness to the conductor and performer remains undiminished.

"Accent means contrast, and vice-versa." [5] The structural role of accent is to fix or mark off those points in time which either establish, confirm, challenge, or overthrow the meter. Sessions's definition implies that accent has no duration. It is the fact of contrast or change that constitutes accent. A harmonic change per se has no duration; only the constituent harmonies have it. A dynamic change must be instantaneous if it is to create accent; dynamic changes involving duration (crescendo or diminuendo) have the effect of deferring accent until some decisive *point* is reached. The species of melodic accent called agogic—whereby a tone receives accent by virtue of its longer duration—is only an apparent exception to the rule, for our perception of the longer duration has the effect of causing us retroactively to place the accent at the point of attack. The same thing can be said for the accentual effect of placing a dynamic "swell" on a given tone.

Meter is established in the mind of the listener by those patterns of accentual recurrence that allow him to perceive a higher order. We have seen that two different kinds of recurrence can produce two alternative meters, especially on higher levels of organization. And especially at these higher levels, the recurrence need not be absolutely regular. It is perhaps necessary to emphasize this point, in view of a common and widespread assumption to the contrary. As has just been observed, the test for meter is simply that the sense of recurrence is present, and that such recurrence allows us to perceive a higher order. Regularity of recurrence is, of course, the surest way in which accents can be metrically oriented. But regularity on lower levels inevitably (at least in Beethoven) gives way to flexibility at higher levels of structure.

According to Edward Cone in *Musical Form and Musical Performance* (page 26, my italics):

> The classical phrase has often been analyzed as an alternation of strong and weak measures, on an analogy with strong and weak beats

---

[4] Grosvenor W. Cooper and Leonard B. Meyer, *The Rhythmic Structure of Music* (Chicago, 1960). See, for example, the discussion of accent on pp. 7–8, and such statements as: "Unaccent is an as- pect of accent, and a rhythmic group is an accented shape" (p. 119).

[5] Roger Sessions, *Harmonic Practice* (New York, 1968), p. 83.

within a measure. In other words, the larger rhythmic structure is treated simply as metric structure on a higher level. Now, I do not deny that such an alternation often occurs, especially in the case of short, fast measures; but I insist that on some level this *metric* principle of parallel balance must give way to a more organic *rhythmic* principle that supports the melodic and harmonic shape of the phrase and justifies its acceptance as a formal unit.

This insight into flexibility at higher levels is achieved at the expense of a blurring of the distinction between meter and rhythm. The idea that once an organization in time becomes flexible rather than mechanical it thereby becomes rhythmic rather than metrical stems from the notion that meter has to be absolutely regular. In my opinion, the distinction between meter and rhythm lies elsewhere, and we should now try to define it.

In the foregoing discussion of the opening of Op. 10, no. 3, the attempt was made to show that all accents are to be heard as occurring on specific beats—regardless of whether these accents are of local or of general significance. It was never claimed that an entire measure or group of measures was accented with respect to any other comparable unit. It is easy—and, therefore, tempting—to speak of "accented measures" rather than to use clumsy expressions like "measures on whose first beats the primary metric accents fall": yet the difference in meaning is important. The same semantic confusion exists in musicians' everyday use of the word "beat." Sometimes we treat it as if it meant a unit of duration, as in the expression "the second half of the beat." At other times we treat it as if it meant simply a point in time, as in "off the beat."

It is this distinction that I believe to be crucial to our understanding of the difference between rhythm and meter. For the present analysis, I shall stipulate that rhythm is the patterning or proportional arrangement of sounds and silences with respect to their durations, while meter is the measurement of the distances between points in time. Distance and duration are not synonymous: the former is the measure of the latter. (Compare the spatial distance between two points in geometry with an actual line drawn between or through them.) In studying a composer's manipulation of metric structure, it is important to be able to treat accent as the specific agent responsible for the fixing of instants, or points, in time; and to keep this function clearly separated from the essentially motivic function of a rhythmic, or durational, pattern, which may be placed in various positions with respect to such points in time. It is true that the motivic pattern may be one of the elements whose accentual content helps to establish the meter, but many other accentual factors (e.g. harmonic, linear) must also be taken into account.

Cone remarks that "there is a sense in which a phrase can be heard as an upbeat to its own cadence," and that "larger and larger sections can also be so apprehended." [6] In my opinion, this statement describes our apprehension of musical phrases and sections very well, provided that the term *upbeat* is understood as referring to a *durational* unit, and *cadence* as the *point* in time at which the primary metric accent occurs. *Upbeat,* in this context, would mean a *rhythmic* element characterized by a sense of preparation for a forthcoming *metrical* event.

It might be nice to have a terminology that could distinguish an *upbeat* (in the sense of a relatively lightly accented point) from, let us say, an *anacrusis* (in the sense of a passage of music perceived as building toward an imminent downbeat). Cone is using *upbeat* for *anacrusis,* as hypothetically defined here. In similar fashion, theorists sometimes refer to durational units (motives, phrases) as being *accented.* Since it is true that an important downbeat accent may impart a generalized sense of greater heaviness to an entire rhythmic unit, perhaps this phenomenon could be described by some such term as *weighting,* to distinguish it from accentuation itself. *Weighting* would then be the opposite of the "upbeat quality" (*Auftaktigkeit*) attributable to what we have just called *anacrusis.*

Let us return now to the question of regularity and flexibility. It has already been proposed that our sense of metrical organization depends not upon regularity as such, but more generally upon a sense of recurrence. The importance of recurrence lies in its ability to establish and to distinguish hierarchical levels of structure. The degree to which, and the levels at which, an approach to regularity will be felt as necessary in order to bring about the effect of recurrence will vary greatly among composers, among individual works according to the relative complexity of their formal requirements, and, of course, among styles and eras. Having said this much, I believe that it is only fair to acknowledge that meter acts as a conservative force. It is the principle that attempts to reduce to "law and order" the protean rhythmic complexities of the musical surface. It is the frame of reference by which we try to measure and judge the relative values of the changes taking place in the music. Our desire for security prompts us to accept the simplest, most nearly regular interpretation of events, unless and until they force us to seek the next simplest. And our desire for order leads us to seek as many higher levels of metrical organization as our powers of attention and synthesis will allow.

---

[6] Cone, *op. cit.,* p. 26.

III

These observations should help to throw light on problems such as that of the "extra" measure. The laws of "conservation of simplicity" and "separation of levels" should account for the fact that, for example, a $\frac{1}{4}$ measure occurring in a prevailing metrical context of $\frac{4}{4}$, tends to be understood as an elongation of the measure preceding or following it, rather than as a measure in its own right. Perceived in this way, the departure from regular metric reccurence is much less extreme, and the separation between the levels of organization (quarter-note level and measure level) remains undisturbed. To state it another way, if two strong metric accents succeed one another at an uncharacteristically close interval of time, we attempt to hear one as taking precedence over the other (i.e. as occurring at a higher level).

Heinrich Schenker, in his discussion of the development of the first movement of the Fifth Symphony,[7] asks us, in effect, to accept measure 208 as an "extra" measure. Up to this point, his analysis of the entire movement has clearly shown the operation not only of a two-measure module, but in addition, of a norm of four measures that is indispensable to the proper understanding and performance of the principal rhythmic motive. In Schenker's analysis, compound groupings of eight or twelve measures are common, and departures from the four-measure module occur in multiples of two to form occasional extended groupings of six, ten, or fourteen. The only exceptions, so far, occur at measures 6 and 25, which are treated as independent anacruses and are not counted. The justification for this is that both of these measures are immediately preceded by fermate, which in turn, by lengthening the end of the motive, dramatize its independent character at the outset, and hence facilitate its later recognition as a unit. In fact it is this very independence, in the case of the first four measures, that provides Schenker with a strong argument in favor of the metric as well as rhythmic importance of the four-measure unit throughout.

Measure 208, however, he regards as the fifth (relatively accented)

---

[7] Heinrich Schenker, "Beethoven V Sinfonie," *Der Tonwille,* I (1921). The bulk of the chapter on the first movement has just been reprinted in translation in Elliot Forbes, ed., *Beethoven: Symphony No. 5 in C Minor,* Norton Critical Scores (New York, 1971). This excerpt leaves out, among other things, some pieces of advice to the performer and some rebuttals of statements by other theorists. I shall quote the Forbes-Adams translation wherever possible, but for the quotations from the latter part of the chapter I shall be obliged to rely on my own translation.

measure of a six-measure group which then *overlaps* by one measure
with the beginning of another six-measure group at measure 209. His
diagram shows it in this manner:

Ex. 3

Measure 209 is treated as simultaneously weak and strong, depending
on which of the two overlapping groups is being considered.

Assuming the validity of the rule proposed above, requiring the
precedence of one of any two closely contiguous strong accents, we
would be obliged to assign precedence to the downbeat of measure 209,
since it initiates the subsequent metrical grouping (just as the first beat
of a measure is, metrically, the strongest of that measure). Thus measure
208 would be "extra," and would become, in fact, the last of a five-
measure group. Example 4 shows this by metric reduction.

Ex. 4

Schenker's diagram, as we have seen, portrays the groupings as though
they were six-measure units. These, then, intersect at a junction that
marks off the melodic completion of the outline of the fourth, F–B♭:

> By reinterpreting m. 209 as a strong measure (although it was origi-
> nally weak) followed by a weak m. 210, the nodal point becomes
> especially underlined, so that from here on there is no longer any
> difficulty in recognizing that only the winds have the strong measures.

. . . When Beethoven places the diminuendo for the strings already at B♭ in measure 210 as against C♭ in the following measure for the winds, he thereby establishes the character of that measure as weak with respect to 209—what a profound stroke of genius! [8]

The question arises, however, whether the reinterpretation of a single measure provides explanation enough for the effect of this passage as perceived from the metric point of view. That a metrical shift takes place there can be no doubt. Unlike the "extra" measures of Op. 10, no. 3, the one in the Fifth Symphony cannot be even provisionally explained out of existence through regrouping. It can only be relocated—and, as Schenker has shown, this has been attempted (Müller-Reuter, for instance, places it at measure 216 [9]). The problem is that there is an odd number of measures separating the downbeat of measure 126 (the beginning of the development) from that of measure 249 (the recapitulation), and this fact must be explained somehow in metrical terms. But relying on any single measure to account for the phenomenon is a little like putting an excessive number of rather delicate eggs in one basket.

The listener's intuitive response to the passage in question is that of one who has been led step by step into a precarious position. The motives have been liquidated; the texture has been radically simplified and now consists of the raw alternation of chords between winds and strings; the harmonies seem to have traveled far from the home tonic. (The actual logic of their relation to the basic key has, of course, been thoroughly demonstrated by Schenker.) The rhythms, too, I believe, have been deployed throughout the preceding measures in such a way as to prepare the ear gradually for the metrical dislocation. Both preparation and dislocation are accomplished through metrical ambiguity on a large scale.

To demonstrate this, it will be necessary first to allude briefly to the exposition, and to examine a simpler ambiguity. Schenker's analysis establishes the four-measure module as the metric basis for all the music from measure 44 through measure 79, after which he postulates a fourteen-measure unit, to bring the music to the clear downbeat at the beginning of measure 94.

An advantage of this reading is that by placing the downbeat of a four-measure unit on the E♭ of the horn call (measure 60), it emphasizes the motivic resemblance between this and the opening subject. For the two can then be shown to be identical not only in general contour and in length, but also in placement with regard to the metric accent. This

---

[8] Schenker, *op. cit.*, pp. 13 (= Forbes, *op. cit.*, pp. 178–79), 18.

[9] T. Müller-Reuter, *Lexikon der deut-* *schen Konzertliteratur, Nachtrag* (Leipzig, 1921), pp. 22–23.

Ex. 5

consideration weighs heavily with Schenker.[10] But he also makes much of the fourteen-measure extension that follows (measures 80–93), stating that its cumulative power partly depends on its having exceeded what he regards as the eight-measure span of the preceding groups. One could mention another reason why the listener might be disposed to hear the passage according to Schenker's interpretation: the inherent resistance to change in every listener will cause him to cling to the four-measure module as long as possible; thus the end of the fourteen-measure unit is the latest point at which a change can be made in recognition of the primacy of the structural downbeat at the beginning of measure 94.

Of course, this is not the first time that the four-measure module has been violated: the ten-measure extension (measures 34–43) has already provided a prototype. Furthermore, the distortions and rhythmic displacements of the motive that immediately follow (measures 44 ff.), and that are associated with the modulation, increase the sense of stress, as Schenker has shown. He regards the E♭ at measure 60 as the point at which all this tension is released: "The introductory motto of the second subject, with its emphatic expression, re-establishes contact with the metrical scheme that had been broken during the modulation: the half notes E♭ and B♭ appear again in the first and third measures of the group." [11]

But is it not possible also to hear the second subject in another way? The stresses developed in the course of the modulation may just possibly prove too powerful to admit of an instant resolution on the tonic of the new key, falling within a re-established four-measure scheme. Consider, then, the alternative of a six-measure group preceding a structural downbeat on the B♭ at measure 62.

Ex. 6

This, by the way, is also Riemann's interpretation, to which Schenker objects only on the ground that it does not reflect any awareness of a motivic correspondence with measures 1 through 4.

---

[10] Tovey also scans the passage in this way: see his essay on the Fifth Symphony in *Essays in Musical Analysis* (London, 1935), I, 38–44, reprinted in Forbes (cf. especially p. 146, ex. 2).

[11] Schenker, *op. cit.*, p. 9 (= Forbes, p. 173).

One effect of this interpretation is to change the cadence in E♭ from full to half—which, in my opinion at least, is more consistent not only with an effective dramatic deployment of the resources of tonality (the deferment of a decisive cadence in the new key until a later point) but even with Schenker's own linear analysis, which reveals the crucial importance of B♭ at this moment. Besides, the B♭ is strongly emphasized by the fact that it initiates a thirteen-measure pedal point. The B♭ is also clearly favored by Beethoven's dynamics: the *ff* marking at measure 59 applies to the entire horn solo; the *sf* on all three half-notes assures their equality of emphasis, except that the sudden diminuendo after the attack on the B♭ marks it off as more "interesting," an impression confirmed by the contrast of the subsequent *p, dolce, legato* in the strings. In this connection it is curious to note that here, and only here, Schenker recommends to the performer a distortion of Beethoven's dynamics: "If the meaning of measures 63 ff is to be rendered, the following articulation must be applied: 4 | 1 2 3 4 | 1 in measures 63–74, and 4 | 1 2 3 4 | 1 in measures 75–82." [12] By stressing the first (weak) measure of the violin melody, he not only contradicts the spirit of Beethoven's *dolce* but cancels out the effect of the horn diminuendo, which places the accent at a point unacceptable to Schenker.

As a final argument in favor of this interpretation, one might add that the placement of the principal metric accent on the last note of the motive does not really conceal its correspondence with the original motive of measures 1–5. In fact, one could regard it as an exploitation of a metrical ambiguity already inherent in the original motive—an ambiguity enhanced rather than destroyed by the lengthening of the second fermata (measures 4 and 5). And the distortions of the motive beginning at measure 44, far from merely providing tension to be released all at once, can be explained as helping to prepare the ear for a transfer of accent to the last note.

If this interpretation is accepted, it will have the further effect of nullifying the irregularity of Schenker's fourteen-measure extension (measures 80–93), and bringing it into line with the four-measure module. The sense of broadening is still present, however, to the extent that three fairly distinct four-measure units (measures 70 ff.) are followed by a homogeneous twelve-measure unit (measures 82 ff.).

The point of the comparison of these two readings is, once again, not to make a final decision as to which is correct, but to show that both are

---

12 *Ibid.*, p. 18.

Ex. 7

possible. The ambiguity raised in the exposition has its consequences in the development, to which we should now return. Upon the reappearance of the horn-call motive, this time in the violins, Schenker places his structural downbeat at the beginning of measure 180. This is consistent with his earlier decision, and plausible in its context. It is made possible, among other things, by the previous foreshortening of the last member of a sequence of large-scale anticipations, beginning at measure 158 and leading to a downbeat at measure 168. Schenker has shrewdly drawn attention to the increase in velocity of the downward bass movement at measure 167, which has the effect of precipitating this downbeat and inhibiting us from accepting it as the beginning of another two-measure anticipation. Thus the group ends up containing fourteen rather than sixteen measures, and is followed by a twelve-measure group leading into measure 180.

Once the primary metric accent of the motive has been unequivocally assigned to its first measure (180), the consequences drawn by Schenker are inescapable: motivic and metric consistency demand equivalent downbeats at the beginnings of measures 188 and 196. By continuation of this logic, the succeeding patterns of paired chords must then be perceived as having accents at the beginning of each pair. Thus we are led to the confrontation that must be resolved before the end of the development, by which time the accents clearly fall at the beginnings of odd-numbered measures. Schenker's solution, already described, has at least the virtue of locating the reversal of accent at the most inconspicuous possible place.

Let us now entertain the other alternative, suggested for the horn-call motive in the exposition, by placing the primary accent at measure 182. This has one immediate and perhaps surprising consequence: it removes the need for Schenker's foreshortening of the two-measure anticipation. The four-measure module, firmly established from the beginning of the development, may be clung to with relative impunity until it brings us to our downbeat at measure 182. I mention this only in order to suggest that there may be a deeply buried, ultraconservative layer of our consciousness as listeners which will persist in interpreting our experience for us as long as possible within an established framework, even in the face of increasingly disturbing events. If this is so, it can perhaps be said to contribute, somewhat obscurely, to our predilection for an accent at measure 182.

Not that Schenker's argument for an accent at measure 168 can be dismissed; this metrical shift of two measures is only the first of that series of disturbing events which, in my opinion, prepare the ear to accept the still more disturbing disruption of the two-measure module itself.

The accent at measure 168 is separated from our downbeat at measure 182 by another fourteen measures, the first eight of which form a separable part by virtue of their divisibility into two rhythmically identical subunits of four each.

Ex. 8

The remaining six measures would then be analogous to our six-measure group beginning at measure 56 in the exposition, in its function of introducing the horn-call motive. In the present instance, the metrical situation *within* the group (measures 176–181) has become unstable as a result of the liquidation of the preceding rhythmic figure, so that we can imagine it as either three groups of two or two groups of three measures. The former interpretation is, of course, the conservative one; but the latter is crucial to the eventual absorption of the "extra" measure into the metrical scheme. One indication of the plausibility of this grouping is the accent created by the bass when it cuts off at the F♯ in measure 179 (note that the analogous D of measure 58 occurs at the third measure of the group, whereas the present F♯ initiates the fourth measure of the group). Another factor that adds to the importance of measure 179 is the melodic completion of the double-neighboring-note motion around D. (There are emphatic Ds in the melody at measures 176, 179, and 182, a fact that encourages still more our hearing groups of three measures.)

So far the primacy of the accent at measure 182 has not been questioned. If we do not do so, we shall be obliged by reason of consistency to supply a similar accent at measure 190 and, by analogy, at measure 198. We would then find ourselves, as Schenker did, with the accent on the first of each pair of chords, and would face the same dilemma in trying to sense some subsequent one-measure shift.

If, however, instead of counting from measure 182 we count from measure 179, everything comes out smoothly. The analogous accents at measures 187 and 195 confirm us in our choice by marking strong cadences, and the subsequent grouping of the chords into end-accented pairs proceeds without further difficulty.

What is proposed, then, is the metrical reinterpretation, not of a single measure, but of a three-measure group: measures 179–181. This group should be understood, simultaneously, as the last half of a six-measure group and the first part of an eight-measure group. Such an interpretation, if acceptable on other grounds, would be desirable because of its greater smoothness and its more organic integration into the larger metrical scheme. Smoother because it has a less disrupting effect on the listener's perception of the periodicity of metric accents, and more organic because the listener's acceptance of the three-measure group in question

Ex. 9

has been prepared in advance and confirmed by subsequent reiteration. The advance preparation consists, in part, of the matching of the two three-measure groups within the ambiguous six-measure unit, measures 176–181, which resembles the matching of the two four-measure groups of measures 168–175. (The shift from fours to threes is reflected in the rhythmic condensation at measures 176–179.) Confirmation by subsequent reiteration is achieved through matching the two eight-measure groups, subdivided each into three plus five (measures 179–194). The acceptance of all these odd-numbered groupings is facilitated by just such parallelisms, on the principle that two odd numbers add up to a larger even number. (Compare the two seven-measure groups in the first movement of Op. 10, no. 3: measures 53–59 and 60–66.) The entire operation is summarized in the following diagram:

Ex. 10

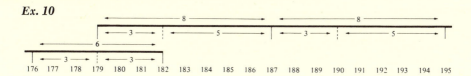

Two final observations may be of interest. First, the grouping of the chords into end-accented pairs (measures 196 ff.) seems, to this listener at least, intuitively more satisfying in itself than the opposite grouping. Among a number of possible reasons for this is, perhaps, a "subliminal" association with the pattern of the accompaniment to the *dolce* violin melody (measures 63 ff.), which also occurs immediately following the horn-call motive.

Second, just as an attempt has been made here to push the "conservative" interpretation of events as far forward as possible in order to see how long one could cling to an established pattern, it might be interesting to see how far back one could push a "radical" interpretation in order to see how soon one could adopt a new pattern. It might be possible, then, to group measures 168–178 in this way:

Ex. 11

The acceptance of an isolated three-measure group at measures 168-170 is encouraged by the change of harmony on the (syncopated) downbeat of measure 171: note that here, for the first time, the initial pattern of three short notes is identical, both melodically and harmonically, with what follows. Although this interpretation may be difficult to accept per se as the vehicle for the accomplishment of the metrical shift, it may at least contribute to the preparation of the ear for the acceptance of the "real" shift soon to follow. There have been times when I have found myself hearing the passage in this way.

It is my belief, however, that when the experienced listener is at his peak of alertness and receptivity, he is capable of responding on several simultaneous metric levels. It is not so much that he consciously and systematically keeps track of the various metrical interpretations of events, but rather that he responds directly and intuitively to the tensions between or among them—just as he responds directly to both the local and the more general structural significance of a harmony or, on occasion, to its pivotal role. Beethoven, more than any other composer, produced masterworks that engage our sensibilities in this way.

A Reconstruction of
the Pastoral Symphony
Sketchbook

(British Museum Add. MS. 31766)

Alan Tyson

I

✳ THE PUBLICATION in 1961 of Dagmar Weise's transcription of a Beethoven sketchbook from the year 1808, commonly known as the Pastoral Symphony Sketchbook and now in the British Museum, was the signal for a renewed interest in its contents, which had been almost entirely neglected since the time of Nottebohm.[1] Yet one feature of the sketchbook that clearly troubled Nottebohm is not allowed for in Dr. Weise's transcription, and is dealt with somewhat tersely in her introduction: the fact that very many years ago a substantial number of its leaves had been torn or cut out. In a short article called "A Sketchbook of the Year 1808," which he published in 1878, Nottebohm wrote:

> I call it a sketchbook, but it is only a part of one. Today it contains 59 leaves, but originally it consisted of 87 or 88 leaves. At 15 separate places 28 or 29 leaves have been cut out, in other words about a third of the original contents. It is not known who was responsible for this vandalism. That it could have been Beethoven who cut out the leaves

---

[1] *Beethoven: Ein Skizzenbuch zur Pastoralsymphonie Op. 68 und zu den Trios, Op. 70, 1 und 2*, Vollständige, mit einer Einleitung und Anmerkungen versehene Ausgabe von Dagmar Weise, 2 vols. (Bonn, 1961). Cf. in particular the review by Lewis Lockwood of this edition, *The Musical Quarterly*, LIII (1967), 128, and Joseph Kerman, "Beethoven Sketchbooks in the British Museum," *Proceedings of the Royal Musical Association*, XCIII (1966–67), 77.

is unthinkable. In circumstances like these it is clear that the gradual growth of a movement cannot be observed.[2]

Nottebohm quite possibly regarded the missing leaves as lost beyond recovery, although (as we now know) he had described some of them in an article published only ten months earlier.[3] Today there is reason to believe that the location of nearly all these leaves is known; and if we are interested in following "the gradual growth of a movement" we must do our best to restore them wherever possible, at any rate in concept, to their original sites and thus to reconstruct the former condition of the sketchbook. For it should scarcely need saying that such a reconstruction is an essential prerequisite to any comprehensive study of its contents.

II

A general description of the sketchbook's present condition and an account of what is known of its history will be found in Dr. Weise's introduction to the first volume of her transcription. It can, however, be supplemented at a number of points. There now appears to be little doubt about the following sequence of events. The sketchbook remained in Beethoven's possession till his death, and at the auction of his *Nachlass* on November 5, 1827, it was acquired by Anton Gräffer, a member of the firm of Artaria & Co., for 1 florin 15 kreuzer. (The evidence for this will be reviewed later on.) On September 12, 1842, as is explained in an inscription on the cover, Gräffer, in Vienna, gave it to his friend Ferdinand Simon Gassner of Karlsruhe. Gassner died in 1851; the sketchbook remained for a while with his family, but by 1876 it had passed into the possession of the Karlsruhe bookseller Adolf Horchler, where it aroused the interest of Johannes Brahms. Brahms tried to prevent it being put up for sale in England, but on April 23, 1879, it was auctioned in London by Messrs. Puttick & Simpson and acquired by Julian Marshall for 55 pounds.[4] It seems to have been Marshall who had the volume handsomely

---

[2] Gustav Nottebohm, "Ein Skizzenbuch aus dem Jahre 1808," *Musikalisches Wochenblatt*, IX (Aug. 30, 1878), 429; reprinted in a much modified form in N II, ch. XXVIII, p. 252. My reasons for citing Nottebohm's statements from the *Wochenblatt* rather than from the much better known 1887 book, which was assembled and published after his death, are given below.

[3] Nottebohm, *Musikalisches Wochen-*

blatt, VIII (Oct. 26, 1877), 593; reprinted with considerable modifications in N II, ch. XL, p. 369.

[4] At Sale no. 1827 of Puttick & Simpson, lot 110. Cf. the "Catalogue of a most interesting and valuable collection of autograph letters, chiefly musical and literary; also of original manuscript compositions, mostly from the celebrated collection of Aloys Fuchs, including Beethoven's Pastoral Symphony" (copy in the

bound in white parchment. Finally in 1880 it was purchased from Marshall, together with other manuscripts, by the British Museum. It should
be noted that nothing in the above brief history of the sketchbook's ownership throws any light on the removal of the leaves; this is a problem that
we shall have to return to later.

Nottebohm's own account of the sketchbook has considerable importance for us, especially since he evidently had access to a book whose
condition differed in certain important respects from its present state. It
is clear that when he published his first account of sketches for the *Pastoral Symphony* in 1877 he had not yet seen the sketchbook. He described
the extant sketches, which he took from the sketchbook Landsberg 6 and
from the miscellanies Landsberg 10 and Landsberg 12, as "meagre," [5] and
it was his subsequent acquaintance with the London sketchbook that
prompted a second article from him within ten months on sketches for
the same symphony. Unfortunately the relationship between Nottebohm's
two articles (1877 and 1878) has been obscured by their republication
after his death in *Zweite Beethoveniana* (1887). It is not merely that the
article printed on a later page in that collection (Dr. Weise even writes
of "ein späterer Artikel") was in fact written earlier, but that some of the
material first printed in the 1878 article was later transferred to chapter
XI of *Zweite Beethoveniana,* which gives a superficial impression of repro-
ducing the 1877 one. How far the responsibility for this confusion lies
with Nottebohm and how far with Eusebius Mandyczewski, who edited
Nottebohm's posthumous collection, it is now impossible to say. The resulting mélange of imperfectly identified sources (a feature of Nottebohm's writing that we have to learn to live with) is carefully clarified
by Dr. Weise in the course of her introduction (page 11, note 26); but it
needs to be stressed that the original discussion of sketches for the *Pastoral Symphony* in the *Wochenblatt* of 1877 contains no reference whatever to the London sketchbook. I shall, therefore, take the original version of Nottebohm's paper on the sketchbook, in the 1878 *Wochenblatt,*
as my starting point.

Nottebohm states there with admirable precision, but with an exas-
perating lack of supporting data, that at the time that he examined the
book it consisted of fifty-nine leaves (in an old blue cover), but that
originally it had contained eighty-seven or eighty-eight leaves; at fifteen
places twenty-eight or twenty-nine leaves had been excised. Since it still

---

British Museum). Several of the lots
consisted of letters to Gassner from musicians, mostly written in the 1820s, 1830s,
and 1840s.

[5] Nottebohm, *Musikalisches Wochenblatt,* VIII (Oct. 26, 1877), 593: "Skizzen zur Pastoral-Symphonie sind uns
spärlich zugemessen."

contains fifty-nine leaves today,[6] Nottebohm evidently saw the same
leaves as we do. But nothing now remains to indicate that "28 or 29
leaves" have been removed at "15 separate places." All we can see is
that between folios 42^v and 43^r there are the stubs of two missing leaves.
An old foliation of the volume has a gap of two numbers at this point
but at no other place, and it appears that two leaves corresponding to "42"
and "43" of the old foliation must have been removed here, leaving their
stubs behind them, at a later date than that of the other depredations—
though still before Nottebohm counted the leaves late in 1877 or early in
1878.[7] Thus it looks as though Nottebohm must have found the stubs of
many more excised leaves, from which he drew his precise figures. Presumably these stubs, of which there is no sign today (apart from the stubs
of the two leaves "42" and "43"), were removed when Julian Marshall had
the book bound; and perhaps the stubs of "42" and "43" were retained by
the binder since, unlike the other detached leaves, they were included in
the "old" foliation. Unfortunately, apart from telling us that the first four
leaves of the sketchbook (i.e. folios 2 through 5 in the British Museum's
"new" foliation, since the blue cover counts as folio 1) are intact and that
the first break comes after them, Nottebohm gives no further information
that would help us to locate the "15 places" at which leaves have been
removed.

III

Today, however, we are in a better position than Nottebohm to
scrutinize the extant sketch leaves for the *Pastoral Symphony* and for the
Op. 70 trios, the first of which is worked on at some length in this book.
As a result of Dr. Weise's investigations, on lines already hinted at by
Josef Braunstein in 1927,[8] it is now clear that most of the missing leaves
from the Pastoral Symphony Sketchbook have been for very many years
in a Berlin miscellany, the volume known as Landsberg 10. This miscellany was among the books once owned in the last century by Ludwig
Landsberg, and on his death in 1858 it was bequeathed to the Königliche
Bibliothek in Berlin; today it is in the Stiftung Preussischer Kulturbesitz
in West Berlin. Of its total of eighty-seven diverse leaves there are

---

[6] Weise, I, 9, erroneously says that it
still contains "60 sechzehnzeilige Noten-
blätter."

[7] The entry in Puttick & Simpson's
auction catalogue states that the book
consisted of sixty-one leaves ("leaves 42
and 43 cut out"): Weise, I, 10.

[8] Cf. Josef Braunstein, *Beethovens
Leonore-Ouvertüren: eine historisch-
stilistische Untersuchung* (Leipzig,
1927), pp. 38–39.

twenty-eight which, from the identity of their paper, watermark, and rastrology (staff-ruling),[9] and from the similarity in the content of the sketches, are clearly from the London book; they are paginated 103–114, 117–124, and 129–164, and in what follows they will be referred to by these page numbers preceded by the letter L. These leaves were evidently removed from the London sketchbook *before* it was first foliated, since none of them shows any traces of a numbering that preceded their present pagination. We have already noted that at least two leaves were removed *after* the first foliation. The second of these two ("43" in the "old" foliation) was found by Dr. Weise in the Bodmer Collection of the Beethovenhaus in Bonn;[10] the first ("42") has not been traced so far.[11] But the Bodmer Collection in fact contains a further leaf from the sketchbook that still retains its "old" foliation, "62," evidently the leaf with which the sketchbook once concluded; it has been identified only very recently.[12] One leaf which cannot, however, be traced today is pages 115/116 of Landsberg 10, which—according to a note in Landsberg's hand on L 114 —was given away by Landsberg as a present to the wife of the French ambassador, the "Gräfinn von Renevall," on March 6, 1852.[13] Summing up, it appears that we now know the whereabouts of thirty leaves from the sketchbook (twenty-eight in Landsberg 10, and two, "43" and "62" of the "old" foliation, in Bonn); and two leaves, evidently once part of the book, are still untraced ("42" of the "old" foliation and the ambassadorial L 115/116). It will be seen that these figures tally closely with those suggested by Nottebohm; he seems, however, to have made a slight underestimate of the damage.

---

[9] The span of the staffs from top to bottom varies from just over 195 mm. on some pages to just under 197 mm. on others. At the right-hand end of the second staff the middle line is consistently shorter than the other four lines. Both these features are discussed further below.

[10] SV 121; SBH 619; in Max Unger, *Eine Schweizer Beethovensammlung* (Zurich, 1939), pp. 168–69, it is catalogued as Mh 74.

[11] Dr. Weise's identification of it as L 137/138 (Weise, I, 10, n. 25) is unacceptable, not least because those pages clearly belong between 35^v and 36^r. It is in any case unlikely that "42" would find its way into the same miscellany as the leaves that were removed earlier— particularly when we know that "43" did not do so.

[12] SV 178; SBH 712. Cf. Alan Tyson, "Stages in the Composition of Beethoven's Piano Trio Op. 70, No. 1," *Proceedings of the Royal Musical Association*, XCVII (1970–71), 19.

[13] Weise, I, 12, n. 35 (where the name has been misread as "Benevalle"). This was the wife of Alphonse Gérard de Rayneval (1813–58), French ambassador in Rome from 1851 to 1857.

IV

In reconstructing any sketchbook we need to know the places from which leaves have been removed, and we are forced to devise a variety of techniques for determining the original positions of any of the detached leaves that have survived. These techniques will vary in the light of the somewhat different problems that each sketchbook presents. Much the best method for locating the places from which leaves have been lost is via an analysis of the sketchbook's physical structure—or, in bibliographical terms, of its make-up. Such an analysis, if it indicates that the sketchbook was originally constructed on a regular pattern, will at the same time expose the places at which that pattern has been broken and suggest very strongly that leaves have been detached at those points.[14] Unfortunately, in the case of the Pastoral Symphony Sketchbook no *direct* examination of its physical make-up is now possible, since the way in which the volume was rebound in 1879, with very tight stitching, trimming and gilding of the upper margins, and (it seems) the removal of almost all the stubs of torn-out leaves prevents the original gatherings from being distinguished. Here, in fact, we are obliged to reverse the more usual order of reconstruction work and to determine the correct positions of most of the loose leaves by other means before resolving the question of the sketchbook's structure. Two techniques which have proved useful in the present case are the examination of blots and the study of the continuity in the sketch contents. Each merits a short discussion.

(a) The pages of Beethoven's sketchbooks are liberally bespattered with blots and smudges. The connoisseur can distinguish various types. First, there are the inkblots that come from the writing itself—the results of Beethoven closing a sketchbook while the ink of the notes or words that he has just written is still wet. Besides usually smudging the notes or words themselves this is likely to produce a corresponding blot or series of blots, known as an "offset," on the opposite page. Second, there are the blots of ink that have fallen on the page as a result of the composer's clumsy handling of his quill pen. These inkdrops, being larger and "juicier" than most of the written material, might be expected to produce even more conspicuous offsets. But that does not seem to happen much, and it may be that their very size warned Beethoven not to close the book or

---

14 For a fuller discussion of the analysis of the structure of sketchbooks as an aid to their reconstruction the reader is referred to Douglas Johnson and Alan Tyson, "Reconstructing Beethoven's Sketchbooks," *Journal of the American Musicological Society*, XXV (1972), 137–56.

turn the page till they had dried. Whenever we find an offset that clearly mirrors something written by Beethoven we can be certain that the pages in question faced each other in Beethoven's time; and the same is true in the case of those offsets that can be matched with inkdrops from a quill, provided that the drops were made by Beethoven himself (as seems likely) and not by some later owner of the book.

A third type might be called a "dry" offset—a mark produced on the opposite page by a very heavily inked passage long after the original ink is dry. Since dry offsets—which are really smears of dried pigment—can be produced at any time, they cannot be taken as evidence of the relation between two pages in Beethoven's day. Usually it is only the darkest blots of ink that produce a discernible dry offset; but almost anything written with Beethoven's *Rötel*, or red crayon, will rub off to some extent on the opposite page and produce a pinkish tinge there. As in the case of dry offsets from ink, such dry crayon smears cannot be taken as proof that the adjacent pages stood in the same relation in Beethoven's day; but when a pink smear is found opposite a page that contains nothing written in *Rötel* the suspicion must arise that a leaf bearing writing in *Rötel* has been removed at that point.[15]

The process of matching blots with offsets does not call for much comment. In the present instance there is some reason to conclude from a study of the contents (see the next paragraph) that the original sequence of the leaves has not been disturbed, except by pruning. In places this impression is confirmed by blots; we can see, for instance, that the first four leaves (folios 2–5) have always been contiguous, as Nottebohm claimed (above, page 70). It is important to discover which leaves still stand in their original relation to each other and to distinguish the places where a leaf could have been removed from those where one could not have been. With this somewhat negative guideline one can then attempt to intercalate the Landsberg 10 pages at points suggested by similarities in the writing, the color of the ink, the spacing of the notes, and the musical content of the sketches and to confirm one's guesses by finding that blots or smudges or offsets on one page are mirrored on the opposite one.

(b) A century ago, in the course of studies on intact sketchbooks,

---

[15] Some examples of dry offsets from the sketchbook: (a) the inkblot on fol. 10ʳ, staff 8, has produced a dry offset on the page now adjacent, 9ᵛ. But L 157/158 and L 155/156 originally stood between these pages (there is, in fact, a barely discernible dry offset from the *same* inkblot on to L 157); (b) the *Rötel* on fol. 28ᵛ, staff 13, has produced an offset on to fol. 29ʳ, now adjacent—but the two pages were originally separated by L 135/136; (c) there are traces of red on fol. 29ʳ, staff 5, which cannot have come from the page now adjacent—28ᵛ; they came from L 136, which originally lay between them.

Nottebohm noted that *in general* the sketches for the separate movements of a work are to be found in the same order in the sketchbooks as in the completed work, and he guessed, moreover, that the sequence of sketching corresponded to a large extent to the order of the pages. Further investigation of the sketchbooks has tended to confirm Nottebohm's findings (although it is easy enough to find exceptions); indeed, the Pastoral Symphony Sketchbook provides a good example of their over-all soundness, since we find that nearly all the sketches for the symphony's first movement are on folios 2^r–9^r, for the second on folios 9^v–25^v, for the third on folios 26^r–28^v, for the fourth on folios 29^r–40^r, and for the fifth on folios 40^v–48^v. A practical consequence of this is that if a leaf in Landsberg 10 contains sketches for, let us say, the third movement, we are encouraged to try to find a place for it around folios 26–28; and we are not surprised when we discover that L 150/149 and L 135/136, the only leaves in Landsberg 10 with substantial third-movement sketches, fit between folios 26^v and 27^r and between folios 28^v and 29^r, and that both these locations are confirmed by blots.

Sometimes the location of a leaf or the relationship between two pages is indicated more precisely by the direct continuation of a sketch line from one page to another. The melodic line of the sketch may simply pass from one page to the next page, or it may be connected with the next page by a linked pair of the signs that Beethoven employed as private aids to continuity: crosses, double crosses, crossed circles, numbers (such as "No. 1000"), or the divided word *Vi-de*.[16]

Sometimes, too, it is possible to arrange leaves containing sketches for a single movement in an order that acknowledges the progressive development of the sketches, the most rudimentary sketches being placed at the beginning and the most highly developed sketches (or those that correspond most closely to the finished version) being grouped at the end. This arrangement at least has the advantage of being likely to be right more often than wrong. Nevertheless, there are drawbacks in the method as well. For we see from intact sketchbooks that Beethoven sometimes skips two or three leaves, with or without a *Vi-de*, before directly continuing a sketch line, and that he sometimes also turns back several leaves (occasionally, no doubt, simply in order to find a blank page). If we choose to ignore this awkward fact and determinedly impose a logical order on a mass of sketches in reconstructing our sketchbook, we may

---

16 The main difficulty here comes from the profusion of such indications on some of the pages. Fol. 16^v, for instance, has seven crosses, three *Vi*-s, and two *-de*s, while fol. 40^r has five crosses, three crossed circles, two *Vi*-s, and three *-de*s. For the successful intercalation of a leaf (L 151/152) by the matching of linked signs, see Kerman, *op. cit.*, 88, n. 20.

end up with an impeccably logical sequence, but one that has little evidential value when we come to consider how Beethoven did, in fact, sketch and compose.

V

With the help afforded by blots and their offsets and by the continuity of the sketch contents well over half the Landsberg 10 pages already described can be restored to their original sites in the Pastoral Symphony Sketchbook. This puts us in a much better position to investigate the structure of the sketchbook by means of its watermark pattern.

Each of the leaves of the sketchbook, as is easy to discover, consists of one quarter, or "quadrant," of a large sheet of paper with the watermark shown in figure 1 (page 81). The portion of this watermark that an individual leaf carries will identify its quadrant (numbered here from 1 to 4).[17] Study of a number of sketchbooks indicates that the sheets from which they were made were folded first horizontally and then vertically, and that the paper was then cut along the horizontal fold. The two bifolia thus produced from each sheet were subsequently gathered in ways that vary from sketchbook to sketchbook; in some cases bifolia from many sheets were collected into a single gathering, while in other cases gatherings made up of bifolia from one, two, or three sheets are the rule.

How was the Pastoral Symphony Sketchbook made up? This, as has been explained, can no longer be determined by examination. Fortunately, however, the sequence of watermarks permits only one interpretation: the sketchbook was made up of gatherings of two bifolia from a single sheet. This conclusion—the result of examining the watermark sequence in the earlier part of the sketchbook in particular, which has lost fewer leaves than the later part—imposes some fairly strict criteria on any attempts to reconstruct the sketchbook, three of which I propose to discuss here:

(a) The way in which each sheet was folded and then cut results in leaves from the same sheet being found in particular sequences. Only four sequences of quadrants from a sheet are in fact possible. These are:

1 2 3 4   and its reverse: 4 3 2 1

2 1 4 3   and its reverse: 3 4 1 2

---

[17] The quadrants are conventionally numbered from 1 to 4, reading from the bottom-left quadrant in a clockwise direction with the sheet disposed in such a way that the watermark is legible and the mold side of the paper faces the observer.

This physical fact is of value in reconstructing the book. If, for instance, the same quadrant is found twice in succession, the two leaves must be from different sheets (a particularly useful piece of information). Or if we find quadrant 1 being directly followed by quadrant 3, we are forced to conclude either that the leaves are from different sheets, or that at least one leaf has been lost between them (or both of these). The sequence of quadrants within the book enables a whole number of conclusions of this kind to be drawn.

(b) The watermark illustrated in figure 1 is, in fact, found throughout the sketchbook in two very similar, though distinguishable, forms. This is a result of the technical process of papermaking, in which two molds were used in alternation. The differences between the watermarks produced by the two molds (distinguished here as "a" and "b") can be seen most clearly in quadrant 1: in 1a the sides of the 'bend" (*Schrägbalken*) on the shield are parallel, and in 1b they diverge (plate IV). There are similar, though less striking, differences between 2a and 2b, 3a and 3b, and 4a and 4b (plates V–VII), and it is possible, therefore, to identify the mold as well as the quadrant of almost all the leaves in the London sketchbook. The same is also true of the Landsberg 10 leaves that once belonged to it. Each leaf can accordingly be classified as one of eight types: 1a, 1b, 2a, 2b, 3a, 3b, 4a, 4b.[18]

The four quadrants from the same sheet will, of course, be from the same mold, and this fact, too, is a great help in the work of reconstruction. For instance, adjacent leaves that are of different molds are bound to be from different sheets; and missing quadrants from a sheet can only be filled by leaves whose mold is correct. If the watermarks of a sequence of leaves from the same sheet are 4b, 3b, [missing], 1b, the missing leaf must be sought from among those with the watermark 2b, for a leaf with the watermark 2a cannot have come from there.

(c) It will be seen that the watermark pattern of the left half of the sheet—the shield surmounted by a fleur-de-lis—is divided between quadrants 1 and 2, and that the name KOTENSCHLOS on the right half is divided between quadrants 3 and 4 (though falling occasionally only in

---

[18] Pls. IV, V, and VI are based on beta radiographs made in the laboratory of the British Museum under the direction of Dr. A. E. Werner, to whom I am most grateful. Plate VII is a watermark photograph made by transmitted light. There is no need to stress the usefulness of beta radiographs in cases where small differences between two watermarks are of importance.

The name KOTENSCHLOS is normally divided between quadrants 3 and 4; but in some sheets it falls entirely in quadrant 3, quadrant 4 having no visible watermark. Such "blank" leaves can be identified as quadrant 4, but the mold cannot, of course, be determined.

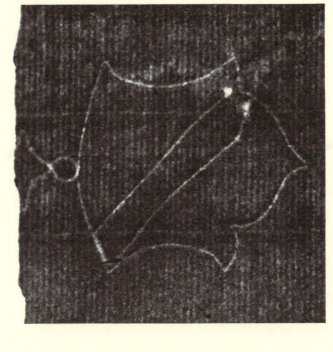

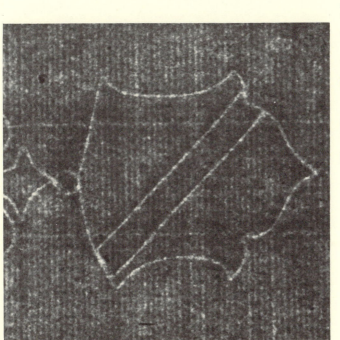

Plate IV ❧ *Watermark of the Pastoral Symphony Sketchbook,*
quadrant 1, the two molds (beta radiographs):
left, mold 1a; right, mold 1b.

Plate V ꕔ *Watermark of the Pastoral Symphony Sketchbook, quadrant 2, the two molds (beta radiographs): left, mold 2a; right, mold 2b.*

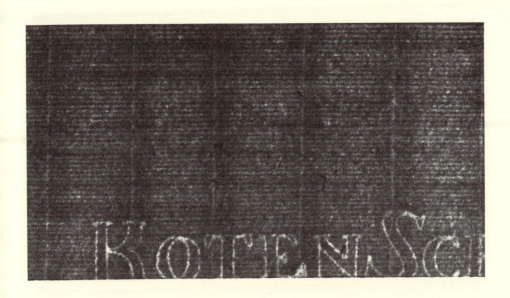

Plate VI  *Watermark of the Pastoral Symphony Sketchbook,*
quadrant 3, the two molds (beta radiographs):
above, mold 3a;   below, mold 3 b.

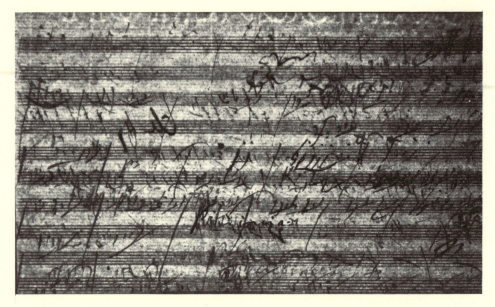

Plate VII ❧ *Watermark of the Pastoral Symphony Sketchbook,*
quadrant 4, the two molds (transmitted-light photographs):
above, mold 4a;   below, mold 4b.

quadrant 3). It is clear that, if the sketchbook had not been trimmed and gilded at the upper edges, we would expect that within a given sheet all the part of the watermark that was not in quadrant 1 would be found in quadrant 2, and vice versa, and all the part that was not in quadrant 3 would be found in quadrant 4, and vice versa.

These expectations may be quantified: in the uncut sheet, in both molds, the distance from the top of the upper ring on the fleur-de-lis to the lowest part of the ball surmounting the shield is between 45 and 46 millimeters, and the distance from the top to the bottom of the initial *K* of KotenSchlos is between 20 and 21 millimeters (see figure 2); and if the sketchbook had not been cut we should expect that (with respect to these measurements) $1 + 2 = 45\text{--}46$ millimeters, and $3 + 4 = 20\text{--}21$ millimeters. In practice the trimming of the sketchbook makes less difference than might be expected. Many leaves, it turns out, escaped trimming altogether while others were trimmed at some points only (indicated by the presence of gilding); most of the Landsberg 10 pages are also untrimmed. In general, therefore, it is a worthwhile exercise to measure the

Fig. 1

Fig. 2

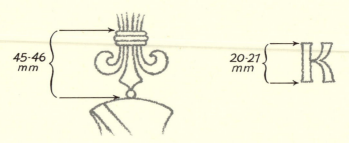

distances described above on leaves that are believed to be from the same sheet, and to see whether $1 + 2 = 45$–46 millimeters, and $3 + 4 = 20$–21 millimeters. In the few cases where the sums are significantly *less* than what was predicted, one or another of the leaves can usually be shown to have been substantially trimmed (e.g. by the presence of gilt along the whole of the upper edge). Where this is not the case, the leaves probably do not belong together. In those instances where the sums are *greater* than predicted, it is clear that the two leaves do not belong together.

An example may make this clearer. If one relied on sketch content and style of writing alone, one might conjecture that L 131/132 originally followed L 133/134 directly; L 131/132 is a quadrant-2 leaf, and one is needed after L 133/134 (a quadrant 1 leaf). But there are two insuperable objections to this arrangement. First, L 131/132 is a 2a leaf, while L 133/134 is 1b; they cannot be from the same sheet. And second, if we measure the parts of the watermark found on the two leaves (as described above), we find that $1 + 2 = 47$ millimeters; this distance is too great for it to be possible for both leaves to be from the same sheet. Either of these arguments by itself would be sufficient to dispose of the possibility that L 131/132 follows directly after L 133/134.

VI

A certain amount of help can also be obtained from rastrology. If the span of the staffs is measured, from the top line of the first staff to the bottom line of the sixteenth staff, it will be found to vary on different pages from just over 195 millimeters to just under 197 millimeters. This variation is not entirely random, for the span appears to be *constant for the same side of any two leaves that originally formed a bifolium*. Once again, an example may clarify the point. Since the first four leaves of the sketchbook (folios 2–5) are intact and originally formed a sheet, it can be shown that the two sides of the bifolium formed by folios 2 and 5 are 2^v and 5^r, and 5^v and 2^r, and that the two sides of the bifolium formed by folios 3 and 4 are 3^r and 4^v, and 4^r and 3^v. When the spans on each side of the two bifolia are measured, the following results are obtained:

2^v and 5^r = 195.5 millimeters (or a little more)
3^r and 4^v = 196 millimeters (or a little less)
5^v and 2^r = 196.5 millimeters
4^r and 3^v = 197 millimeters (or a little less)

An adequate explanation of this phenomenon would no doubt include a description of the piece of machinery (*Rastrum* or *Rastral*) by which the staff lines were ruled. Such a description is surely overdue, but I am not in a position to offer one; however, the presence of a constant rastrological feature on both sides of every leaf of the Pastoral Symphony Sketchbook —a short middle line at the right-hand edge of the second staff—suggests that the same sixteen-staff *Rastral* was used eight times on every sheet in circumstances that permitted the span to vary very slightly. Small as they are, these variations cannot be neglected by anyone who is trying to reconstruct the sketchbook, since they impose a further series of exacting conditions: the spans on each side of any reconstructed bifolia must match.

VII

The following table shows a proposed reconstruction of the Pastoral Symphony Sketchbook that satisfies the criteria described above. The table aims at presenting much (though not all) of the evidence on which the reconstruction is based. The first column lists with Roman numerals the twenty-four sheets from which it is conjectured that the sketchbook was made up; long square brackets, used in the second column, indicate the two bifolia of each sheet. The second column shows the conjectural original sequence of the leaves; those that are now in London are identified by single or double figures corresponding to their present ("new") foliation, and those now in Landsberg 10 in Berlin are identified by their present three-figure pagination (with the page of the original recto given first). Quotation marks are used for the "old" foliation of the sketchbook ("42," "43," "62"). The letters from [A] to [G] record the likely positions of seven leaves that so far have not been traced. A curved bracket linking two leaves indicates that their original contiguity is confirmed by blots or by the sequence of sketch content; it has been omitted in all doubtful cases. The third column records the watermark quadrant together with

SHEET	FOLIO OR PAGE	WATERMARK	PART OF WATERMARK (IN MM.)
I	2 3 4 5	1a 2a 3a 4a	21 24 16 5
II	162/161 123/124 160/159 6	2a 1a 4[a] 3a	25.5 19.5 Nil 20
III	7 8 9 157/158	1a 2a 3a 4[a]	18.5 27 21 Nil
IV	155/156 10 11 12	3a 4[a] 1a 2a	21 Nil 16 29
V	13 14 15 16	2b 1b 4b 3b	28 17 1.5 19
VI	17 18 19 153/154	2b 1b 4b 3b	27 18 1.5 19
VII	20 21 22 23	3a 4[a] 1a 2a	20 Nil 17 28
VIII	151/152 24 25 26	4b 3b 2b 1b	3 17.5 30 16
IX	150/149 27 28 135/136	4b 3b 2b 1b	2 19 29 16.5
X	29 30 119/120 31	4b 3b 2b 1b	2 18 29.5 16
XI	32 33 34 35	3a 4a 1a 2a	17 2.5 21.5 24
XII	137/138 36 37 38	2a 1a 4[a] 3a	26 20 0.5 20

SHEET	FOLIO OR PAGE	WATERMARK	PART OF WATERMARK (IN MM.)
XIII	147/148	3a	18
	145/146	4[a]	3
	139/140	1a	22
	39	2a	24
XIV	40	1a	19
	144/143	2a	27
	[A][? = 115/116]	[3a]	[20–21]
	117/118	4[a]	Nil
XV	114/113	2b	22.5
	141/142	1b	23
	41	4b	5.5
	42	3b	14.5
XVI	163/164	1a	17.5
	[B][= "42"]	[2a]	[27.5–28.5]
	"43"	3a	21
	43	4[a]	Nil
XVII	44	3b	17
	45	4b	4
	46	1b	20
	47	2b	26
XVIII	48	4b	4
	111/112	3b	16
	107/108	2b	26
	122/121	1b	20
XIX	[C]	[3a]	[17–18]
	106/105	4[a]	3
	49	1a	21
	[D]	[2a]	[24–25]
XX	103/104	3a	21
	50	4[a]	Nil
	51	1a	20
	52	2a	25.5
XXI	53	3b	17.5
	109/110	4b	3
	133/134	1b	20
	54	2b	26
XXII	[E]	[1a]	[18–19]
	131/132	2a	27
	[F]	[3a]	[?]
	[G]	[4a]	[?]
XXIII	55	2a	27
	56	1a	19
	57	4[a]	Nil
	58	3a	20
XXIV	129/130	4b	6.5
	59	3b	14.5
	60	2b	23.5
	"62"	1b	22

its mold ("a" or "b"); the mold of some quadrant-4 leaves cannot be determined. The final column records the vertical dimension of an easily measured portion of the watermark, as described on pages 80–82.

The above reconstruction calls for a couple of comments. First, the proposed size of the sketchbook should be noted. Originally, it is suggested, the book consisted of twenty-four sheets, which provided ninety-six leaves; eighty-nine of these survive today in London, Berlin, and Bonn, and there is a past record of two further leaves at present untraced: "42" of the "old" foliation and L 115/116 that was once in Landsberg 10. Thus not more than seven leaves are still missing, and of these only five are completely unknown.

There are sound precedents as well as a general bibliographical plausibility in favor of the number ninety-six. If we consider those of Beethoven's sketchbooks that are made up of a number of regular gatherings we find evidence to suggest that several once had forty-eight or ninety-six leaves. The "Kessler" Sketchbook (SV 263) in Vienna, for instance, which appears to be undamaged in any way, still has ninety-six leaves. Its structure, though a little more complex than that of the Pastoral Symphony Sketchbook, is perfectly regular, since its gatherings consist of bifolia from two sheets, with a single-sheet gathering at the beginning and end of the book. The "Wielhorsky" Sketchbook (SV 343) in Moscow has eighty-seven leaves today, but there is no doubt that it has lost some, and it is likely that six leaves now in Bonn (SV 116–118; SBH 635–637) and a bifolium now in Modena were once part of it.[19] If it once had ninety-six leaves, only a single leaf would still be unaccounted for. So far as can be judged from the watermark sequence,[20] this sketchbook —like the London book—is made up of single-sheet gatherings, but— unlike the London book—they are from papers of two (possibly more) distinct types, identically ruled. The Berlin sketchbook Landsberg 6 (SV 60) has been missing since 1945, so its structure cannot be determined by inspection or derived from its watermarks. But some of the leaves have eighteen staffs, while others have sixteen staffs; and from their distribution it is possible to discover that the sketchbook is regularly constructed out of two-sheet gatherings. When Nottebohm examined it he found that it had ninety-one leaves and that five more had been lost;[21] thus in spite

---

[19] Cf. Alan Tyson, "The 1803 Version of Beethoven's *Christus am Oelberge*," *The Musical Quarterly*, LVI (1970), 576.

[20] For information concerning the watermarks of the "Wielhorsky" Sketchbook I am very grateful to Mme. E. N.

Alekseeva, the director of the Glinka Museum, Moscow, and to Dr. N. L. Fishman.

[21] Gustav Nottebohm, *Eine Skizzenbuch von Beethoven aus dem Jahre 1803* (Leipzig, 1880), p. 4. The distribution of sixteen-staff and eighteen-staff leaves can

of its present unavailability there is every reason to include Landsberg 6 among the ninety-six-leaf sketchbooks with a regular structure. Other sketchbooks constructed along similar lines seem originally to have been exactly half the size of those already discussed. It is probable that the two earliest sketchbooks, Grasnick 1 (SV 45) and Grasnick 2 (SV 46), and a sketchbook of the year 1809, Grasnick 3 (SV 47), each originally had forty-eight leaves, although their present number of leaves is, respectively, thirty-nine, forty-two, and forty-three.[22]

Second, it will be observed that the damage that the sketchbook has suffered is not distributed in a way that can be regarded as random: most of it has fallen on the latter part. In the first half of the sketchbook—the first twelve sheets—it will be seen that only eleven leaves have been removed; none of these is lost, and the locations of the single leaves taken from sheets VI, VIII, IX, X, and XII are fixed beyond all possible doubt by blots and sketch continuity.[23] But in the second half of the sketchbook twenty-six leaves have been extracted—more than the number left untouched—and seven of these are still missing. This has inevitably made a reconstruction of the latter half of the book more problematical.

A particular difficulty arises in the case of sheet XXII. If the reconstruction is correct, only one of the four leaves from this sheet can be identified for certain—L 131/132, with the watermark 2a. Its exact position in relation to the other three (untraced) leaves cannot, therefore, be determined; since it does not appear either directly to follow folio 54[v] or directly to precede folio 55[r], I have provisionally assigned it to the inner bifolium of the sheet.[24]

VIII

Who removed the leaves, and when and why did he do so? The finger of suspicion points to Anton Gräffer, and if he was responsible the date or dates must fall within the period that he owned the sketchbook —i.e. between November 5, 1827, and September 12, 1842. As for a motive, we need to look no further than the desire to provide collectors of musical autographs (whether friends or potential buyers) with material of interest to them. At that date it was simply not regarded as "vandal-

be discovered from a microfilm of the sketchbook which is in the DStB.

[22] For an analysis of the structure of these three sketchbooks see Johnson and Tyson, op. cit.

[23] Much the greatest uncertainty attaches to the location of L 123/124, but

I am satisfied that the leaf is placed correctly.

[24] For the possibility that a leaf now in the Stadtbibliothek, Vienna (SV 393), once belonged to this sheet, see section X below.

ism" to break up sketchbooks and to distribute or rearrange their leaves; and collectors, for their part, seem scarcely to have been interested in acquiring intact volumes.

At the *Nachlass* auction something like half the lots loosely classed as "sketches and sketchbooks" were purchased at very low prices by a single firm, that of Artaria & Co. Anton Gräffer's relations with that firm, of which he was a member, and the catalogue that he compiled at some date between 1838 and 1844 of the complete Beethoven autograph material then in the possession of the Artarias (Autograph 47a, now in the Deutsche Staatsbibliothek, Berlin), are discussed in great detail elsewhere within these covers (pages 174–236) and need not be recapitulated here. Gräffer officiated at the auction as "Schätzmeister und Ausruffer," [25] and himself purchased the first lot, described as "Notirungen und Notirbücher." (Perhaps he felt obliged to open the bidding.) It was his only recorded purchase, and I see no reason to doubt that lot 1 was (or included) the Pastoral Symphony Sketchbook.

The question, of course, arises whether the sketchbook was then intact; and one's answer to the question will be colored by one's view of the way that Beethoven treated his sketchbooks. It would not be surprising if a leaf or two had been lost, here and there, from some of the sketchbooks in the days of their use, and perhaps later in the accidents of changing lodgings (one might expect the first and last leaves of a book to be especially vulnerable). But it goes against all we know of Beethoven's careful hoarding of his sketchbooks (in some cases for half a lifetime) to suppose that he made a practice of tearing leaves out—a sure way, if it were done on a large scale, to ensure their disintegration. To Nottebohm, with his vast experience of the sketchbooks (some of which he must have known when they were a little closer to their original condition than they are today), it was "unthinkable" that Beethoven could have defoliated the London book. Hard as it is to suggest a possible reason why he might have done so, it is even harder to explain how thirty of the detached leaves—that is, all but seven of them—would, nevertheless, have managed to survive without further damage, twenty-eight of them now being contained within the very same volume. The whole weight of probability is on the leaves still being in the sketchbook at the time of Beethoven's death in March, 1827, and although there may have been certain irregularities surrounding the arrangements for the November auction, it has

---

[25] According to the title of Aloys Fuchs's copy of the auction catalogue, quoted in Georg Kinsky, "Zur Ver- steigerung von Beethovens musikalischem Nachlass," *Neues Beethoven-Jahrbuch,* VI (1935), 75.

never been alleged that those included an assault on the integrity of the sketchbooks.[26]

The presumption, then, is that Gräffer acquired an intact sketchbook. But it now seems certain that by the time that Gassner obtained it from him in September, 1842, many of its leaves had already gone elsewhere. That is the only possible conclusion from evidence such as the following:

(a) The miscellany Landsberg 10, into which twenty-eight of the leaves found their way, was formerly in the possession of Artaria & Co. (no doubt it was, in fact, assembled by that firm) and formed Notirungsbuch T in their alphabetical series of the collections of sketch leaves that they owned (see pages 185–86).[27] Although it is not known precisely when Ludwig Landsberg acquired the miscellany from Artaria & Co., Notirungsbuch T is *not* included in the Autograph 47a catalogue, and we can only assume that by the time the catalogue was compiled—at some date between 1838 and 1844—the miscellany had already been sold. Since it is hardly thinkable that Gassner, upon receiving the sketchbook as a present from his friend Gräffer in September, 1842, would himself remove twenty-eight leaves and give them to Artaria for inclusion in one of their miscellanies, the inescapable conclusion is that it was Gräffer who supplied Notirungsbuch T with the twenty-eight leaves at some time before he gave the torso to Gassner.

(b) The "old" foliation of the sketchbook, which numbered the leaves from "1" to "62," has already been referred to several times. It is still to be seen in London today, though the numbers have been neatly crossed out.[28] Clearly this foliation was added *after* the Landsberg 10 leaves (and a few others as well) had been taken out of the book. The numbers are boldly written and are individual in their forms—the figure

---

[26] Such an activity would, of course, be illegal. It is perhaps noteworthy that Ignaz Sauer, who dismembered a sketchbook and sold the leaves individually, was careful to attach a note to each leaf explaining that he had legally acquired the book and citing the date of the auction and the lot number.

[27] The cover of Landsberg 10 is inscribed: "Notirungen/T/78." This cover was provided some time before 1835 (see p. 186), at which time the collection evidently contained seventy-eight leaves (excluding those that were blank on both sides). Today it has eighty-seven

leaves, of which three are blank on both sides; and a further leaf, L 115/116, was removed in 1852. Thus it looks as though seven leaves were added to the collection (by Artaria? by Landsberg?) at an undetermined date after the original cover was provided. Since that is a far smaller number of leaves than the twenty-eight (twenty-nine) from the Pastoral Symphony Sketchbook, it suggests that those leaves were already there before 1835.

[28] No doubt the "old" foliation was crossed out when the "new" foliation was added by the British Museum, probably in 1880 or soon after.

"1," for example, is almost always made with a conspicuous initial upward stroke. On each leaf, moreover, the numbering is rendered more prominent by being surrounded by a roughly semicircular loop.[29] It seems certain that it was Gräffer himself who numbered the sketchbook in this style. The same forms of the numbers—though not the characteristic semicircular loops—are found throughout Gräffer's own copy of the *Nachlass* auction catalogue [30] and throughout Autograph 47a which (as is argued in detail on pages 179–80) is also in his handwriting (cf. plates XV–XVII). Thus the sketchbook must have received its "old" foliation during the period in which it was still with Gräffer in Vienna—i.e. no later than 1842. And since the "old" foliation was added after the leaves had gone, they must have gone by 1842.

Pagination or foliation by Gräffer is found on some other Beethoven manuscripts that Artaria had purchased at the *Nachlass* auction—e.g. on the autographs of the two Op. 70 trios, of the *Missa solemnis*, Op. 123, and of the *Pastoral Symphony*, Op. 68.[31] Op. 70 had been lot 73 and Op. 123 had been lot 126; Op. 68 seems to have been represented at the auction only by its second movement (lot 106) and its finale (lot 80), and how and when Artaria acquired the other movements is not known.[32] Since the complete symphony was sold by Artaria to Baron J. M. Huijssen in 1838, and since the Kyrie of Op. 123 is said to have been disposed of to the Berlin collector Georg Pölchau for four gold ducats as early as the autumn of 1828,[33] at least some of these manuscripts were evidently numbered by Gräffer fairly soon after Artaria had acquired them in 1827.

(c) A few pages of the sketchbook have neat penciled identifications of the sketch contents; they will be found on fols. 2^r, 9^v, 26^r, 29^r, 31^r, 31^v, 39^r, 39^v, 40^v, 49^r, and 60^v, and the wording of each is duly recorded in the notes of Dr. Weise's first volume. The argument that follows depends on

---

[29] Illustrated in Weise, II, pls. [1] and [2].

[30] Some pages of this are illustrated in Robert Bory, *Ludwig van Beethoven: His Life and his Work in Pictures* (Zurich–New York, 1960), pp. 222–23.

[31] For illustrations showing these encircled page numbers and folio numbers, see Joseph Schmidt-Görg and Hans Schmidt, eds., *Ludwig van Beethoven* (London, 1970), pp. 42 (Op. 68, 2nd movment), 122 (Op. 70, no. 2, 1st movement), 199 (Op. 123, Kyrie); *Catalogue of the Mary Flagler Cary Music Collection. The Pierpont Morgan Library* (New York, 1970), pls. IX, X (Op. 70, no. 1, 2nd and 3rd movements); and the facsimile edition of the Op. 123 Kyrie (Tutzing, 1965).

[32] By "finale," the 4th and 5th movements may have been meant. The fact that the pagination of the 3rd through the 5th movements of Op. 68 is continuous seems to rule out the possibility that it was added during the preparations for the auction.

[33] See Schindler (1860), II, 369; Eng. trans., p. 505. The information comes from a letter of Aloys Fuchs to Schindler dated Sept. 30, 1851.

the correctness of the claim I make here—that these penciled phrases are also by Gräffer; they should be compared with the penciled words in Autograph 47a, plates XVI and XVII. The first five of them record the pages on which the first obvious sketches for the five movements of the *Pastoral Symphony* are to be found; and the earliest material relating to Op. 69, Op. 70, no. 2, and Op. 70, no. 1 (in that order), is also scrupulously recorded. The only redundancy, in fact, is contained in two further jottings recording the fourth and fifth movements of the symphony after the unexpected presence of Op. 70, no. 2, on folio 39^r. It seems to me that, granted the precision and the economy of these identifications, they would not have been placed on those pages if the Landsberg 10 leaves had still been in the book. The storm, for instance, would have been minuted on L 149 (or, at any rate, on L 136) rather than on folio 29^r; [34] the *Hirtengesang* on L 119 or L 120 rather than on folio 31^r; Op. 70, no. 2, on L 140 rather than on folio 39^r; and Op. 70, no. 1, on L 106 or L 105 rather than on folio 49^r. We must, I think, assume once again that the Landsberg 10 leaves had already gone when Gräffer penciled in his identifications of the sketch contents.

IX

If we accept the general proposition that Anton Gräffer is likely to have felt no more scruples than Domenico and August Artaria over removing leaves from a sketchbook, is it possible to go further and suggest why it was these particular leaves and not other ones that were removed in the present instance?

Here I am aware of entering rather deeper into a labyrinth of speculation. Nevertheless it seems possible to divide the Landsberg 10 leaves into two groups:

(1) One group was apparently removed because each of its leaves carried some words or phrases in Beethoven's hand or some other feature of interest that (it was believed) would make it attractive to collectors. Thus, for example, L 104 has a number of jottings on it that include the words "ma[e]stoso," "geschwind," and "Vieleicht durch aus Triolen." This group forms the first sixteen of the leaves in Landsberg 10—i.e. L 103–114, 117–124, 129–140. Apart from three leaves (107/108, 113/114, 121/122) that more or less defy identification, the recto or verso of each leaf carries a brief comment in pencil (L 135–140, in ink) below the bottom staff; this is plainly in Ludwig Landsberg's hand and identifies

---

[34] For a facsimile of fol. 29^r, showing the word *Sturm*, see Weise, II, pl. [2].

the contents as being from the *Pastoral Symphony* or from the "Trio in D." [35] Only three out of the leaves that I assign to this group fail to have "interesting" specimens of Beethoven's word writing—L 105/106, 121/122, and 131/132. The first two, however, contain a variety of melodic scraps, a feature that might make them appear more attractive to a superficial viewer than specimens of sustained sketching; while the third, apparently the only survivor of its sheet, may have been lying loose in the book.

(2) A second group, one of eleven leaves, seems to have been selected exclusively from that part of the sketchbook devoted to the *Pastoral Symphony*. In Landsberg 10 these leaves are now paginated from 141 to 162. None carries any identification by a later hand except the first, which has "Pastoral Symph" in pencil—not at the bottom, but in the top-left-hand corner of the page (L 142). The point to which I want to call attention is their order: it is the exact reverse of the order in which they originally stood in the sketchbook. This can hardly be a coincidence, and it suggests that a sequence of leaves chosen to represent the *Pastoral Symphony* as a whole—but *not* selected in particular for the words that they carried—simply became reversed at some stage. At any rate the sequence in which the leaves now stand is quite correct (apart from some confusions of recto and verso) if one is prepared to start at page 162 and to work one's way backward to page 141. What of the final leaf from the sketchbook in Landsberg 10, L 163/164? This, it seems to me, is the only leaf of the second group which did *not* get reversed; its proper place is, indeed, last of all, and it belongs after page 141. Some of the leaves of the second group, in particular L 149, 150, 161, and 164, have interesting inscriptions; but many more do not, and I believe that the two groups, as described here, are distinct and represent two different assaults on the sketchbook. I doubt if more can at present be said concerning the extraction of the leaves that found their way into Landsberg 10. Nor can any light be thrown on the later removal of folios "42," "43," and "62" (in the "old" foliation); these leaves may have disappeared at any time between the date at which the sketchbook was first foliated and the time that Nottebohm examined it late in 1877 or early in 1878.

X

Finally, what are the chances of tracing the seven leaves of the sketchbook (lettered [A] to [G] in the table) that are shown still to be

---

[35] See the facsimile of L 133, with "Trio D adagio" at the bottom, in Paul Bekker, *Beethoven* (Berlin-Leipzig, 1911), pl. 65.

missing? Here, if they have been preserved at all—for all of them, except for [B], must, like the Landsberg 10 leaves, have left the book before it was first foliated—everything depends on their being recognized. Fortunately it is now possible to issue a detailed description of them.

(1) All seven leaves will be on sixteen-staff paper, with a span (from the top line of the first staff to the bottom line of the sixteenth staff) of from 195 to 197 millimeters. A consistent feature of the rastrology is that the middle line of the second staff is shorter than the other four lines of that staff at its right-hand end.[36]

(2) Each of the seven leaves will consist of one of the four quadrants of a sheet having the over-all watermark shown in figure 1 and characterized by the details shown in the plates. By a coincidence, none is of mold "b." [E] = 1a; [B] and [D] = 2a; [A], [C], and [F] = 3a; [G] = 4a. The portion of a watermark that is likely to have fallen on an individual leaf is indicated in the table; in the case of [F] and [G], which share the word KotenSchlos, separate estimates are not possible, although if one leaf is recovered it will be possible to calculate the portion on the other.

(3) Certain predictions can be made about the approximate span of the staffs on some of the leaves. Thus the span of [A] recto is likely to be about 196 millimeters (matching L 143), and that of [A] verso is likely to be about 196.5 millimeters (matching L 144); similarly, the span of [F] recto is likely to be about 195.5 millimeters (matching L 132), and that of [F] verso to be about 196.5 millimeters (matching L 131).

(4) [A] is likely to be numbered "115" in Landsberg's hand, and may possibly also carry a presentation inscription from him; [B] is likely to be numbered "42," with a semicircular loop around the number.

(5) The contents of the sketches are a less sure guide to identification, since at least some of the missing leaves have come from a part of the sketchbook that followed the completion of the symphony but preceded any solid work on the Op. 70 trios. Still, one might hope that [A] and [B] would show some traces of the fourth and fifth movements of the symphony, and that among [C], [D], [E], [F], and [G] there would be identifiable portions of Op. 70, no. 1 or perhaps no. 2.

At present only one leaf is known to me that answers to all the points in the above description—a leaf in the Stadtbibliothek, Vienna (SV 393).[37] Both sides are entirely filled with sketches for the first, the last, and probably the second movement of Op. 70, no. 2; the watermark is

[36] This feature is visible in pl. 65 of Bekker and in the plates in Weise, II.

[37] It was acquired in 1925 from the widow of Nikolaus Dumba (1830–1900). (Information kindly supplied by Dr. Fritz Racek.)

quadrant 4 (the mold cannot be determined). It is tempting, therefore, to identify it as the missing leaf [G]; nevertheless, the fact that the contents are devoted exclusively to the second trio (one side is even headed "2tes Trio"), and the progress that the first-movement sketches are making on it (the introduction, for instance, is virtually complete), make me hesitate to assume that the leaf was once part of the sketchbook, and I have not included it in the present reconstruction.[38] But whether there are still seven or only six leaves at present untraced, I am hopeful that the detailed description of their physical characteristics provided here will bring some of them to light. Only a reconstructed sketchbook is going to be of much use to serious students of Beethoven; and in fact the observations of Gustav Nottebohm in discussing the sketches for the *Eroica Symphony* in 1880 remain equally true of the *Pastoral Symphony* and, indeed, of any other work of Beethoven today:

> In order for it to be possible to watch the evolution, origins, growth and coming into being of the work that especially interests us here, the sketches for a movement or a section that is to be examined must be presented so far as possible in their entirety, and in their proper context.[39]

APPENDIX

Contents of the Leaves Removed from the Pastoral Symphony Sketchbook

What follows is intended as a brief guide to the main identifiable musical contents of the leaves that were formerly part of the sketchbook. In addition to recognizable sketches many pages have other jottings on them that cannot be related to any work and therefore remain unidentified. These are not listed here, though if the page in question contains no other identifiable sketch a broad description of them (such as "instrumental music") has been attempted. The leaves are listed here in what is believed to be their original order.

---

[38] It is noteworthy, however, that L 132 contains a few fragments in $\frac{6}{8}$ time that resemble the main figure (in its earlier form, with eighth notes in a descending triad in the second half of the first measure) of the first movement of Op. 70, no. 2—a movement for which no other sketches appear to have survived in the sketchbook or in Landsberg 10, though [E] and [F] may, of course, have included them. For the difficulties of reconstructing sheet XXII, see p. 87. With three leaves apparently missing here little help can be obtained from blots; moreover the surviving leaf L 131/132 cannot be adjacent to [G].

[39] Nottebohm, *Ein Skizzenbuch von Beethoven aus dem Jahre 1803*, p. 3.

PAGE	OP. 68 AND OP. 70, NO. 1	OTHER WORKS
L 162	I	
161	I, II, III, IV, ?V (early idea) [40]	
123	I (with ?introduction, $\frac{2}{4}$)	
124	I	
160	—	Piano music
159	I	
157	II	
158	I	
155	I, II	
156	II	
153	II, ?V (early idea)	
154	II	
151	II	
152	II	
150	III, IV	
149	III, IV	WoO 59
135	III	
136	III, IV	
119	IV, V	
120	IV, V	
137	IV, V	
138	IV	
147 *Op.68* (?) IV, V	
148	IV, V	
145	V	
146	V	
139	V	
140	V	Op. 70, no. 2/IV
144	IV, V	
143	V	
117	IV, V	
118	—	Orchestral music
114	—	Blank
113	IV	
141	—	Orchestral music: cf. Op. 125/IV
142	V	
163	IV, V	
164	V	
"43" r	V	
"43" v	V	
111	V	
112	V	

PAGE	OP. 68 AND OP. 70, NO. 1	OTHER WORKS
107	—	?Op. 70, no. 2/IV (early idea) Instrumental music
108	—	?Op. 70, no. 2/IV (early idea) Instrumental music
122	—	?Instrumental music
121	—	?Piano music
106	I	
105	I	
103	I	
104	—	Op. 70, no. 2/IV
109	I	
110	II, ?III (early idea) [41]	
133 *Op. 70,*	II	"Macbeth" [42]
134 *no. 1*	II	
131	II	
132	II, ?III (early idea) [41]	Op. 70, no. 2/I
129	III	Op. 70, no. 2/IV
130	III	
"62" r	III	
"62" v	III	
SV 393 (Vienna) [43]	—	Op. 70, no. 2/I, probably II and IV [40]
SV 393	—	Op. 70, no. 2/I, IV

[40] These may be what I have called "concept" sketches, in which ideas for a number of movements are briefly noted on the same page. Cf. Tyson, "The 1803 version of Beethoven's *Christus am Oelberge*," 570–71.

[41] For this see Tyson, "Stages in the Composition of Beethoven's Piano Trio Op. 70, No. 1," 8, n. 18.

[42] Cf. N II, p. 225–27.

[43] This side, which is headed "2tes Trio," was perhaps the original recto.

Beethoven's Sketches
for *Sehnsucht*

(WoO 146)

Lewis Lockwood

I

❊ NOTHING in the broad span of Beethoven biography or historiography has found a wider and more uncritical acceptance than the view of his creative work as being normally a process of assiduous labor by which once commonplace musical thoughts were transformed by gradual stages into artistic substance. This is often contrasted with the supposedly automatic flow of creative imagination characteristic of a Mozart. Thus the poet Stephen Spender, in an essay first published in 1946, says:

> Some poets write immediately works which, when they are written, scarcely need revision. Others write their poems by stages, feeling their way from rough draft to rough draft, until finally, after many revisions, they have produced a result which may seem to have very little connection with their early sketches.
>
> These two opposite processes are vividly illustrated in two examples drawn from music: Mozart and Beethoven. Mozart thought out symphonies, quartets, even scenes from operas, entirely in his head—often on a journey or perhaps while dealing with pressing problems—and then he transcribed them, in their completeness, onto paper. Beethoven wrote fragments of themes in note books which he kept beside him, working on and developing them over years. Often his first ideas were of a clumsiness which makes scholars marvel how he could, at the end, have developed from them such miraculous results.
>
> Thus genius works in different ways to achieve its ends. . . .[1]

---

[1] Stephen Spender, "The Making of a Poem," originally published in *Partisan* *Review* (summer, 1946), and reprinted in B. Ghiselin, ed., *The Creative Process*

The basis for this prevailing view is, needless to say, the sketchbooks; or rather, those essays about the sketchbooks that have filtered out into the popular literature about Beethoven—few scholars and even fewer amateurs have actually worked closely with the inner contents of even one Beethoven sketchbook, and scholarship in this field since the late nineteenth century has been remarkably monolithic.

The standard view, repeated by Spender, is drawn, no doubt indirectly, from Nottebohm's pioneering essays, which were first published in the 1870s and 1880s[2] and have been supplemented since then by all too few later studies and transcriptions.[3] And although the distant outline of the larger terra incognita of the sketchbooks is beginning to be visible to scholars and students on a broader scale, the prevailing view will probably hold until a substantial number of the sketchbooks become accessible in complete facsimile and accurate transcription, thus making it possible to assimilate their contents into Beethoven scholarship and to establish a more accurate perspective on those few well-known examples of single ideas in consecutive elaborations that have largely induced the prevailing view. In many particular cases this view may, indeed, turn out to be valid and entirely convincing, but in the absence of close study of particular works and their genetic backgrounds it lacks depth and substance. Enough is known of the chronology of Beethoven's works to suggest not a single mode of compositional procedure but a broad spectrum of structural problems to which a variety of approaches must have been necessary. At one end of the spectrum is, for example, a work allegedly composed in a single night—the Horn

---

(New York, 1955), p. 114. For a balanced and informed view of the evidence for Mozart's methods of composition see Erich Hertzmann, "Mozart's Creative Process," in P. H. Lang, ed., The Creative World of Mozart (New York, 1963), pp. 17–30. To the generally known indications of Mozart's rapidity in composition and the apparent absence of drafts (Hertzmann believes that Constanze Mozart may have disposed of a good many after his death) one may add this line from a letter of Mozart's to his father, dated July 31, 1778: "You know that I am, so to speak, soaked in music, that I am immersed in it all day long and that I love to plan works, study and meditate."

[2] N I and especially N II. To these must be added Nottebohm's valuable extended essays on single sketchbooks: his Ein Skizzenbuch von Beethoven (Leipzig, 1865), on the "Kessler" Sketchbook, and his Ein Skizzenbuch von Beethoven aus dem Jahre 1803 (Leipzig, 1880), on the "Eroica" Sketchbook.

[3] For a brief review of publications in facsimile or transcription since Nottebohm see Lewis Lockwood, review of the Beethovenhaus publication of the Pastoral Symphony Sketchbook, in The Musical Quarterly, LIII (1967), 128–36. To these should now be added Joseph Kerman, ed., Beethoven: Autograph Miscellany from circa 1786–1799. British Museum Additional Manuscript 29801, ff. 39–162 (the 'Kafka Sketchbook'), 2 vols. (London, 1970).

Sonata, Op. 17—and the other is the Ninth Symphony, the first hints for which (at least the idea of a setting of the "Ode to Joy") date from even before the period of Beethoven's arrival in Vienna in the early 1790s, and which in a more specific sense was sketched for at least eight or nine years before its completion in 1824.[4] The purpose of this essay, then, is to take a close look at one of the most frequently mentioned examples of Beethoven's elaboration of a single thematic idea in a single sketchbook—his sketches for the song *Sehnsucht,* WoO 146. In doing so I hope to raise some questions not merely about previous interpretations of these sketches but also about issues that have a wider bearing on this sector of Beethoven studies.

II

Despite the conservative and even recessive character of the German song literature as Beethoven approached it, this piece shows considerable breadth of conception and careful modeling of details; it is one of Beethoven's most interesting achievements in what was for him a secondary genre up until the writing of *An die ferne Geliebte*—which seems to have followed directly on the composition of this song. *Sehnsucht* was written in 1815 and was first published in June, 1816. It was based on a poem by C. L. Reissig, a professional military man and dilettante poet of idiosyncratic character, whose works were used by Beethoven for as many as seven songs written between 1809 and 1815; this is the last of the group.[5] In the familiar jargon of lieder categories, as used by Hans Boettcher in his useful survey of the Beethoven songs, *Sehnsucht* stands halfway between the extremes of the purely strophic and the thoroughly *durchkomponiert.*[6] Boettcher labels it, appropriately enough, "variierte

---

[4] In a letter of Jan. 26, 1793, Beethoven's Bonn acquaintance Bartolomäus Fischenich sent Beethoven's song *Feuerfarb'* (later published as Op. 52, no. 2) to Charlotte von Schiller and described it as "by a young man whose musical talents are universally praised and whom the Elector has sent to Haydn in Vienna. He also proposes to set Schiller's 'Freude' and indeed all stanzas of it"; see Ludwig Schiedermair, *Der Junge Beethoven* (Leipzig, 1925), pp. 221 f., and Thayer-Forbes, I, 121 f. The first sketches directly attributable to the Ninth Symphony are also found in the "Scheide" Sketchbook and refer to the opening of

the scherzo.

[5] On Reissig see Otto Erich Deutsch, "Der Liederdichter Reissig, Bestimmung einer merkwürdigen Persönlichkeit," *Neues Beethoven-Jahrbuch,* VI, (1936), 59–65; also Kinsky-Halm, pp. 602 f. Beethoven's settings of Reissig texts are the songs WoO 137, 138, 139; Op. 75, nos. 5 and 6; WoO 143 and 146.

[6] Hans Boettcher, *Beethoven als Liederkomponist* (Augsburg, 1928), pp. 64 f., 95 f. Boettcher's few remarks on Beethoven's treatment of meter in *Sehnsucht* sketches are based entirely on Nottebohm's examples.

Strophenlied" of the type in which variation is most prominent in the successive patterns of figuration with which the instrumental component accompanies repetitions of the melody. As Boettcher observes, this type is represented by only a few of Beethoven's vocal compositions, all relatively late works: the present song; the *Abendlied,* WoO 150, of 1820; and the *Opferlied,* Op. 121b, of 1824 (a work that also goes back to early antecedents).

The text of *Sehnsucht* is laid out in three double stanzas of eight lines each: 4 + 4 lines regularly alternating seven and six syllables with three main stresses per line (iambic trimeter) and an alternating rhyme-scheme: *a b a b, c d c d,* etc. The image evoked is that of a sleepless lover whose inner torment contrasts with the calm peace of night:

1a   Die stille Nacht umdunkelt   1b   Verstummt sind in den Zweigen
       erquickend Thal und Höh',   die Sänger der Natur;
       der Stern der Liebe funkelt,   geheimnissvolles Schweigen
       sanft wallend in dem See.   ruht auf der Blumenflur.

2a   Ach, mir nur schliesst kein   2b   Sanft trockne mir die Thränen,
         Schlummer   gib' süsser Freude Raum,
       die müden Augen zu: komm, täusche hold mein Sehnen
       Komm, lindre meinen Kummer,   mit einem Wonnetraum!
       du stiller Gott der Ruh'!

3a   O zaub're meinen Blicken   3b   Du Holde, die ich meine,
       die Holde, die mich flieht,   wie sehn' ich mich nach dir;
       lass mich an's Herz sie drücken,   erscheine, ach erscheine
       dass edle Lieb' entglüht!   und lächle Hoffnung mir!

This type of four-line stanza is less frequent in earlier Beethoven songs than a pattern alternating eight and seven syllables (e.g. Op. 52, no. 1, the very early song *Urians Reise um die Welt*) or eight and six (Op. 52, no. 8, *Es blüht ein Blümchen irgendwo*) [7] but he had set this pattern at least twice before. One example is his equally early setting of Goethe's *Flohlied* from *Faust* (Op. 75, no. 3); another, perhaps significantly, is an earlier setting of another text by Reissig, *Der Zufriedene,* Op. 75, no. 6, of 1809. [8] In both earlier settings of 7 + 6-syllable verse Beethoven had used the conventional $\frac{2}{4}$ meter in a moderate to fast tempo, thus contributing to what we now see as the larger background for Schubert's masterpieces in

---

[7] Op. 52, no. 1, probably dates from the early 1790s; the date of Op. 52, no. 8, is still in doubt.

[8] For sketches for Op. 75, no. 3 (perhaps from 1791–1793), see N II, p. 563, and Kerman, *op. cit.,* II, 69; for references to sketches for Op. 75, no. 6 (written in 1809), see N II, pp. 274 f., and 281.

this verse pattern, such as *Die Forelle* and *Wohin*. The declamation of the earlier examples furnishes a basis for comparison with *Sehnsucht:*

Ex. 1 Declamation in Op. 75, no. 3, and Op. 75, no. 6.

(a) Op. 75, no. 3.

Poco Allegretto

Es war ein - mal ein Kö - nig   der hatt' ei - nen gros - sen Floh

(b) Op. 75, no. 6.

Froh und heiter, etwas lebhaft

Zwar   schuf das Glück her - nie - der, mich we - der reich noch gross

From the relative simplicity of Op. 75 it is a long step to the unhackneyed choice of triple meter in *Sehnsucht,* with its concomitant effect of enjambment for paired lines, its subtle differentiation of accent for parallel words and syllables, and the many delicate rhythmic features by which Beethoven elaborates not only the pianoforte figurations but selected bars in the vocal strophes themselves (compare the vocal part in bars 11 and 22, bars 6 and 27, bars 9 and 30). Essential to the conception of the song is its completely syllabic text-setting and its larger organization in parallel phrases of four bars each (eight bars each strophe) with introductory units of two bars each preceding the main strophes (except at bar 23, where it is one bar long) and with one bar between half strophes (bars 7, 18, 28). Both the upper line and its harmonic underpinning are so tightly confined to the functional domain of E major that the piece lacks scope for all but the lightest suggestion of a tonicization of the dominant (bars 8, 19, 29), while the only other chromatic inflection anywhere is the passing A♯ at bars 10, 21, and 31.

Boettcher is surely right in associating a strophic variation song of this type and period with Beethoven's continued use of variation procedures in such works as the *Archduke Trio,* Op. 97, and the Piano Sonata, Op. 109.[9] Not only in key and meter but also in initial thematic contour this song has come to be seen as foreshadowing the variation movement of Op. 109.[10] Apart from its variation form and unusual meter the basic

---

[9] Boettcher, *op. cit.,* p. 64.

[10] Most recently by Leslie Orrey in his chapter, "The Songs," in Denis Arnold and Nigel Fortune, eds., *The Beet-* *hoven Companion* (London, 1971), p. 432. The sketches quoted by Orrey are also based wholly on Nottebohm.

layout of the song is simple enough, and its strophic design is an essential background condition for the sketches. For when we find that Beethoven doggedly explores a wide variety of linear, metrical, and rhythmic formulations for the opening of the song, we need to keep in mind that he was, in effect, testing a formulation that would decisively determine the form of the entire piece. This is a substantially different situation from those in which he reworks a single subject that can form only a fractional segment of a diversified musical continuum. The point needs emphasis precisely because the many reshapings of this material—and even these sketches themselves, as incompletely presented by Nottebohm—have been taken as typical examples of Beethoven's sketch process as a whole, while in fact it would be safer and saner, in the light of present knowledge of the vast source material, to take them as sketches definitely linked only to the working out of this single strophic song, thirty-four measures in total duration.

III

In his essay in *Zweite Beethoveniana* entitled "Ein Skizzenbuch aus den Jahren 1815 und 1816," Nottebohm published a series of melodic entries for *Sehnsucht* that have since remained the exclusive basis for comments on the sketches for the piece.[11] The sketchbook from which they are drawn was one that Nottebohm had studied in Vienna, since in the mid-nineteenth century it was the property of a private collector, Eugen von Miller; later it passed into the collection of Louis Koch; and recently it has been acquired by Mr. William Scheide.[12] It is Beethoven's major sketchbook for 1815 and at least the early part of 1816, to judge from the completed works for which it contains preparatory studies; these include not only *An die ferne Geliebte,* Op. 98, on which Joseph Kerman writes elsewhere in this volume, but also the Piano Sonata, Op. 101, and the last of Beethoven's violoncello sonatas, Op. 102, no. 2. It also contains material for a number of projects that remained incomplete, among them a D-major piano concerto [13] and an F-minor trio. On pages 60–65, directly following ten pages of sketches for Op. 102, no. 2, and preceding six pages

---

[11] N II, pp. 332–33.

[12] The sketchbook is extensively described in N II, pp. 321–48, and more briefly in G. Kinsky, *Manuskripte, Briefe, Dokumente . . . Katalog der Musikautographen-Sammlung Louis Koch* (Stuttgart, 1953), pp. 69–71. It is now housed in the Scheide Library at Princeton University.

[13] See Lewis Lockwood, "Beethoven's Unfinished Piano Concerto of 1815: Sources and Problems," *The Musical Quarterly,* LVI (1970), 624–46, reprinted in Paul Henry Lang, ed., *The Creative World of Beethoven* (New York, 1970), pp. 122–44.

of sketches for Op. 98, it contains six pages devoted solely to material for this song.

From these sketches for *Sehnsucht* Nottebohm printed some sixteen entries. His transcriptions exhibit the high degree of musical insight we learn to expect from Nottebohm, but they are presented with the limitations characteristic of his methods. First, the material is by no means complete and it lacks all indication of the basis for selecting some items but omitting others. Second, there is no hint of the basis on which the order of the transcriptions was decided, beyond a tacit common-sense inference that they probably occur on the sketchbook pages in a top-to-bottom, left-to-right order, corresponding to what Nottebohm gives us (as will be seen, this is a most difficult and crucial point). Here, as elsewhere in Nottebohm, there is no mention of the entire problem of spatial grouping in the source material or of the possibility of devising various possible genetic orderings in the light of spatial arrangements. Third, the entries are not given in diplomatic transcription: stems are reversed, clefs are tacitly entered without indication of whether they were in the original or not, there are no footnotes indicating doubtful readings (this may be the fault of Nottebohm's editor, Mandyczewski), and words of text are regularly included whether or not they appear in the original.[14]

If one defines as an "entry" any intelligible unit that is not the continuation of preceding material, there are not sixteen but thirty-one entries for the song spread over five pages of the sketchbook (pages 60–64) plus jottings on a sixth page (page 65). Even after subtracting from these what might be considered truly minor variants, we can distinguish twenty-three entries on pages 60–64, all but three of which include portions of the vocal line. As a first means of establishing the scope of the material I have tried to codify the entries in the following table, in which the capital letters at the left represent what I take to be the major units that can be distinguished as individual entries.

The crudity of such a table is all too obvious once one has made it, yet it nevertheless supplies a tabulation that makes possible direct reference to particular entries and their possible interrelations. I am well aware that one category in the table is particularly gross: the terms "right," "left," and "center" as indications of location of entries on individual staffs. Perhaps open to question, too, in a few cases is the assignment of

---

[14] For more on the problem of the original and later versions of Nottebohm's essays see the brief remarks in Lewis Lockwood, "On Beethoven's Sketches and Autographs: Some Problems of Definition and Interpretation," *Acta Musico-* *logica*, XLII (1970), 41, n. 13; see also the "Papers of the Colloque at Saint-Germain-en-Laye: Studies on Music of the 19th Century," *Acta Musicologica*, XLIII (1971), 86 f.

	SKETCHBOOK		NOTTEBOHM (N II)	CORRESPONDING	
ENTRY	PAGE	STAFF	PAGE & ITEM NO.	BARS IN WoO 146	COMMENTS
A	60	1 left	332 (no. 1)	3–4	
B	60	2 left	332 (no. 2)	3–4	
C	60	1 right +			
		2 right	332 (no. 3)	3–4	
D	60	3 right	—	3–4	
E	60	4 right	—	3–4	
F	60	5 right	332 (no. 4)	3–4	
G	60	6 left	332 (no. 5)	3–4	
H	60	7 right	332 (no. 6)	3–4	
	60	8 left	—	4?	= alternative for H?
I	60	9 right	333 (no. 1)	3–6	
		10			
		11			
J	60	12–13 + 14	333 (no. 2) incomplete	3–6	
	60	15	—	5–6?	= alternative for J, bars 5–6?
K	61	1 center	333 (no. 3)	3–4	
L	61	3 center	—	3–4	
M	61	4 center	333 (no. 4)	3–4	
N	61	6 center	—	3–4	
O	61	8 center	—	3–4	"oder C" [$\frac{4}{4}$]
P	61	9 center	333 (no. 5)	3 (4 implied)	related to O
Q	61	10–11	—	3–4?	
R	61	12–13	—	3–6	
S	62	1–2 left	333 (no. 6)	3–6	in E♭
	62	2 right + 3	—	5–6 (twice?)	= alternative for S?
T	62	5–8	333 (no. 7) incomplete	3–11	
U	62	11	333 (no. 8)	3–4	
	63	1 (fragment)	—	pfte., bar 2?	
V	63	3–4, 5–6, 7	333 (no. 9)	3–11	
	63	10	—	10–11?	variant of bars 10–11 for V?
	63	12	—	10–11?	variant of 10–11 for V?
	63	13	—	14 (pfte.)	fragment of pfte. part
W	64	1–2–3–4–	333 (no. 10) incomplete	3–11	
	64	5 (two fragments)		11?	
	64	10, 12, 13, 14, 15, 16 (all right side)	—	16 ff., pfte?	
X	65	1–2, 3–4, 5–6 plus other fragments	—	3–4 (plus others)	fragments of pfte. part

an entry to particular bars of the finished version, though here I think the attribution of most of the entries to the opening bars of the vocal line (bars 3–4) is unequivocal once one has seen the larger organization of the song. Much more arbitrary, and inevitably so, is the precise basis for setting up the alphabetical order in the way I have done. A close look at the page, staff, and "Nottebohm" columns, however, should indicate that the primary ordering follows the material across and down each page, while also holding to Nottebohm's ordering of his examples, to facilitate comparison. What cannot be grasped from the table at all are the spatial relations and graphic character of pairs and groups of entries (for example, the proximity of A and B, or the close similarity in size and writing style of C, D, E, and F) as well as many more subtle nuances. For this my defense is that these can hardly be grasped from any transcription, even an exact diplomatic one, without close comparison with the original, as recent publications of sketchbooks have shown; effective judgments in such matters can only be made on the basis of access to good-quality facsimiles.[15] The table and the transcriptions given here and in Nottebohm should be compared with plates VIII and IX (of pages 60 and 61).

Grouping on paleographic criteria. In broad terms there is a basic distinction between pages 60–61 and 62–64. The first two pages present numerous elaborations of segments of the basic theme as well as some full statements of it, while pages 63–64 present, essentially, only complete versions of the subject, one to a page. If we attempt beyond this to group the entries by some sort of paleographic criteria, the first observation to be made is that pages 60–61, with the sketches, and pages 62–63, with the complete subject, are all in ink; while page 64, again presenting the full theme in a broad and central position on the page, is entirely in pencil. Pages 64 and 65 are the only pages in pencil in this part of the sketchbook, and they are two of only five in the entire sketchbook that are wholly in pencil.[16] The importance of this point is purely negative: it establishes that we have no reason to think that pages 60–63 were done at different times, times when quite different implements and ink could have been at hand and could have created quite different appearances for certain entries on these pages.

(*Please continue on page 113.*)

---

[15] On this point, see Lockwood, review of the Beethovenhaus publication of the Pastoral Symphony Sketchbook, in *The Musical Quarterly*, LIII (1967), 128–36.

[16] The "Scheide" Sketchbook is one of the large type used at the writing table, in which Beethoven normally wrote in ink —as opposed to the folded or smaller notebooks or sheaves which he was accustomed to carrying in his pockets while out of doors and in which he normally wrote in pencil.

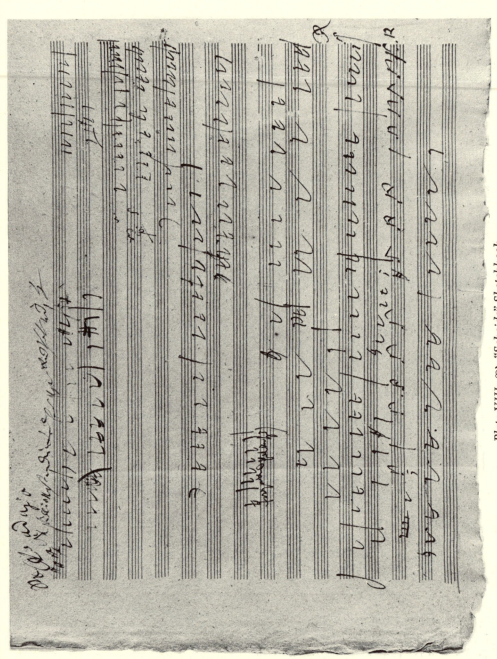

Plate VIII ❧ "Scheide" Sketchbook
(library of Mr. William Scheide, Princeton), page 60.

107

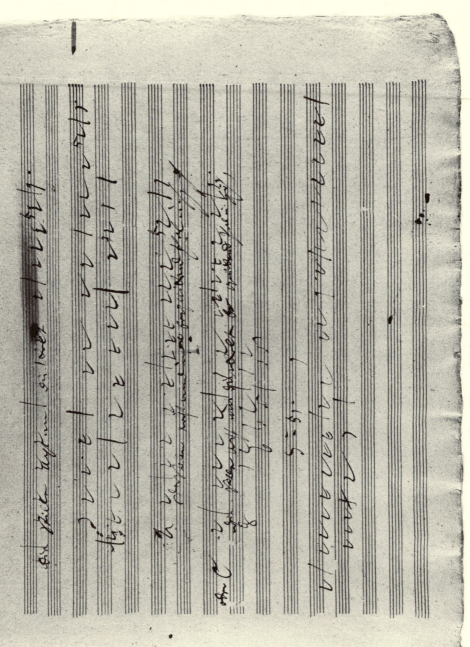

Plate IX ❧ "Scheide" Sketchbook
(library of Mr. William Scheide, Princeton), page 61.

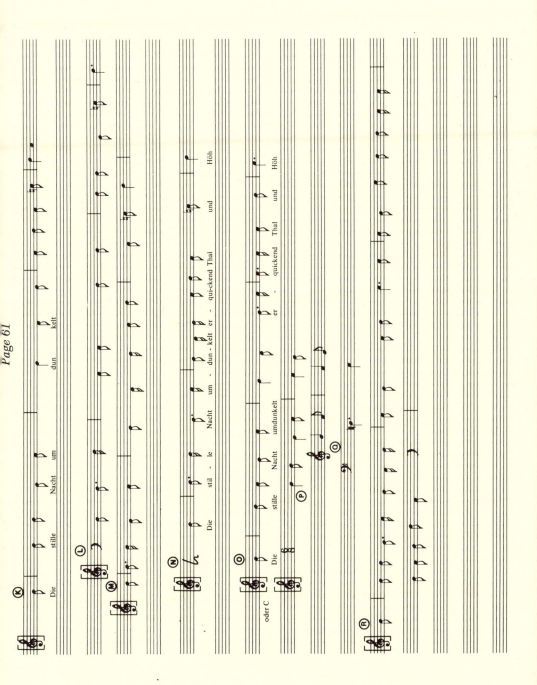

Die stille Nacht umdunkelt er quickend Thal und Höh der in dem See Ver-

Stern der Liebe funkelt sanft wallend Sänger der Natur ge

stummt sind in den Zwei gen die

heim nis volles Schweigen

ruht auf der Blumen flur

NOTES TO TRANSCRIPTIONS

P. 60, st. 4, item E, notes 3–6.

The rhythmic values here are not fully clear but were probably intended to be ♪. ♪ ♪. ♪, as in entry D.

P. 60, st. 6, item G, bar 2, note 4.

The upper stroke above this note is not transcribed here as a separate notehead.

P. 60, st. 7, item H, first note after barline.

The note here can be read as A or G♯.

P. 60, st. 7, item H, second note after barline.

The note here can be read as F♯ or E.

P, 60, st. 10, item I, first note on staff.

An apparent dot after the first note is not transcribed here.

P. 60, st. 12, item J, bar 3, first note.

I follow Nottebohm in reading A–G♯ here, but it could be read as G♯–F♯.

P. 60, st. 14, item J, last noteheads of this entry.

It is unclear what note was intended here.

P. 61, st. 1, item K.

A large smear partly obscures bar 2, second beat.

P. 61, st. 1, item K, penultimate note.

The symbol here is doubtless ♮.

P. 61, st. 8, item O, second bar.

Beethoven evidently intended the rhythm ♪ ♪ ♪. ♪ in this bar.

P. 61, st. 12, item R, second bar, notes 5–6.

This is doubtless intended to be a ♪., not a ♩.

P. 62, st. 3, item S, seventh note before the last.

Beethoven doubtless intended a ♪, although it is written ♪

P. 62, st. 6, item T, seventh note.

This F♯ is only partly visible.

P. 62, st. 7, item T, notes 6–7.

These two notes were doubtless intended to be sixteenths.

Quite the contrary: the whole appearance of these pages suggests much more strongly that they were written rapidly and consecutively. Since they evidently represent a highly concentrated effort to explore various possibilities for the organization of the opening phrase (and its declamation) they could, indeed, be plausibly interpreted as the product of a very short span of time—and would thus represent not long and tedious labor, but the rapid tumbling out of ideas, one after another.[17]

Perhaps the principal paleographic problem in these entries is the spatial layout of page 60. Here I would propose an attempt to classify the material into "primary" and "secondary" groups, both with regard to location and with regard to possible ordering of writing. For page 60 Nottebohm's ordering moves across the first two staffs, so that his A and B are followed by the four short entries in the upper-right-hand area which I am calling C–F, even though these units are quite different in manner of writing (they are smaller and more crowded in comparison to everything else on the page). Starting at staff 6 the writing once again becomes bold and centrally spaced, resuming the character of A and B. It seems at least plausible to imagine that the entire group in the upper-right-hand area of page 60 could have been quite literally a secondary group, and that it could have been inserted into an available space after the remainder of page 60 had been filled out. Against this is the coincidence that the "primary" group resumes directly after it on staff 6. Yet even if one holds fast to Nottebohm's inference that the group C–F follows directly from A–B, it is well to realize that there would have been room for entry A to go on into the remainder of the main theme, if Beethoven had not then begun to experiment with just the first two measures of that theme; entries C–F represent, on the other hand, small–scale jottings that rework the same two bars (3–4) of the theme but lack the bold spacings of the other entries and, located at the margin, lack even the possibility of continuing on with the theme. These entries, then, are "subsketches," and in that sense, too, seem to be "secondary" items. On the remaining pages no such anomalous group appears. On page 61 everything is in the same broad style of writing as the primary group of page 60; the only secondary units here—secondary on internal, not paleographic grounds—are P and Q, which may possibly be immediate alternatives to O. On page

---

[17] Little, if anything, can actually be said about the length of time Beethoven devoted to any particular body of sketches. The exact chronology of the "Scheide" Sketchbook is still uncertain in details and is based on a few relatively fixed external points, such as the dating of the autograph manuscripts of Op. 102, no. 2 ("anfangs August 1815"), of Op. 98 ("1816 im Monath April"), of the March in D Major, WoO 24 ("3ten Juni 1816"), and of Op. 101 ("1816 im Monath November"). One song in the sketchbook, WoO 145 (*Wo blüht das Blümchen*), was published in a Vienna periodical as early as Feb. 28, 1816, just four months before the publication of *Sehnsucht* (WoO 146) by Artaria. While Nottebohm attributed the entire sketchbook to the period "May 1815 to May 1816," he then emended this hypothesis to limit the sketchbook to 1815 (N II, p. 348). For critical comments on this view of the dating and especially on the date of Op. 101, see A. Levinsohn, in *Vierteljahrsschrift für Musikwissenschaft*, IX (1893), 163–65.

62 everything is primary; on page 63 all the material from staff 3 to staff 7 is primary, the remaining staffs having local variants. I should repeat here that page 65 contains a set of jottings for the pianoforte part alone, and may be thought of as leading on to the autograph, where extensive revisions of the accompaniment are also found but in which the vocal line is fully established in its final form.

Metrical and rhythmic variants.   With the spatial groupings in view we are prepared to look more closely at the material itself, particularly the variants of bars 3–4 that are spread through pages 60 and 61—the "sketch pages." Although the separation of metrical and rhythmic features from those of contour is inevitably arbitrary it will simplify the discussion and make possible a synthesis of details at a later point. Again, it must be kept sharply in view that the piece for which these variants are proposed is a short strophic setting of a $7 + 6$-syllable verse pattern, for which the choice of meter determines not merely the autonomous musical shape of the line but the declamation of the text. If we tabulate once more, a more comprehensive view is possible, and these entries should be examined with the words of lines 1 and 2 in mind (see example 2, page 116).

Immediately striking in larger terms is a general parallel between the two pages of sketches: on page 60 the material begins with two units in $\frac{2}{4}$ and only reaches $\frac{3}{4}$ at entries H, I, and J; this is so whether or not the sketch group C–F is regarded as an interpolation. On page 61 the process is virtually the same: a series of $\frac{2}{4}$ elaborations leads to $\frac{6}{8}$ and finally to $\frac{3}{4}$ After this point in the material, the remaining pages contain only entries in $\frac{3}{4}$—the final metrical form has been decided.[18] The larger parallelism of the two sketch pages suggests, beyond this, that what I am calling A and K, both of which are boldly written entries at the tops of their respective pages and both of which have text, could have been written as deliberately conventional points of departure for the excursions which follow upon each one. If this is not so it is an astonishing coincidence that of the $\frac{2}{4}$ entries these two—and only these—are rhythmically identical to one another; the only major discrepancy is the

---

[18] For an approach to the meter of *Sehnsucht*, largely derived from the standpoint of Riemann's theory of "Vier-hebigkeit," see Arnold Schering, "Metrische Studien zu Beethovens Liedern," *Neues Beethoven-Jahrbuch*, II (1925), 30–31. The predictable result of this approach is that the final $\frac{3}{4}$ meter is considered "really" a series of $\frac{2}{4}$ bars in which bars 2, 4, 6, and 8 are shortened by half—e.g. each bar consists of $\frac{2}{4} + \frac{1}{4}$, and Beethoven chose the $\frac{3}{4}$ notation only to avoid an awkward change of meter signature too frequently. From this standpoint the $\frac{2}{4}$ of the sketches is regarded not merely as the "original" conception but as the underlying one, transformed only for notational convenience.

Ex. 2 Rhythm in the sketches for *Sehnsucht* (entries A to R).

*Written as a quarter-note in the sketchbook.

"molto adagio" before A, while K has no tempo marking. One could even imagine that A and K could have been written first, for some reason, at the tops of the pages; and the remainders filled in. But while this can be imagined, it cannot be verified.

That Beethoven is systematically exploring a range of possibilities in meter and rhythm is further made clear when we separate the entries into $\frac{2}{4}$ and $\frac{3}{4}$ groups and their subdivisions. Entry A opens the $\frac{2}{4}$ series with a simple treatment of the text in which the first weak syllable is on the upbeat; this is followed in B, K (as we have seen), and then consecutively in M, N, and O. The alternative in $\frac{2}{4}$, beginning on the second eighth of the bar, turns up first in entry F, and is followed by G (with sixteenth-note offbeat), and then by L. On page 60, entry C shows a first trial of $\frac{6}{8}$, but this is not followed up until the next page in the fragmentary entries P and Q. The next major phase is the $\frac{3}{4}$ group, in which an interesting point is the arrival at the final rhythmic version of bars 3–4 fairly early in the series. Entry E seems to apply in $\frac{3}{4}$ the opening with weak beat following the downbeat, as does H; but at I the final version is reached. On page 61, R is the only $\frac{3}{4}$ reading at all, and has the complete rhythmic form of the final version. The metrical state of affairs between pages 60 and 61 strongly suggests the hypothesis that in writing out page 60 Beethoven worked his way through to the $\frac{3}{4}$ meter and then, on page 61, returned to an exploration of $\frac{2}{4}$ before settling once and for all on $\frac{3}{4}$.

The inner rhythmic intricacies of some of the entries are best considered in the light of their contours, but a few points can come up here. The difference between bar 2 of entries A and K and almost all the others (whether in $\frac{2}{4}$ or $\frac{3}{4}$) is very striking. A and K give a half-measure agogic accent to the first beat of bar 2 ("um-*dun*-kelt") that is more in the manner of Beethoven's earlier declamation than of the refinements he is seeking in this song. In all later entries, this syllable is reduced in length and integrated into the rhythmic flow, propelling the motion forward without extension or pause on the accented syllable.

Contour variants.[19]   Although the variants of pages 60 and 61 cover as wide a span of possibilities in inner contour as in rhythmic design, they are more constrained in choice of their initial melodic point of departure and local melodic goal (equivalent to the first tone of bar 3 and the last of bar 4 in the version). The ultimate decision, of course, in bars 3–4 is to begin the upper line on 3 and establish a motion to 5 at end of bar 4 (on the word "Höh' "), but a 5 of which the harmonic support is a weak position of the pre-established tonic triad, producing a quite different and far less active effect than 5 supported by even a passing dominant harmony in root position. The result in the final version is to render the melodic 5 on "höh" essentially subordinate to the strong 3 from which it emerged. In a first reduction, the motion of bars 3–4 of the final version can be represented as shown in example 3 (page 118).

If we attempt to follow the sketches of pages 60 and 61 on the basis of choice of initial and final tone for bars 3–4, some rather surprising results emerge. The first is that not just many but nearly all of the

---

[19] In this discussion italicized arabic numbers are used exclusively to refer to scale steps, while Roman numerals have their conventional meaning of tonal harmonic functions.

entries open on *3;* the only ones that do not do so are D, F, and J, which attempt fresh starts on *1* and move in rising direction to a first goal at the end of the next bar. Of these, J is the most developed. That there are no versions at all beginning on *5* is important. It seems clear that from the outset Beethoven had *3* in mind as initial melodic tone, and that essentially he held fast to it through other transformations, giving only passing consideration to the alternative of an opening on *1*. The opening vertical relationship of upper-line *3* over the tonic triad in root position is, therefore, essentially a fixed point against which variants are played out over the remaining entries.

Ex. 3 Reduction of *Sehnsucht,* bars 3–6.

If we try to see the larger mapping-out of the various motions that evolve from initial *3,* another tabulation will help:

	ENTRY	INITIAL SCALE STEP (BAR 3)	CLOSING SCALE STEP (BAR 4)
p. 60	A	3	5
	B	3	5
	C	3	5
	E	3	4
	G	3	3
	H	3	3
	I	3	4
p. 61	K	3	5
	L	3	5
	M	3	5
	N	3	5
	O	3	4
	P	3	incomplete
	Q	3	incomplete
	R	3	4

Again, a broad cyclic parallel emerges between the sketches of page 60 and those of 61, just as it did for metrical organization. Starting from A

and progressing to I, we can see an almost pedantically systematic alteration of the closing step. In the first three entries (A, B, and C) Beethoven
takes the line to 5; in the next (E) to 4, and in the next pair (G, H) to 3.
In entry I, closing the group on page 60, he leads it to 4 once more. On
page 61 the situation is parallel. The first four entries (K–N) again re-
vert to 5, and then the next (O) employs 4; while the next pair are incomplete (P, Q), R uses 4 once more. In both series the sketch page
itself constitutes an apparent framework for the elaborative procedures
used, and the larger direction of the procedures on each page is, in this
respect, substantially identical. Important, too, in the 3–5 group so far
(A, B, C, K, L, M, N) is that *all* the entries at the top of page 60 and all
those at the top of page 61 (K–N) move toward 5 by means of its leading
tone (sharped 4), implying a light tonicization of 5 at the end of bar 4.
This brings up a crucial point about the notation of page 61 which con-
tradicts Nottebohm but seems to me valid: in entries K, L, M, and N the
penultimate note seems to have not a sharp sign but a natural sign, while
on page 60 it had been a sharp; this would mean that the entries on the
top of page 61 (K–N) are intended to be in E♭ major, not E major, and
that they anticipate the explicit signature of E♭ major of the full melodic
version at S (page 62). While the change of key has no effect on the
linear details themselves, it helps to reinforce the sense of fresh beginning
which is conveyed by entry K and what follows it.

If we look a step beyond pages 60 and 61 to the larger contours of the
vocal line that were written out on pages 62 (S, T, and partly in U) and
63 (V) we can see the remaining step prior to the final choice of linear
direction.

While S returns to 5 as closing goal, it seems regressive in its first bar,
in which it reintroduces the passing-tone 2 between 3 and 1, which had
gradually been disappearing and would not re-emerge in the final version; also it implies a wholesale change of harmony at bar 2 that is retro-
spective in these sketches. In T the opening motion is reduced again
to a minimum (the sustained repetition of the opening 3 before step motion to 1) and recalls the simplicity of repetitive openings of the entries
A, B, and C but is quite distinct from K, where the final opening motion
is actually anticipated. The same line of direction is further pursued in
bar 1 of entry V, which resembles T in having 4 as its goal and has just
as little motion in bar 1. At last, in W, with the apparent exception only
of the second note of bar 2 (still a passing-tone 2) the ultimate contour
of the upper line is achieved.

Although I shall not attempt here to comment on the complexities of
inner contour of each entry—which would require a vastly expanded discussion—a few points can be noted. One is that the course of events after

the initial 3 can have many different forms and emphases, resulting in the attribution of different degrees of importance and melodic "weight" to the principal tones in the unit—3, 2, 1, and 5. For example, in A the motion from 3 to 1 is subordinated in two ways: by the repetition of 3 and by a strong motion to the dominant at bar 3 of the entry. In K, step 3 moves decisively and immediately to 1 (as in the final version), then ascends again to 5 through the dominant of the dominant. As was seen earlier, by the time Beethoven has come to the bottom of page 61 he has reached the final rhythmic formulation of the line but has yet to establish its definitive contour. When he does so, the total assembling of the details will produce a text setting that gives maximum attention to the vowel pitch-distinctions between the opening words "Die stille" and the following "Nacht"; the tone repetition of opening 3 (G♯) reflects the close similarity and high placement of the vowels of the first two words, while the drop to 1 (E) reinforces the lower vowel of "Nacht." A similar refinement in the next pair of lines is brought about by the tone repetition for "der Stern der" with motion then a step higher for the open vowel ie of "Liebe." This goes beyond anything in Beethoven's declamation in songs of an earlier period.

Finally, a passing glance at the autograph, which is preserved in Berlin (DStB, Grasnick 18).[20] As mentioned earlier, the only revisions of

Ex. 4 Sehnsucht, bars 1–6, from Beethoven's autograph manuscript (Berlin, DStB, MS. Grasnick 18).

[20] See E. Bartlitz, *Die Beethoven-Sammlung in der Musikabteilung der Deutschen Staatsbibliothek* (Berlin, 1970), p. 37.

any real consequence are in the pianoforte part, and especially in the rhythmic location of the punctuating chords separated by rests, as in bars 5 and 6 (see example 4). But also one detail in the voice part is revised: the last beat in bar 4, on the first word of the group just mentioned, "der Stern der"; the B for the first "der" is changed from a sixteenth to a eighth note. Thus an exact parallel is made between upbeats (cf. measure 2, last beat), and the contrasting functions of dotted and even eighth-note pairs in bars 3 and 4 are clarified and carried over also into bars 5 and 6.

IV

In his remarks on the sixteen variant entries for *Sehnsucht* which he published, Nottebohm wrote:

> The song *Sehnsucht* is not at all the product of a moment, but the result of assiduous, continuous labor. The melody is gathered together from portions of the whole, and is built up in a steady metamorphosis. Only gradually and by means of steady industry do the emerging fragments weld themselves together and group themselves, first into a smaller, then a larger entity.[21]

This is an entirely characteristic sample of what I called earlier the "prevailing view" of the composition process in Beethoven's sketchbooks. It reflects not only the traditional type of statement that grew out of the evidence first discovered by Nottebohm, but is obviously also designed to rebut an earlier nineteenth-century view of composition as being the spontaneous product of unpremeditated art. It is not so much that Nottebohm's paragraph is "incorrect" as a commentary on these entries, but that it stands at so lofty a level of abstraction above the particular compositional problems entailed by the material that it can hardly be more than a panoramic generality. To speak of a series of variants merely as being gradually "gathered together" to form a melodic totality means little without careful discrimination between those elements in the series that remain more or less constant and those that are decisively subjected to transformation. Nor does Nottebohm's comment suggest the possibility that there is a way of viewing these sketches other than as embodying a gradually emerging series of variants whose goal is only discovered en route. One might, for example, be persuaded that Beethoven had in mind from the beginning one or more fixed points in the conceptual scheme, and that against these fixed points he proceeded to develop variant possibilities, emphasizing different dimensions of the final scheme, dimensions that are brought to realization not simultaneously but in consecutive phases and in the order displayed by the sketches.

---

[21] N II, p. 332.

One such fixed point, I would contend, is the text—not merely its sentimental content and imagery, though these are by no means negligible contributors to the genre of which the song is a mature example for Beethoven—but more essentially its stanza structure, its rhyme scheme, and it $7 + 6$-syllable verse form. The poetic factors are directly and, I believe, crucially related to the metrical and syllabic organization of the setting. In determining the final choice of meter Beethoven seems to have elaborated on these pages two sets of entries which begin with a fully conventional choice and develop toward the unconventional $\frac{3}{4}$; in the process he fixes the metrical, and even the inner rhythmic, aspects *before* determining finally the details of contour. This last point implies that the problem of syllable length and agogic stress is solved before the problem of vowel pitch. In turn, decisions about contour are also bound up with the linguistic characteristics of the song and serve to reinforce it; and our evaluation of the "better" or "worse" linear alternatives considered in the sketches inevitably entails declamatory correctness and refinement as criteria of value.

To the extent that this fragile reed—a single series of entries on five pages of a single sketchbook—will bear a thesis, it is that the traditional notion of Beethoven's simply "building up" a structure from fragmentary sketches remains inadequate without an attempt to uncover the direction and purpose of the building up along with consideration of the prior constraints from which the process has begun. To do less is to fall back upon what may now be regarded as merely a traditional pious acknowledgment of the importance of Beethoven's sketches— namely, that they show us how allegedly lacking in distinction his original ideas were, and much hard work he needed to do to bring them to realization. The alternative is to come down to cases and to encourage serious and close-grained examination of particular problems that will focus instead on the variety of specific structural purposes the sketches seem to have been designed to fulfill.

An die ferne Geliebte

Joseph Kerman

I

❋ AN AFTERTHOUGHT by Anton Schindler tells us how Beethoven esteemed the poets of some of his songs. To the shadowy Count Haugwitz, author of the song *Resignation*, Beethoven conveyed or sought to convey

> his gratitude for giving him such a "happy inspiration." He had honored only a few poets in this way before: Matthisson for *Adelaide*, Tiedge for *An die Hoffnung*, and Jeitteles for his song cycle.[1]

Beyond this, nothing is known of Beethoven's relations with Alois Isidor Jeitteles, the poet of *An die ferne Geliebte*. Jeitteles was a young Jewish medical student who achieved some prominence in Vienna around 1815 to 1820. "A brilliant youth," according to Thayer, he later became a noted physician in Brno, his home. His literary career was encouraged by Beethoven's friend Ignaz Castelli, who published several poems by Jeitteles—one of them thirty-two pages long—in his almanac *Selam* for 1815, 1816, and 1817, and collaborated with him in writing a highly successful parodistic play called *Der Schicksalsstrumpf* in 1818. In spite of statements that have sometimes been made to the contrary, it does not appear that the poems of *An die ferne Geliebte* were ever published apart from the music, so the composer must have obtained them from the poet. It is a natural inference that the two men were brought together by Castelli.

The literary text, never having been published separately, exists only in musical sources. The transcript below follows Beethoven's careful orthography in the autograph.[2]

---

[1] Schindler (1860), II, 156; Eng. trans., p. 337.

[2] Beethoven's erratic capitalization is preserved. A few emendations have been made: 3, l. 5, Beethoven writes "denn" —the first edition reads "dann"; 4, l. 12, Beethoven puts the quotation mark at the start of the previous line. This is

An die entfernte Geliebte.
Sechs Lieder von
Aloys Jeitteles
in Musik gesezt
Von L. v. Beethowen

1. Auf dem Hügel si[t]z ich spähend
    In das blaue Nebelland
    Nach den fernen Triften sehend,
    Wo ich dich Geliebte fand[.]

    Weit bin ich von dir geschieden,
    Trennend liegen Berg u. Thal
    Zwischen unß u. unserm Frieden,
    Unserm Glück u. unsrer Quaal.

    Ach den Blick kannst du nicht
       sehen,
    Der zu dir so glühend eilt,
    Und die Seufzer, sie verwehen
    In dem Raume, der unß theilt.

Will denn nichts mehr zu dir
   dringen,
Nichts der Liebe Bothe sejn?—
Singen will ich Lieder singen,
Die dir klagen meine Pein!

Denn vor Liedesklang entweichet
Jeder Raum u. jede Zeit,
Und ein liebend Herz erreichet,
Was ein Liebend Herz geweiht!

2. Wo die Berge so blau
    Aus dem nebligen grau
    Schauen herein,
    Wo die Sonne verglüht,
    Wo die Wolke umzieht,
    Möchte ich sejn!

    Dort im ruhigen Thal
    Schweigen Schmerzen u. Quaal
    Wo im Gestein
    Still die Primel dort sinnt,
    Weht so leise der Wind,
    Möchte ich sejn!

Hin zum sinnigen Wald
Drängt mich Liebes Gewalt
Innere Pein.
Ach mich zög's nicht von hier,
Könnt ich, Traute! bej dir
Ewiglich sejn!

---

followed in all early editions; 6, Beethoven writes the numeral erroneously as IV; 6, l. 8, Beethoven writes "jenen." This is followed by the first edition but changed to "jener" in the second issue. For other such corrections in the second issue—many of them involving the capitalization, which obviously worried Beethoven—see Alan Tyson, "Beethoven in Steiner's Shop," *The Music Review*, XXIII (1962), 120–21.

3. Leichte Segler in den Höhen,
   Und du Bächlein klein u. schmal
   Könnt mein Liebchen ihr erspähen,
   Grüßt sie mir viel Tausendmal!

   Seht ihr Wolken sie dann gehen
   Sinnend in dem Stillen Thal,
   Laßt mein Bild vor ihr entstehen
   In dem Luftgen Himelssaal.

   Wird sie an den Büschen stehen,
   Die nun Herbstlich falb u. kahl
   Klagt ihr wie mir ist geschehen
   Klagt ihr, Vöglein! meine Quaal.

   Stille Weste bringt im Wehen
   Hin zu meiner Herzenswahl
   Meine seufzer, die vergehen
   Wie der Sonne lezter Strahl.

   Flüstr' ihr zu mein Liebesflehen
   Laß sie Bächlein klein u. schmal,
   Treu in deinen Wogen sehen
   Meine Thränen ohne Zahl[.]

4. Diese Wolken in den Höhen,
   Dieser Vöglein muntrer Zug
   Werden dich, o Huldin! Sehen—
   "Nehmt mich mit im leichten Flug!"

   Diese Weste werden spielen
   Scherzend dir um Wang und Brust
   In den Seidnen Locken wühlen—
   "Theilt ich mit euch diese Lust!"

   Hin zu dir von jenen Hügeln
   Aemsig dieses Bächlein eilt
   Wird ihr Bild sich in dir spiegeln—
   "Fließ zurück dann unverweilt!"

5. Es kehret der Majen, es blühet die Au
   Die Lüfte sie wehen so milde, so lau,
   Geschwätzig die Bäche nun rinnen;
   Die schwalbe die kehret zum wirthlichen Dach,
   Sie baut sich so Aemsig ihr bräutlich Gemach,
   Die Liebe soll wohnen da Drinnen.

   Sie bringt sich geschäftig von kreuz u. von queer
   Manch weicheres Stück zu dem Brautbett hieher,
   Manch wärmendes Stück für die Kleinen.
   Nun wohnen die Gatten bejsammen so treu,
   Was winter geschieden verband nun der Maj,
   Was liebet das weiß er zu einen.

   Es kehret der Majen, es blühet die Au,
   Die Lüfte sie wehen so milde so lau,
   Nur ich kann nicht ziehen von Hinnen;
   Wenn alles was liebet der Frühling vereint,
   Nur unserer Liebe Kein Frühling erscheint,
   Und Thränen sind all ihr Gewinnen.

6. Nim[m] sie hin denn diese Lieder   Und du singst was ich gesungen
Die ich dir, Geliebte sang,   Was mir aus der vollen Brust
Singe sie dann Abends wieder   Ohne Kun[st]gepräng erklungen
Zu der Laute süßem Klang.   Nur der sehnsucht sich bewußt:

Wenn das Dämmrungsroth dann   Dann vor diesen Liedern weichet,
   ziehet   Was geschieden unß so weit,
Nach dem Stillen blauen See,   Und ein liebend Herz erreichet
Und sein lezter strahl verglühet   Was ein Liebend Herz geweiht!
Hinter jener Bergeshöh;

The last stanza of song number 1, which is so similar to the last stanza of number 6, was almost certainly an addition by the composer. Beethoven is known to have tampered with his original literary material in other cases,[3] and there are several reasons for thinking that he did so here. A fifth stanza in number 1 breaks the rigid symmetry established by Jeitteles in the stanza count and general layout of the poems:

SONG NO.	1	2	3	4	5	6
NUMBER OF STANZAS	4(+1)	3	5	3	3	4
			8			
METER	trochaic	anapaestic	trochaic	anapaestic	trochaic	
NUMBER OF LINES PER STANZA	4	6	4	6	4	

The first, middle, and last poems contain 4, 8, and 4 stanzas of 4 trochaic lines each,[4] and the intervening poems contain 3 stanzas of 6 anapaestic lines. This symmetry appears if we treat numbers 3 and 4 as a unit—as Beethoven did by setting them to music both in the same key; and indeed, although in its poetic content number 4 moves in a somewhat new direction, it shares verse structure, imagery, and even an interlocking rhyme with number 3. It is even possible that Jeitteles wrote this pair of poems as a single entity and Beethoven split it at a logical point because eight stanzas were too many for a strophic setting. Ludwig Nohl actually printed the two poems as a single number as though he were following some independent text, but without offering a word of explanation.[5]

[3] Hans Boettcher, *Beethoven als Lie-derkomponist* (Augsburg, 1928), p. 50.

[4] This "vierfüssige Trochäus" was a favorite line with Jeitteles, according to Castelli, who considered it to be a verse form of Spanish origin; see his *Memoiren*

meines Lebens, ed. Josef Bindtner (Munich, 1913), II, 278.

[5] Ludwig Nohl, *Eine stille Liebe zu Beethoven* (1875), 2nd ed. (Leipzig, 1902), pp. 128–29. There are so many plain errors of wording in Nohl's tran-

Apart from the question of symmetry, the fifth stanza in number 1 has a false sound. Jeitteles was quite sensitive to half rhymes, arranging them systematically between all the stanzas of the early songs; he placed them *within* stanzas only at the end of the final song, presumably as a means of achieving climax.[6] In song number 1 he would not have wanted the surfeit of *ei* sounds produced by the rhymes *entweichet/erreichet* and *Zeit/geweiht* (stanza 5) right after *eilt/teilt* (stanza 3) and *sein/Pein* (stanza 4). Moreover, if the cycle is read closely, I think it will appear that the thought introduced in this stanza belongs logically in song number 6, not in song number 1.

In number 1, read as a four-stanza poem, the poet sets the stage: separated from his beloved, the lover will sing songs to tell her of his pain. Then in the set songs that follow, an obvious sense of continuity is established by images carried over systematically from one to the next. The "Berg" and "Thal" of number 1 carry over into number 2, and the "Wolke" and "Wind" of number 2 turn into three of the five insistent images of number 3 (one per stanza) and number 4: "Wolken," "Segler," "Weste," "Vöglein," and "Bächlein." These are still present in number 5, where the "Weste" reappears as "Lüfte," the "Bächlein" as "Bäche," the "Büschen" as "Au," and—most startlingly—the "Vöglein" as a "Schwalbe" with a complete family. Besides continuity, there is a crescendo in feeling and fantasy-making as the songs proceed. First the lover dwells nostalgically (but realistically) on the spaces separating him from his beloved, spaces filled by mountain, valley, and wood (number 2). Next he begins to dream of agents that will bridge space for him. In number 3, these agents are to convey to the beloved *his* greetings, *his* image, *his* sorrows, sighs, and numberless tears; in the markedly warmer number 4, he wishes to be

---

script (which includes the fifth stanza of song no. 1) that one dare not take it seriously as an authority. Yet lumping two poems together is not the sort of thing that happens through an error nor, one would think, through editorial whim. As for the "Six Songs" mentioned in Beethoven's title, I do not think that constitutes evidence one way or another. He could have been following Jeitteles or he could have been pointedly recording a new numeration of his own.

The term "Liederkreis" first appears in the first edition, probably at Beethoven's instigation and certainly with his approval.

[6] Half rhymes between stanzas: in no. 1, *spähend/sehend, sehen/verwehen; Nebelland/fand, Tal/Qual; eilt/teilt, sein/Pein.* In no. 2, *Tal/Qual, Wald/Liebesgewalt; verglüht/umzieht, hier/dir.* In no. 4, *Zug/Flug, Brust/Lust; spielen/wühlen, Hügeln/spiegeln.* In no. 5, *rinnen/drinnen, hinnen/Gewinnen; Kleinen/einen, vereint/erscheint.* In no. 6, *Lieder/wieder, ziehet/verglühet,* and within stanzas (the two final stanzas) *gesungen/erklungen, Brust/bewusst; weichet/erreichet, weit/geweiht.* In no. 3 half rhymes do not come into consideration because there are true rhymes between all stanzas.

taken to *her* (by the bird), to fondle *her* (with the wind), and to see *her* image (in the brook).[7] Fantasy runs riots in the picture of the Bieder-meier love nest, number 5, with its heady anapaestic meter. The relentless way in which Jeitteles pursues his images repels, but perhaps he earns a few points by contriving to combine the sense of continuity with cre-scendo throughout the cycle of poems. He achieves a fairly genuine effect of spontaneous emotional outpouring.

Number 5 is a lyric of a standard category, in which the lover's dis-tress is placed in sharp relief against the general burgeoning of spring-time. One famous prototype familiar to musicians is Petrarch's *Zefiro torna;* the pathetic turning point "Ma per me, lasso" becomes "Nur ich kann nicht ziehen von hinnen," the fantasy collapses with a bump, and the lover returns to the realization that only songs can bridge space on his behalf, not birds or brooks. And number 6—a poem of the *Gitene canzonette* category—introduces a new thought. The songs are now sung not to convey the lover's pain but in order to be sung back by the beloved; the "logical" conclusion is drawn in the final stanza—separation will be eased by songs experienced in common. This small fresh insight has emerged from the modest drama of fantasy and sublimation played out in numbers 2 to 6. By adding a near-duplicate of this climactic stanza to song number 1, Beethoven achieved an obvious tightening of the "cyclic" effect: a stanza sung at the beginning is sung again at the end (to the same music, of course). But he lost something in the way of a logical unfolding of ideas.

Jeitteles also devoted considerable care to the modulation of spatial and temporal imagery in the cycle. The first two poems concentrate on the space between the lovers and the next two on agents that bridge space. However, numbers 3 and 4 also include some temporal images ("den Büschen . . . Die nun herbstlich falb und kahl . . . Wie der Sonne letzter Strahl"), and such imagery dominates numbers 5 and 6. Number 5 is about May, winter, and spring, and in number 6 the singing of songs takes place at evening, "Abends":

> Wenn das Dämm'rungsrot dann ziehet
> Nach dem stillen blauen See,
> Und sein letzter Strahl verglühet
> Hinter jenen Bergeshöh . . .

This rather surprising emphasis on evening imagery, consuming an entire stanza—a stanza set by Beethoven in a rather surprising way, too—is to

---

[7] This conceit, with its faintly erotic or voyeuristic overtones, occurs in other Beethoven song poems: *Sehnsucht* (*Was zieht mir das Herz so?*) and *Ruf vom Berge.*

be explained as the climax of a tendency gradually increasing through the six poems. There is only one clearly spatial image left in the whole of number 6, "Bergeshöh'."

It is easy to get impatient with the young man on the hill. If his beloved is really within "spying" distance, or close to it, he might well set about crossing the intervening landscape rather than making up mawkish songs. We can perhaps take the cycle a little more seriously if we are prepared to regard space-distance as a metaphor, gradually clarified by the poet, for time-distance. The poet is celebrating a past love affair. And this would accord better with Beethoven's own situation in April, 1816, when the cycle was composed. To Beethoven, if I am right, we owe the one line that frankly brings together space and time:

> Denn vor Liedesklang entweichet
> Jeder Raum und jede Zeit . . .

This brings us to the delicate question of Beethoven's own identification with the lover of Jeitteles's poems, and the identification of "The Distant Beloved" with "The Immortal Beloved" or some other one of his actual amours.

II

The figure of a Distant Beloved, adored from afar, is not exactly rare in lyric poetry. Still, it turns up in what would appear to be more than a statistically fair share of Beethoven's song poems.[8] In broad terms, this may be seen as reflecting the quality of Beethoven's actual relationships with women all through his life—or at least, what little he has allowed us to piece together about those relationships. The construction by Editha and Richard Sterba in *Beethoven and His Nephew* has influenced most recent biographers in their treatment of this matter. Martin Cooper writes:

[Beethoven's] attitude to women was always ambiguous, as is shown by the conflicting accounts of his contemporaries and his known abortive relationships with a series of generally aristocratic girls. . . . The attraction that he felt towards his aristocratic pupils—among the most famous Therese von Brunsvik, Josephine von Deym, and Giulietta Guicciardi—often seems to have thrived in proportion as it

---

[8] *Adelaide, An den fernen Geliebten* (*Einst wohnten süsse Ruh*), *Sehnsucht* (*Was zieht mir das Herz so?*), *Lied aus der Ferne, Andenken, Der Jüngling in der Fremde, Ruf vom Berge, Gedenke mein.* For Paul Bekker, "Beethoven's whole lyric output might almost be regarded as a series of variations upon the *An die ferne Geliebte* theme" (*Beethoven* [Berlin, 1912], p. 361; tr. M. M. Bozman [London, 1925], p. 256).

was unrealisable in fact and the letters to the Immortal Beloved, even
if they were ever sent and were not simply a literary effusion, show
him retreating behind vague excuses and finding reasons in advance
why his passion could never be consummated.[9]

Beethoven was attracted to many women, but so far as we know he with-
drew from a full commitment to any of them. He either chose his women
at a safe distance or, when necessary, placed them there.

Other features of the poems would have invited identification on
Beethoven's part. The aptness of the lover who makes songs, in numbers
1 and 6, is obvious. The domestic bliss recorded in number 5 corresponds
to a nostalgic wish that he often voiced.

Indeed, it is hard not to go one step further and surmise that *An die
ferne Geliebte* refers to a specific woman. Even Thayer remarked that the
piece was composed shortly before Beethoven wrote to Ries, "I found only
one, whom I shall doubtless never possess" (May 8, 1816), and not long
before he told Giannatasio del Rio that he had been in love, hopelessly,
for five years.[10] No one can hear the songs "adequately sung," added
Thayer in a rare burst of innuendo, "without feeling that there is something more in that music than the mere inspiration of poetry." The conversation with Giannatasio is reported by his daughter Fanny, in her
diary entry for September 16, 1816:

> My father asked him if he did not know anyone, etc. I listened with
> the utmost attention, at some distance, and learned something which
> threw my inmost soul into turmoil, which confirmed a long foreboding
> —he was unhappy in love! Five years ago he had become acquainted
> with a person, a more intimate union with whom he would have con-
> sidered the greatest happiness of his life. It was not to be thought of,
> almost impossible, a chimera. Nevertheless, it is now as on the first
> day. I have still not been able to get it out of my mind, were the
> words which affected me so painfully.[11]

---

[9] Martin Cooper, *Beethoven: The Last
Decade 1817–1827* (London, 1970), pp.
13, 32.

[10] Thayer-Deiters-Riemann III (1911),
547, 564–65; Thayer-Forbes, II, 647.
Anderson's version of the letter (no.
632—footnoted, "This is a literal translation of the original German"!) renders
"Ich fand" as "I have found," a little
twist that manages to strengthen the impression that Beethoven was still in love.

[11] Thayer-Deiters-Riemann IV (1907),
534. One hesitates, perhaps, before a report of a conversation overheard as precisely as this. But although Fanny was
more than half in love with Beethoven,
her diary entries in general seem accurate, sensitively observed, and transpar-
ently honest, and are generally credited.
It has been suggested by some popular
biographers that Beethoven was deliberately exaggerating his feelings as a way
of scotching matchmaking overtures on
Giannatasio's part; but this does not feel
like Beethoven's style.

The phrase "five years ago" rings a bell for anyone who knows of the letter to "The Immortal Beloved" of July, 1812. Fanny did not, of course.
Thayer misdated it. But now that the 1812 dating is accepted, most biographers conclude that the letter and the song cycle were addressed to
the same lady.

There is something else striking about the conversation reported by
Fanny. Beethoven says that he cannot get the five-year-old affair out
of his mind ("noch nicht aus dem Gemüth bringen können"), but the
signs are that he was trying to accomplish exactly that. Always a poor
judge of his own feelings and motives, Beethoven tells Giannatasio "it
is now as on the first day" and he may very well have thought so; but
from his actions of the time I think we can infer otherwise. For the first
time in five years (so far as we know) he now begins to talk about his
secret love, to a relative stranger such as Giannatasio. He drops hints
about it to the Giannatasio girls in another conversation recorded in
Fanny's diary.[12] He writes about it, albeit cryptically, in a letter to Ries.
He composes songs about it which will be dedicated to Prince Lobkowitz,
sold to Steiner, and broadcast to the world at large. We also know that a
decisive new turn was taking place in Beethoven's emotional life at
exactly this period. As was clear to sensitive observers of the time—such
as Fanny [13]—his affections were converging intensely on his nephew
Karl, whose guardianship he had assumed a few months earlier, following the death of his brother in November 1815.

Music had often provided Beethoven with a field for the working out
of emotional conflicts. A brief but impressive article by Alan Tyson has
traced this mechanism in reference to the crisis memorialized by the
"Heiligenstadt Testament." [14] It seems probable that something of the
same kind was happening now in reference to a crisis of another kind,
recorded by another famous document, the letter to "The Immortal Beloved." By bringing his feelings into the open, Beethoven was renouncing
or abandoning them. Projecting himself into Jeitteles's poems, he was
saying that love was removed from him in time as much as in space: distant from him, and also well behind him.

If we "read" *An die ferne Geliebte* in this way, it may throw more
light on Beethoven's inner life than if we join the hunt for the particular
lady to whom it was secretly (and hypothetically) dedicated. Possibly it
served as a literal love offering; more probably it served as a nostalgic
hymn to past love in general. On the other hand, I believe that in another

---

[12] *Ibid.*, 539.   Phase," *The Musical Times*, CX (1969),
[13] *Ibid.*, 532.   139–41.
[14] Alan Tyson, "Beethoven's Heroic

respect a literal reading can be more illuminating than a general one. Beethoven, through Jeitteles's lover, seems to be saying that only through art could he achieve loving communication; the beloved is unreachable except through songs. There is therefore some justification for regarding the cycle as an act of renewed dedication to music, to the artist's mission in general.[15] But we would also do well to recall what, quite literally, Beethoven and his time understood by

> . . . Lieder
> . . . aus den vollen Brust
> Ohne Kunstgepräng' erklungen,
> Nur der Sehnsucht sich bewusst.

The renewed dedication to art turns out to be a dedication to a new artistic ideal—new, and not altogether expected.

III

Our term "art song" is miserably confusing as far as the modern German song in its early years is concerned.[16] The lied grew up in reaction to the "art music" of Italian opera, cantata, and canzonet, and also in reaction to the artifices of mid-eighteenth-century poetry. Simple, direct verses were to be kept in balance with simple, direct melodies. Goethe, in his review of Des Knaben Wunderhorn, conceived of no distinction between a Volkslied and a newly composed song:

> But best of all, may this volume rest upon the piano of the musical amateur or the professional, so that the songs contained within it may either be done justice to by means of familiar traditional melodies, or may be matched to their individual proper tunes, or—God willing —may elicit notable new melodies.[17]

As for Goethe's own activity as a lyricist, Frederick Sternfeld has put his finger on one of its most significant aspects by showing how frequently the lyrics were "parodies," written out of enthusiasm for some simple melody that the poet heard and felt impelled to provide with verses of his own.[18] A man who writes poetry from this standpoint will have little patience with complex musical settings; Goethe's well-known championship of strophic as against through-composed songs stemmed inevitably

---

[15] Bekker calls the last song Widmungsgesang (p. 364).

[16] For an introduction to the vast literature on the lied, see the MGG articles "Lied," by Kurt Gudewill, and "Goethe," by Friedrich Blume.

[17] Johann Wolfgang von Goethe, review of Des Knaben Wunderhorn, Deutscher Taschenbuch Verlag Gesamtausgabe, XXXII/21 (Jan., 1806).

[18] Frederick W. Sternfeld, Goethe and Music (New York, 1954).

from his devotion to the *Volksweise* ideal. In this he was seconded by his "house composers" Reichardt and Zelter. By his emphatic support of this ideal, Goethe lent it prestige at the very time it was being questioned by a new generation of composers, and by writing his own superb lyrics with this ideal firmly in mind, he raised it to a level of artistic dignity that they could not easily brush aside.

Beethoven seems to have been caught between an innate allegiance to *Kunstgepränge* on the one hand and a growing sensitivity to the attractions of *Volksweise* and strophic setting on the other. In the best songs of his early years, he tried to inject musical complication of the same order as that of his instrumental music. *Adelaide* has something like a whole tiny sonata squeezed into its four Sapphic stanzas; *Neue Liebe, neues Leben* and the *Mailied* employ aria forms; the Gellert *Busslied* does much violence to the stanza structure before changing mode, tempo, and style halfway through. But in the eight years prior to the composition of his song cycle Beethoven had repeatedly been brought face to face with the contrary aesthetic of song composition. He had been setting many Goethe poems, including *Sehnsucht* (*Nur wer die Sehnsucht kennt*) four times, in a spirit of experiment. He had associated with people close to the great man, and in 1812 had actually met him. Goethe the poet he admired unequivocally—we have no reason to doubt his statements to this effect—and somewhat more equivocally, he admired Goethe the man: a dominating, revered figure in the world of letters such as Beethoven wished to become (and soon did become) in the world of music.[19] Furthermore, in the years in question Beethoven was spending a lot of time on Thomson's behalf making folksong arrangements. A folksong melody is written out on one of the sketch pages for *An die ferne Geliebte*.[20] A few months later he composed *Ruf vom Berge*, WoO 147, modeled on a folksong.

Beethoven's ambivalence on the question of simple or complex song setting appears in his two versions of Tiedge's *An die Hoffnung*, works that he put considerable store by even though they are never sung today. Op. 32 (1805) is strophic, the three stanzas being sung to a single carefully fashioned melody. Op. 94 (1813?) is through-composed, beginning with a recitative and proceeding to an intense, highly inflected, furiously modulating treatment of the same three stanzas. The only way Beethoven could get the piece on an even keel was to make a literal da capo of stanza 1, words and music, at the end. This action, and the resulting

---

[19] How characteristic is Beethoven's superscript over the autograph of the fourfold *Sehnsucht* setting—"Sehnsucht von Göthe und Beethoven"! (Kinsky-Halm, p. 598).

[20] See N II, p. 340.

musical form, both have their parallels in *An die ferne Geliebte*.

What Beethoven saw about the Jeitteles poems was that they gave him the opportunity to eat his cake and have it too. The issue of musical complication, which in *Adelaide* and the second *An die Hoffnung* had been worked out on the level of the relationship among stanzas, could be shifted onto a higher level, the level of the relationship among the six songs. The individual songs could be treated very simply while a plan of some subtlety and power was put into operation for the cycle as a whole. Perhaps Beethoven also realized that this was a "special" solution of the problem of strophic versus through-composing, a solution that was not likely to bear issue. Still, those were lean years, and he was interested enough to try the notion out. Work went swiftly, to judge from the sketches.

Schlesinger in Berlin and the Bureau des Arts et d'Industrie in Vienna published Zelter's songs in four volumes between 1810 and 1816. Did Beethoven have the idea of beating Zelter at his own, or rather Goethe's, game? It is possible, though if this had been a major incentive he would presumably have used poems by Goethe, not Jeitteles. However this may be, *An die ferne Geliebte* really ought to have mollified the old poet, for many aspects of the piece seem tailor-made to validate his own theories of song writing. The melodies are simple, direct, *volkstümlich*. The piano accompaniment is held down to a most unobstrusive role; the figuration becomes only slightly agitated to reflect increasing agitation in successive strophic stanzas, as Goethe allowed and, indeed, encouraged. Beethoven marked numerous ritardandos, fermate, and the like in order to bend the melodies to match successive stanzas, just as Goethe had recommended to the singer Eduard Genast in their famous session on the song *Jägers Abendlied* in 1814. Changing mode for certain lines or stanzas—as in songs numbers 2, 3, and 5—was also a resource that Goethe and Zelter admitted.[21] Singing a stanza on a monotone while the piano plays the tune, as happens in Beethoven's number 2, was an admired (and imitated) feature of Reichardt's *Erlkönig*.[22] *Erlkönig* was probably Beethoven's model, in fact, for his own song.

---

[21] Though, in fact, Zelter does not appear to have employed the resource often in his own songs. Among those available in modern editions, only the Schiller *Berglied* and *Kennst du das Land* (*Mignon I*) involve mode changes (*Fünfzig Lieder*, ed. Ludwig Landshoff [Mainz, 1932]). From the dissertation on Zelter by Gertraud Wittmann one can infer that this also happens in *Künstlers Abendlied* and Schiller's *Der Taucher* (*Das klavierbegleitete Sololied C. F. Zelters* [Giessen, 1936], pp. 44, 56).

[22] *Das Erbe deutscher Musik*, LIX, 2–4.

Technical matters apart, what was central for listeners of the time was the elusive folklike quality of the tunes. And this was not something they would have expected to find in the latest new Beethoven opus. Power, complexity, overwhelming feats of construction and development, motivic unity, high drama—these, rather than artless strains, were qualities associated then (as now) with the composer of the *Eroica Symphony*. His contemporaries can be forgiven, too, if they viewed the turn toward simplicity in the song cycle as a sport in the composer's output. He did not continue writing such songs, and the great sensation of the next opuses—Op. 101, 102, and 106—was a turn toward fugue of a particularly gritty kind. Today we can hear in the music of Beethoven's late period not only new complexities but also a new and determined effort toward simple, direct expression. I have spoken of this tendency elsewhere [23] and shall return to it briefly later in this essay. Beethoven's dedication to songs "without the adornment of Art" had lasting consequences for his artistic development in his last decade.

In 1823 Marianne von Willemer seems to have sent Goethe a copy of *An die ferne Geliebte:*

> . . . ask someone with a beautiful, gentle voice to sing you Beethoven's song to *die Entfernte;* the music seems to me unexcelled, comparable only with that to *Egmont,* and the words correspond very well to a loving, youthful-feeling spirit; however, it must be sung simply and calmly and must be played very well. How I should like to know that it has given you pleasure, and what you think of it.[24]

Goethe was, of course, at least as equivocal in his attitude toward Beethoven as the other way around. His admiration for the *Egmont* music is well known (to Marianne as well as to us), and so is his sharp objection to the setting of *Kennst du das Land* in Op. 75. In the present instance the old poet found it expedient to fall back on silence, as was not infrequently his way. He would not have agreed about the Jeitteles poems, and the operatic ending of the cycle was just the sort of thing he had always disliked about Beethoven's songs. As Frau von Willemer must have seen, *An die ferne Geliebte* represents a large step toward Goethe, whether or not this entered at all into Beethoven's calculations. Goethe, one suspects, was not really disposed to meet him halfway.

---

[23] Joseph Kerman, "Voice," Ch. 7 of *The Beethoven Quartets* (New York, 1967).

[24] *Marianne und Johann Jakob Willemer: Briefwechsel mit Goethe,* ed. Hans- J. Weitz (Frankfurt, 1965), No. 123. Weitz takes it for granted that this letter was accompanied by a copy of the work as a gift.

IV

Both content and form of Jeitteles's cycle of poems would have interested Beethoven, then: the subject matter, with its yearning for a distant love blending into nostalgia for past love, and the poetic structure consisting of six separate but closely linked lyrics. On the level of structure, it was very likely the hint of "cyclic" form—the plain invitation in poem number 6 to make a da capo of song number 1—that started him thinking. This was the thread around which the large-scale musical form of the song cycle would rapidly crystallize. It is not surprising that Beethoven's idea of how to handle this da capo can be seen to have been refined through several stages in the process of composition.

The sketches for *An die ferne Geliebte* known today are the same as those described by Nottebohm.[25] An isolated early sheet is bound into a sketch miscellany at the British Museum, Add. MS. 29997, folio 9 (SV 187). Written in pencil, doubly folded, and scribbled with street addresses, this was one of those casual sheets that Beethoven carried around on his walks. Then there is a compact set of six pages in what is now the "Scheide" Sketchbook at Princeton, pages 68–73 (SV 364). Here, sketches cover the essential work on the first five songs. Two sketches also appear in the autograph, recently published in a fine facsimile by the Henle Verlag.[26] They are found on the last (back) page, page 28, and refer to the concluding piano passage of the cycle on page 27.

In the sketchbook, as Nottebohm did not fail to point out, the tune we now know for song number 6 is entirely absent while stanza 1 of poem number 6 appears with the tune of number 1.[27] So evidently the

---

[25] N II, pp. 334–39. Though Nottebohm speaks of early sketches found on "single sheets" ("auf einzelnen Blättern"), only one such sheet is known today—the very one from which his (single) example is taken. He may have seen others, which have since disappeared from view; but I do not think we can be quite certain that he did.

On the vagaries of Nottebohm's transcription of song sketches, see the remarks by Lewis Lockwood on p. 103. To these may be added the observation that Nottebohm generally presented only the clearest sketches, skipping those that are problematic to transcribe. He could doubtless have puzzled these out brilliantly, but I suspect that he disliked dealing in conjecture and especially presenting conjectures to his readers. Given his determination to survey all Beethoven's surviving sketches, Nottebohm may also have made the decision not to take the time for puzzle solving. It should also be remembered that his time with the sketchbooks was limited; most of them were in private hands at that period.

[26] *Beethoven. An die ferne Geliebte: Faksimile nach dem im Besitz des Bonner Beethovenhauses befindlichen Original* (Munich-Duisburg, 1970). For a description of the autograph, see SBH 561.

[27] Two sketches show this (N II, pp. 336–37, 339). The first is found among sketches for song no. 1 (p. 69) and is headed "Nim̃ sie hin lezter Vers." This

original plan for the last song was to bring back the old tune for all four stanzas. At some later point Beethoven decided to restrict the da capo to the final stanza only, stanza 4. To begin the song he wrote a new tune which recalls the original one in a rather subtle way; we shall return to this point presently. It was now, presumably, that he also decided to reinforce the musical da capo with a textual da capo, and "planted" that final stanza (or something very much like it) at the end of song number 1. Restricting the tune to a single stanza at the end was doubtless good insurance against overexposure. It also provided the final stanza with the emphasis and freshness it needed if it was going to provide an effective concluding *stretta*.

(A problem of declamation that Beethoven seems to have overlooked in the sketch stages may now have started him off in modifying his original plan. In poem number 1, the first syllable is weak in most of the lines, including—and this was crucial—the very first one, "Auf dem Hügel sitz' ich spähend." The scansion ⌣⌣ — ⌣ — ⌣ — ⌣ fell into patterns in $\frac{3}{4}$ time beginning on beat 2 or 3. But in poem number 6, although most of the first syllables are still weak, there are awkward exceptions: the first line "Nimm sie hin denn, diese Lieder," and another line which I believe interested Beethoven particularly, "Ohne Kunstgepräng' erklungen." The triple-meter patterns of song number 1 would not do for "Nimm sie hin" and would sound flabby on the word "Ohne." In a situation like this a composer is well advised to hedge his bets. After choosing a basic $\frac{2}{4}$ meter with each line beginning on beat 1, Beethoven also lead the first melodic phrase up to an agogic accent on the third syllable, so that lines such as "Und du singst was ich gesungen" would work as well as "Nimm sie hin denn, diese Lieder.")

A second refinement in the da capo plan was made after the autograph had ostensibly been completed. In fact, this refinement counts as the most significant addition to the autograph, which is a very clean one, by Beethoven's standards, incorporating relatively few additions or major corrections. But in the final song the quiet, tentative-sounding piano recollection of the single line "Auf dem Hügel sitz' ich spähend," just before the voice brings back the whole of the tune, was a last-minute inspiration. The two bars in question were squeezed into the space originally occupied by the following one bar. It is even possible Beethoven had a momentary temptation to mirror this piano statement at the

heading might admit of two interpretations, but Beethoven's meaning is clarified when text words from stanza 1 appear: "die ich dir Geliebte sang ~~Zu der~~ ~~Laute~~ Sin[ge]." "Nim̃ sie" are the sole words accompanying the second sketch, which appears with the sparse sketches for song no. 5 and the coda (p. 72).

very beginning of the cycle; at bar 1, song number 1, there is the relic of
an erased "caret" (⊠)

This little piano passage has interesting parallels in two instrumental
compositions written within months of the song cycle, the Cello Sonata
in C, Op. 102, no. 1, and the Piano Sonata in A, Op. 101. These sonatas
are twins, standing together and apart from other pieces by Beethoven
in a number of ways. They both open with an unusually gentle lyric
statement, followed by a forceful vivace movement in one of the submediant keys. Then comes an adagio in the original tonic key (tonic
minor in Op. 101); this turns out to be an extended introduction to the
coming finale. In both sonatas the transition to the finale is a sort of
meditative miniature cadenza centering on a return of the first bars of
the opening movement. Such returns are, of course, rare in Beethoven, and
here they have a surprisingly romantic cast, seeming much more like
momentary nostalgic recollections than like recapitulations in the approved
classical style. The effect stems from the subtle tonal placement of these
returns. Coming within cadenzalike passages, they sound as if they are
hovering on the dominant, even though in Op. 102, no. 1, the music looks
as though it is in the tonic and, in fact, no dominant pedal is present.
A few years earlier Beethoven had achieved a similar effect in a true
cadenza (or what starts out like a true cadenza), with the return of the
horn theme in the cadenza of the first movement of the Piano Concerto
no. 5. In all these passages, actual tonic arrival or establishment waits
for a later juncture—in the concerto, for the final ritornello, and in the
sonatas, for the first downbeat of the finale themes.

The parallel passages in the sonatas and the song cycle illuminate one
another, at least to my way of thinking or apprehending the music. The
returns in the sonatas help us hear the piano return in *An die ferne
Geliebte* as a tiny cadenza or fermata, introduced by an arpeggio and
perched over a dominant which Beethoven takes care not to clarify too
rapidly. The slowly reiterated B♭ at the beginning of the tune is directly
to the purpose here; the arpeggio is also a slow one, surely; tonic arrival
waits for the vocal statement of the complete tune, with its cadence.
Furthermore, the fact that the return in the song cycle is directly symbolic
—the beloved echoing the songs sung by the lover—conveys something
about the quality or the mood of the sonata passages. They, too, are
distant half-visions, unexpected, muted, nostalgic in effect. And like the
echo of the lover's song in *An die ferne Geliebte,* they seem to inspire
directly the forthright, affirmative music that follows.

Then at the very end of the cycle, the last two bars of the piano postlude contain the melody of *Auf dem Hügel* once again, played in a compressed version an octave higher, this time forte. The passage appears

in the autograph, but as a correction; something has been scratched out under certain of the notes. Thanks to the sketches on the back of the autograph, we can see that this thematic return, too, was an afterthought. The sketches run as follows:

Ex. 1

Beethoven must have thought of this final piano statement of *Auf dem Hügel* in conjunction with the earlier one, though the autograph does not make it clear whether or not they were both done at the same sitting.

What the piano does as its final gesture here is to interpret the first fragment or motif of a longer melody as a self-contained cadential unit. This device, with its inherent quality of paradox, had been used occasionally by all the classic composers: by Haydn in the Quartet in G, Op. 17, no. 5 (the earliest example?), and in the Op. 33 quartets; by Mozart in the Overture to *La finta giardiniera* and in Symphony no. 39 in E♭; by Beethoven in the Op. 12 violin sonatas and recently in the Eighth Symphony.[28] In most earlier cases the melodic outline of the motif is what one would expect—a descending fifth from dominant to tonic (5 to 1). The situation in *An die ferne Geliebte* is richer in that the fragment arches from 5 up to 1 down to 3 and leaves ambiguous which interval is "functional," 5–1 or 1–3 or 5–3. The result is more aphoristic and arresting

---

[28] Incidentally, the idea of ending the first movement of the Eighth Symphony in this way was, again, a last-minute refinement of Beethoven's original plan; compare the early version in Willy Hess, *Beethoven: Supplemente zur Gesamtausgabe*, IV, 70.

In considering this device in general, a distinction is worth making between those cases in which the truncated figure is played several times to make the cadence, and the more unexpected cases in which it is played just once.

in effect than paradoxical or witty.[29] The scherzo of the *Hammerklavier Sonata* is interesting to consider in this context, and so is the cavatina from the Quartet in B♭, Op. 130:

Ex. 2

V

We have seen how the "cyclic" idea in *An die ferne Geliebte* grew from a simple da capo of the opening tune in the final song to a recapitulation of considerable subtlety. For the intervening songs, Beethoven followed a relatively simple plan. On the evidence of the sketches, he hit upon this at once in almost all particulars. The songs are set in different keys, except for numbers 3 and 4, which Beethoven treated as a unit in this respect: the keys are E♭, G, A♭, A♭, C, and E♭. Between them come short, sometimes abrupt piano transitions which take care *not* to establish the new keys with the force of a true modulation. Internally, too, most of the songs shun modulation. Exceptions are number 2, in which the second stanza shifts to the subdominant, C, and number 6, in which the second stanza modulates to the dominant, B♭.

Two striking things about this key scheme are the strength of the mediant, G, shadowed by the submediant, and the weakness—almost the nonexistence—of the dominant. The subdominant, though it is the key of two songs, numbers 3 and 4, is also weakened. In number 3, the cadence to each stanza comes on one of Beethoven's characteristically quirky $\frac{6}{4}$ chords, root-position triads occurring only at the beginnings of the fol-

---

[29] In his article, "Kleine Beiträge zur Beethovens Liedern und Bühnenwerken," *Neues Beethoven-Jahrbuch*, II (1925), 55–56, Hans Joachim Moser noted a special "Schlussdevise" in Beethoven's songs *Andenken, Adelaide, Wonne der Wehmut, An die Hoffnung*, Op. 94, and *An die ferne Geliebte*. For Moser the effect was "like a dreamlike echo." However this may be, I find fewer similarities between the end of *An die ferne Geliebte* and those other songs than differences—in thematic content, dynamics, phrasing, even scoring (voice or piano), and certainly in the over-all quality of the gesture. On the other hand, the ending of the cavatina in Op. 130 (ex. 2) seems to me close in spirit to that of the songs.

lowing stanzas. In number 4, the beginning of the tune is over a dominant pedal, and although the end of it does cadence on a root-position
tonic triad, this is undercut by a preceding *échappée* figure supported
once again by a $^6_4$ chord. All this confirms the feeling that in large structural terms the subdominant, A♭, is an upper neighbor to the important
mediant degree, G.

The prominence of the mediant appears more clearly yet from a
consideration of the tessitura of the six songs. In the diagram below
(example 3) small notes indicate the initial notes of the various tunes,
stemless "chords" their over-all vocal ranges, and circled notes their
cadential tonics: [30]

Ex. 3

The tessitura rises steadily, mirroring the emotional crescendo we have
noted (and Beethoven noted) in the poems. While the songs in E♭ and
A♭ remain, in general, within the E♭–E♭ octave and those in G and C
remain within the G–G octave, the cadence notes themselves rise from
low E♭ to C. Then, after the da capo, the coda makes a cadence for the
cycle as a whole on high E♭, within the G–G octave. Both the last cadence
in the voice and the last cadence in the piano stress the note G strikingly:
the voice by means of the *échappée* figure G–F–G–E♭,[31] and the piano by
means of the recollection of "Auf dem Hügel" (B♭–C–D–E♭–E♭–G) discussed above. The last treble note heard is G.

The next diagram, example 4, attempts to summarize the articulation
of Beethoven's key scheme and the role played in this by the piano transitions. The large notes represent the tonic keys of the various songs and
the small ones reproduce the transitions, in complete or in skeleton form.
In song number 6 subsidiary bass notes within the piece are also shown.
It will be seen that there are several threads running through these transitions: a pattern of three reiterated notes derived from "Auf dem
Hü(gel)"; semitone steps E♭–D/D–E♭ and especially G–A♭/A♭–G (which

---

[30] Song no. 2 and the first part of no.
6 have no circles because the music remains unresolved melodically, the voice
cadencing not on *1* but on *3* in both
cases (on B and G respectively). The
chord in parentheses in no. 2 refers to the
range of the tune when it is played a

fourth (actually an eleventh) higher by
the piano while the voice sings the words
of stanza 2 on a monotone—the monotone being G.

[31] Compare the *échappée* cadence to
tune no. 4, mentioned above.

places A♮ in a neighbor relationship to G); and a descending-third motif ("Ewiglich dein!"; "Es kehret der Maien"), which, as we shall see, has some larger importance for the cycle as a whole. It is significant, perhaps, that Beethoven pulled none of these threads very tight.

Ex. 4

However, he definitely had the piano transitions very much in mind from the start. This is one thing that is not clear from Nottebohm's extensive and otherwise fairly effective display of the Scheide sketches in *Zweite Beethoveniana*. The following sketch(es), for example, which record an early idea for song number 2, may show a transition from numbers 1 to 2 and perhaps also the germ of a transition from numbers 2 to 3:

Ex. 5

An even earlier notation for number 2 hints at a different sort of transition:

Ex. 6

The next idea for this transition was a passage of up-and-down triplet scales—as Nottebohm should have shown but did not at the beginning of his transcription of a large-scale ink draft of number 3; he did, however, show the scales as they recur to form the interlude between stanzas, and they can be inspected in *Zweite Beethoveniana*, page 338, lines 10–11. Another sketch suggests cloudily how these scales were going to hook in with the end of number 2:

Ex. 7

To return to the transition between numbers 1 and 2: an obscure, different idea for this precedes a large-scale draft of number 2:

Ex. 8

On the previous page, but seemingly written later, is a corrected sketch approaching the final version. The bass semitone is there and also some kind of reiteration:

Ex. 9

The absence of transition between numbers 3 and 4 was decided on at
the start, as is indicated by an early sketch for number 3 (this sketch
precedes the large-scale draft mentioned above):

Ex. 10

Next, a large-scale ink draft of number 4 is followed by pencil squiggles
which can be interpreted (with hindsight) as gestures toward the long
piano introduction to number 5:

Ex. 11

Pencil sketches for this transition on the previous page were, again,
evidently written later:

Ex. 12

Number 5 is sketched less than the earlier songs. There does not seem
to be any indication of a piano transition (or retransition) after it.

It should be said that the transcriptions in examples 5–12 are, to a
considerable extent, conjectural; these sketches are mostly hard or im-
possibly to read exactly. Indeed, that was one reason why Nottebohm
skipped them.

VI

The Insel Verlag in 1924 brought out an elegant little 12mo edition of *An die ferne Geliebte,* edited by the great lied scholar Max Friedlaender. Friedlaender's presentation copy to Dr. and Mrs. Alfred Einstein, now in the library of the University of California at Berkeley, has on the flyleaf an obvious-enough quotation from Jeitteles: "Nehmt sie hin denn, diese Lieder." Less obvious is the music written above this, a conflation of tunes numbers 1 and 6 that is definitely *not* a quotation from Beethoven:

Ex. 13

Nehmt sie hin denn, diese Lieder

This was a slip stemming from a deeper wisdom, perhaps. It was probably many, many years previously that similarities between the two tunes had lodged in some corner of Friedlaender's brain.[32]

The last song of the cycle is the most interesting, and one feels more than one twinge of regret that sketches for it are not present in the Scheide group. Its melody is modeled on tune number 1, which emerges in its final form only at the end of the extensive series of sketches in the sketchbook. The richest feature of tune number 1 is the memorable drop of a sixth, E♭–G, on the word "spähend"; harmony comes into play as well as melody, for within the stylistic limits of this music the C-minor chord is striking in itself and the more so for being approached by a leap in both outer voices.[33] All this conspires to stress the note G, the importance of which in the cycle as a whole has already been indicated. Also important is the interval of a descending third, B♭–G, between dominant and mediant degrees (5 and 3). This interval encloses both phrases 1 and 3; in one case the path from 5 to 3 is arpeggiation of the tonic triad, in the other chromatic step motion, but the echo is still clear (even without

---

[32] Few commentators seem to have noticed these similarities, an exception being Romain Rolland in *Beethoven. Les grandes époques créatrices,* III (Paris, 1937), 197. But, in fact, I know of only two serious or extensive studies of *An die ferne Geliebte*—Rolland's and that of Moser, in *Das deutsche Lied seit Mozart* (Berlin, 1937), II, 16–24. It is beyond belief how much musicologists can write —the last of the *Beethoven-Jahrbuch's* five-year Beethoven bibliographies has 504 entries—without looking hard at important composition.

[33] An improvement over the most advanced sketch, in which the space between E♭ and C in the bass is dutifully filled in by a D. Nottebohm's transcript of this sketch, p. 337, l. 8, omits the D.

listening to the rhymes in the verses). Things become even clearer in song number 6, where the same interval reappears as a direct echo between the cadences of phrases 1 and 4.

The descending third 5–3 is also prominent in the two mediant-submediant songs, numbers 2 and 5. Number 2 ends with this interval in the voice on the words "Ewiglich dein!"

The relationship of tunes numbers 1 and 6, and the role of the descending third in this relationship, can be seen from the following composite example:

Ex. 14

Phrases 1, 2, and 4 of the later song mirror phrases 1, 2, and 3 of the earlier one in terms of initial, final, and peak notes. The "spähend" minor sixth is still there, though by being filled in it is made quieter (this can be said also of the other phrases). The cadences of phrases 1 and 4, which are identical, consist of the descending third B♭–G filled in diatonically. Ending on 3, the tune does not come to a thorough cadence; resolution waits for the da capo and the coda.

Beethoven was sufficiently interested in the interval 5–3 to echo it in the piano after stanzas 1 and 3—doubtless as a *Nachklang* of "der Laute süssem Klang" mentioned rather gratuitously by Jeitteles in stanza 1 (but the publisher gratefully seized on this lute as the subject of his title-page vignette). As late as at the time of writing the autograph, Beethoven actually contemplated multiplying these piano echoes: there are extra, canceled bars in the autograph after stanzas 1 and 3 and after the piano introduction, too (see example 14). They would certainly have sounded saccharine and flabby. The double echo in stanza 3, in particular, would have spoiled the effect of the vocal echo on the words "Nur, nur der Sehn(sucht)," which carries the voice up to high F.

The one phrase of the new tune that is not modeled on the old one, phrase 3, consists of the eight notes F–F–F–F–F–G–G–F. Beethoven seems to have been playing a dangerous game of quiet here. One can adduce some mitigating circumstances—the ostinato F points toward the dominant, B♭, soon to be introduced for the first time in the cycle; the phrase comes on F no more than twice; the other time it comes, in the piano introduction, it sounds less dull because it is transposed up to B♭ and provides a springboard for a melodic climax on high F in the phrase that follows. (This climax would not have been good to bring into the song itself; as we have just noted, high F was being saved for the words "Nur der Sehnsucht sich bewusst.") Another explanation for the brute simplicity of this fragment of music may perhaps be found in the words ultimately joined to it in stanza 3, "Ohne Kunstgepräng' erklungen." Did Beethoven take this statement so seriously that he fashioned a musical line for it that would sound almost pre-artistic? It is a remarkable fact that he also "simplified" the word "Kunstgepräng'" when he copied the Jeitteles poems in the autograph—the sole word that is garbled in his careful transcript (see page 126).

Stanza 2, "Wenn das Dämm'rungsrot dann ziehet," is the only through-composed stanza in the cycle. One reason for this special treatment was the text, obviously; Beethoven may have been moved by the idea of temporal distance suggested by the rich evening imagery in this stanza, or he may have been responding to the richness for its own sake. The throbbing triplet chords are in his best pantheistic vein. Another reason was probably a desire to find a position, at last, for a clear dominant in the total key scheme of the cycle. We can refer back to example 4 on page 142. By beginning song number 6 on the subdominant, Beethoven was doing a number of rather elegant things. He was making possible a common-tone link between songs numbers 5 and 6; he was referring for the last time to the key of numbers 3 and 4 and to the large-scale semitone pattern G–A♭–G enclosing them; and he was placing the dominant, which is finally to emerge, in maximum—though, at the same time, very delicate—relief. After stanza 1 ends on G in the voice, stanza 2 heads back to a major triad on G; G is everywhere in evidence in *An die ferne Geliebte,* and perhaps the "Berge so blau" of number 2 are now finding their reflection in the "stillen blauen See." From here a circle of fifths produces a clear but peaceful modulation to the dominant, B♭. Beethoven gets out of it by means of one of those extraordinary compressed gestures that become more and more frequent in the third period:

Ex. 15

The hollow, molto adagio B♭ evokes the slowly reiterated B♭s of "Auf dem Hü(gel)"; then the solemn two-part counterpoint in octaves gingerly picks out the chords of E♭, G major, A♭, even A♭ minor, as well as the semitone G–A♭ which had joined (or, rather, disjoined) the earlier songs. This bar seems to hold the entire tonal dynamic of the composition in a nutshell. It also stresses the key words "und du singst," words which record the psychological turning point of the poem, and it associates tune number 6 more closely than ever with tune number 1 (see examples 13 and 14).

Without much doubt the expressive climax of the song cycle comes at the through-composed stanza of the last song and the molto-adagio bar following it. The discharge of tension represented by this climax—the full resolution of the dominant—is delayed for quite a considerable length of time. The next stanza, stanza 3, returns to the tune, which begins on the subdominant and which never comes to a thorough cadence (when coming to cadences with the tonic in the bass, the voice always settles not on *1* but on *3*, via the descending-third figure we have just been discussing). At the end of the stanza the voice repeats the last line, "Nur der Sehnsucht sich bewusst," and the music hovers, cadenzalike, as the piano tentatively recalls "Auf dem Hügel," half in the tonic and half over the dominant. Resolution is accomplished only at the end of the vocal da capo of this tune, at the end of stanza 4.

Thereafter, in the coda or *stretta,* the voice and the piano concentrate on the phrase of tune number 1 in which the descending third B♭–G is filled in chromatically. The cadence zone resounds with thirds hinging on G. After the voice ends with the *échappée* figure G–F–G–E♭, the piano plays the chromatic motif from B♭ to G one more time before ending with the last recollection of "Auf dem Hügel" and the descending sixth E♭–G.

VII

It may be of interest to take up a few more points about the sketches and the autograph.

The early sheet of pencil sketches in London is only minimally informative. Seven of the total ten lines on one side contain some music, roughly written and faded, about twenty bars in all, and it is not clear that more than four of these bars are consecutive at any one point. For example, here is the complete line from which Nottebohm took his transcription:

Ex. 16

It is perhaps safe to infer from this that the unfortunate "up the hill" beginning of the tune, still present in the Scheide sketches, was one of the original notions, and that Beethoven had not yet seen that the climax of the first phrase should be on "spähend" rather than "Hügel." A somewhat clearer line of sketches suggests that the last phrase of the tune was the earliest fixed into something like its present state:

Ex. 17

This impression is confirmed by the Scheide sketches. There are no identifiable sketches for any of the other songs on this early sheet.

In the "Scheide" Sketchbook, the six pages devoted to *An die ferne Geliebte* follow closely on the sketches for *Sehnsucht* (*Die stille Nacht umdunkelt*) discussed by Lewis Lockwood elsewhere in this volume. As with the *Sehnsucht* sketches, the first page-opening for *An die ferne Geliebte* (pages 68–69) consists mainly of dense work on a single tune, *Auf dem Hügel*.[34] Then the other four pages are devoted essentially to large-scale drafts—though, in this case, not drafts of the same piece but of the other songs in the cycle.[35] All three stanzas of song number 2 are drafted consecutively on page 70. Number 3 is mapped out in full on page 71 and runs into the first bars of number 4, which continues (on two staffs) overleaf, page 72. Page 73 has full drafts of the tunes of numbers 5 and 6, the latter being simply the tune of *Auf dem Hügel* with an indication of the new words. In short, a different method of sketching was

---

[34] The page-opening was not quite clean when Beethoven started the song. Line 1 of p. 68 has a two-bar sketch in A major, and ll. 1–2 of p. 69 have a copy of the folksong *Es ritten drei Reiter* (cf. n. 20).

[35] These drafts can be found in N II as follows: no. 2, p. 338 (incomplete, cf. ex. 18); nos. 3–4, pp. 338–39 (incomplete); no. 5, p. 339; no. 6, p. 339.

used for the later songs; they could be roughed out swiftly and surely,
without the careful work of melodic modeling that the first song seems to
have required from the start. It also required later attention, and it is not
an easy matter to see exactly what was written at any one sitting. Pep-
pered over the pages are notions for the piano transitions, as shown in
examples 5–12 above.

Nottebohm printed almost as many sketches for the *Auf dem Hügel*
tune (twelve) as he did for *Sehnsucht*. Consequently the former song has
formed the basis for cloudy or plainly erroneous statements about Beethoven's compositional process as frequently as has the latter. Here, Lockwood's comments on the situation with *Sehnsucht* are exactly apposite.
The aspect of the pages devoted to *Auf dem Hügel* does not suggest long,
tedious labor so much as "the rapid tumbling-out of ideas," and the process of melodic formation can be seen to have been less a matter of random exploration than of trying out options around certain firmly fixed
constants. One such constant was the high note on "spähend," another
was the general form of the last phrase. What was not fixed was that
descending sixth on "spähend" and the resulting low note G. Even though
as we listen to the piece today this leap down to G sounds like the direct
impetus for the move to G major in the next song, the choice of G major
was certainly made first and the descending sixth decided on only later.
It is worth noting that in both *Sehnsucht* and *Auf dem Hügel* a significant part of the problem was the balance of 5 and 3 degrees; Beethoven
can hardly have been unaware of the parallel, for he sketched both songs
for a time in the same key, E♭.

Sketches for the second song, *Wo die Berge so blau,* are in some
ways the most interesting. After two preliminary sketches, given in examples 5 and 6, there comes a series of superimposed drafts that pose a pretty
problem for the transcriber. It seems that on lines 2–6 of page 70 (plate
X) Beethoven first wrote a hasty pencil draft covering all three stanzas,
but with some passages skipped over with "etc." indications. Then he
came back with pen in hand and wrote over this draft, trying two alternative versions one above the other—lines 1, 3, and 5 aligned (and barred)
with lines 2, 4, and 6 respectively. He ran out of space and continued
after a *Vi-de* mark on lines 15–16. The original pencil draft and the ink
revisions are shown separately in example 18, page 152.

The third of these transcriptions is unproblematic, but the second is
conjectural and the first is speculative. I have ventured to set down all
three because, for all their uncertainties, they do establish certain points.
Beethoven had the descending-third figure D–C–B in mind quite early,
although he dropped it momentarily in the second draft (compare also

Plate X   *"Scheide" Sketchbook*
(library of Mr. William Scheide, Princeton), page 70.

Ex. 18

example 7). He contemplated an ostinato for stanza 2 on F♯ rather than on G(!). And taken with the preliminary sketches, the drafts show Beethoven's changing ideas about the declamation appropriate to this poem. Vacillation continued until the autograph stage, where the beginning of the song was first written as shown below in small notes, then corrected as shown in full-size ones:

Ex. 19

The main points of alteration in the autograph have already been discussed in the pages above. Hubert Unverricht, in his valuable study of problems of textual criticism in Beethoven, mentions and illustrates another interesting point, in the piano postlude six bars from the end of the composition, where the autograph reflects the composer's "inner aural conception while the first edition offers a notation that can be realized technically."[36] Since the paper is ruled with twelve staves and they are all filled by four systems of music, Beethoven did not have any space at hand for the composing or recomposing he always found necessary at the autograph stage. As a result, he made many of his smaller corrections by scratching out the original and writing the new version on top; the original is often impossible to reconstruct with confidence. Larger corrections had to be made on separate sheets, a recourse that seems to have been needed only once, in the introduction to song number 5 (page 16). The idea of including two bars of the tune in the piano, just before the voice enters, was either an afterthought or something that slipped

---

[36] Hubert Unverricht, *Die Eigenschriften und die Originalausgaben von Werke Beethovens in ihrer Bedeutung für die moderne Textkritik* (Kassel, 1960). In bar 6 of Unverricht's transcription from the autograph, p. 26, I believe that the second and third notes should be A (natural assumed) and A♭ (the flat written in under the cancel line); compare with the first sketch in ex. 1.

Beethoven's mind as he wrote the autograph. These two bars do not appear there, but from a "caret" (⊠) one can infer that Beethoven was sending along an insert sheet to the copyist. To be precise, the insert (which is now lost) must have covered the last bar prior to the two-bar passage as well; that last bar does appear in the autograph, but it is canceled and the left-hand chords were never put in.

VIII

In the total span of Beethoven's output we can see *An die ferne Geliebte* as a quiet herald of the third-period style. Of the various features discussed in the paragraphs above, two in particular encourage such a view—the surprising assimilation of the *Volksweise* ideal and the treatment of tonality. As I have remarked before, a tendency toward means of immediate communication on the most basic level is very marked in the late music. The tune for the *Ode to Joy* is the famous paradigm for this tendency. But it is also manifested in other works and in other ways: in the late bagatelles, in the songlike sonata and quartet movements entitled "arietta," "arioso," and "cavatina," in the instrumental recitatives which seem to break down controlled discourse in favor of direct communion, and in those naïve country-dance scherzos—movements so different in mood from the scherzos of earlier years. *An die ferne Geliebte* was Beethoven's first emphatic essay in this new genre. It was also the first of his two all-but-explicit ideological statements about it, the other being, of course, the *Ode to Joy*. Songs without the adornments of art can achieve loving communication and brotherhood.

To be sure, the ambivalence in respect to simple and complex utterance that we noted in Beethoven's earlier song writing is still much in evidence in the later music. Even the *Ode to Joy*, starting as an unprecedented, unaccompanied, and utterly unpretentious tune, works its way up through ornamental variations to a double fugue. More quietly, *An die ferne Geliebte*, too, shows that Beethoven could not accept the *Volksweise* ideal in its pure form. Indicative here is the way the piano almost imperceptibly assumes more and more importance as the piece proceeds. In song number 1, all that the piano provides is accompaniment, an introductory chord to give the singer his note, and small self-effacing interludes between the stanzas. In the next three numbers the piano also plays two bars of the vocal melody before the voice sings it. A twelve-bar piano passage of nature illustration begins number 5—bolstered at the last minute, as we have just seen, by a two-bar forecast of the melody as in the earlier songs. In number 6 the piano plays the entire tune before the voice enters, and what is more, plays it in a somewhat different and more emphatic version. During the middle, through-composed stanza of this song it is really the piano that guides the voice, and the da capo of tune number 1 is initiated (and in symbolic terms, impelled) by the piano. The excited coda sees the voice swept along by the piano, which behaves like the orchestra in a miniature cantata or opera finale. Small wonder that the wording of Beethoven's original title page in the edition, "Ein Liederkreis . . . mit Begleitung des Piano-Forte in Musik gesetzt," did not satisfy him and came to be changed in the second issue to the less invidious rubric " . . . für Gesang und Piano-Forte." [37]

It is also the piano that, by carrying through the transitions illustrated in example 4, controls the unusual tonal dynamic in the song cycle. These transitions are arranged so as *not* to make convincing, stable modulations. The new keys G, A♭, and C are simply asserted or, as it were, placed in apposition to the original tonic, E♭; the original tonic is never erased from the listener's memory. It has already been mentioned (page 140) how the cadences in the two middle songs weaken any impression that they have an independent tonality of their own. At the end of the cycle, there is no need for tonic re-establishment by means of anything like a customary Beethovenian retransition passage, with extended dominant preparation and all the rest (it is significant that the tonal return in this composition comes well ahead of the thematic return). As a result of this treatment of tonality, there is a distinct feeling of instability or tension in the way the middle songs "set"; nothing arises to dispel this feeling, since the songs are so utterly simple in themselves. It can be interpreted as a feeling of unreality, perhaps, corresponding to the fantasy-making indulged in by Jeitteles's lover in these middle songs. His reality, in this interpretation, is the E♭ tonic of songs numbers 1 and 6.

The interconnection of all the songs in *An die ferne Geliebte*, accomplished by the piano transitions, is always mentioned by writers on this history of the lied. This feature distinguishes Beethoven's song cycle, the first serious example of the genre, from almost all later ones. What is less frequently mentioned is that this feature makes the inner songs dependent—much more so than the songs of *Die schöne Müllerin* or *Die Winterreise,* or even those of *Dichterliebe,* for all of Schumann's anxious tonality-plotting. Indeed, Beethoven's inner songs hardly have enough lyrical distinction—and they certainly do not have musical distinction of any other kind—to sustain them simply on their own terms. They live by their special tonal placement in the total composition; unlike *Die Post* or *Ich grolle nicht* they would be unthinkable as separate numbers. This was what Hans Boettcher was saying when he described the cycle, in

---

37 Pointed out by Tyson, "Beethoven in Steiner's Shop," 121.

his monograph on Beethoven's songs, as "gleichsam *ein* ungeheuer erweitertes Lied." [38]

Something of the same tonal poise between large musical sections is encountered in certain of Beethoven's last compositions, such as the *Grosse Fuge* and the Quartet in C♯ Minor, Op. 131. We may not wish to describe the quartet as "a single dreadfully extended movement, so to speak," but manifestly Beethoven went further here than ever before in the direction of unifying the members of the cyclic sonata, quartet, or symphony form into a single unit. There are no stops between movements, but instead curt musical transitions which are interesting to compare with those in *An die ferne Geliebte*. Again, the simplicity of certain movements—simplicity, at least, relative to Beethoven's ordinary musical style in quartets—contributes to a sense of tension in the way these movements "set" vis-à-vis the opening tonality of C♯ minor. The famous Neapolitan position of the second movement contributes a great deal to its strange ephemeral quality and is still sufficiently vivid in the listener's memory to validate the Neapolitan echo at the end of the finale. Of another movement, the presto following the A-major variations, Robert Simpson has recently observed that it actually sounds on the dominant of A all the way through, rather than in its own ostensible key of E.[39] And Joachim von Hecker, studying the sketches for the C♯-Minor Quartet, came across a startling analogy to *An die ferne Geliebte*: in place of the G♯-minor adagio prior to the finale, Beethoven once planned a return of the opening fugue theme.[40] Even after dropping this idea, he still made one of the finale themes echo the fugue theme in an unusually direct way, as is well known.

Whether or not the specific analogies drawn above seem convincing or prove to be suggestive, there will probably be little argument on the general proposition that a new quality of tonality emerges in Beethoven's late music. This quality is not easy to characterize, but perhaps one can say that tonality is now treated less as a process and more as a kind of absolute. Movement from one tonality to another, with its concomitant psychological sense of sequence, or direction, or achievement, or whatever—this interests Beethoven less at this stage than tonality as a framework, an orientation, a system. To venture a metaphor from electricity, he is no longer taking tonality as the potential to drive musical currents of all kinds in all directions, but rather as an electrostatic field. It is in

[38] Boettcher, p. 67.

[39] Robert Simpson, "The Chamber Music for Strings," in *The Beethoven Reader*, ed. Denis Arnold and Nigel Fortune (New York, 1971), p. 274.

[40] Joachim von Hecker, "Untersuchungen an den Skizzen zum Streichquartett cis-moll op. 131 von Beethoven," Diss. Freiburg, 1956.

the light of this new attitude that we can best understand his well-known reticence toward the dominant tonality during his late years. The dominant is employed less often, and when it is employed it is handled in a notably quiet, undynamic way. This feature, too, is adumbrated in *An die ferne Geliebte*—more strikingly, I should say, than in any of the earlier music.

After the small burst of song writing in 1815–16 that produced *Sehnsucht* and *An die ferne Geliebte,* Beethoven in effect abandoned song composition. There are only two more significant songs: *Resignation* (1817) and *Abendlied* (1820). Yet the incorporation of song into his large-scale instrumental works became more and more important to him as a compositional impetus. And somewhat paradoxically, these works assimilated certain formal and tonal procedures pioneered in his most ambitious song composition, procedures that evolved in direct response to the quite special conditions imposed by Jeitteles's cycle of poems and the compositional choices open to Beethoven as he approached them specifically as a song writer. In the annals of musicology *An die ferne Geliebte* has a safe place only, it seems, in the history of the lied, and even this place is not always conceded with good grace or good sense. It is also important for its role in Beethoven's own development—in his musical development as well as what Sullivan called his "spiritual development," the musical record of his changing response to life experience. It deserves study in the context of the musical style of his third period, the music of the last decade.

The Authors of the
Op. 104 String Quintet

Alan Tyson

✵ IT WOULD BE SURPRISING if Op. 104—Beethoven's arrangement for string quintet of his C-Minor Piano Trio, Op. 1, no. 3—were anyone's favorite piece, though most of those who have commented on it have found something kind to say about it.[1] If they were puzzled that in 1817 Beethoven should have chosen to concern himself once again with a work he had published over twenty years earlier, they were fortunately spared the necessity of searching for any deep internal motives for his renewed interest, since the presence of an external stimulus at that time is well documented. As for its place in Beethoven's creative output, the summary that is found in Thayer, "the greatest musical labor in the course of this unproductive year [i.e. 1817]," seems (to judge, at any rate, from the number of times that it has been quoted or paraphrased) to have found general favor; and the same may be said of Thayer's unpretentious account of the skill with which the transcription was made.[2] I think it possible, nevertheless, that Beethoven's contribution to his own Op. 104 has been radically misconceived, and that a revised estimate of that contribution will do better justice both to the strengths of the work and to its weaknesses, as well as illuminate some of the problems that it contains.

It is apparent that the external stimulus for the arrangement was Beethoven's dissatisfaction with an arrangement that had been completed by someone else. This much at least emerges from three sources that must be briefly reviewed here: a score, an anecdote, and a letter.

---

[1] See, for instance, Friedrich Munter, "Beethovens Bearbeitungen eigener Werke," *Neues Beethoven-Jahrbuch*, VI (1935), 159–73; Willy Hess, "Beethoven's Revisions of His Own Works," *Miscellanea Musicologica* (Adelaide), V (1970), 1–25.

[2] Thayer-Deiters-Riemann IV (1907), 43–44.

(a) The score is in the Stiftung Preussischer Kulturbesitz in Berlin; known as "Grasnick 11," it is an *Abschrift* made in 1817 by copyists, with extensive corrections by Beethoven. On the title page stood originally the single word "Quintett," written by a copyist; but Beethoven crossed it out and replaced it with the following whimsical inscription (plate XI):

> Bearbeitetes terzett zu einem/3³ stimigen quintett/vom Hr. Gutwil-len/u. aus dem schein von 5 stimen/zu wirklichen 5 Stimen ans Tags/licht gebracht, wie auch aus größter Miserabilität/zu einigem Ansehn erhoben/von Hr. Wohlwollen.—/1817/am 14ten august./ NB: die ursprüngliche 3 stimige quintett partitur/ist den Untergöttern als ein feierliches/Brandopfer dargebracht worden.

i.e. "trio arranged as a 3-part quintet by Mr. Goodwill, and from a sem-blance of 5 parts brought to the light of day as 5 genuine parts, and at the same time raised from the most abject misery to some degree of respectability, by Mr. Wellwisher. August 14, 1817. NB: the original 3-part quintet has been ceremonially sacrified as a burnt offering to the gods of the underworld."

(b) Much that is mystifying in this inscription is explained in an anecdote about Beethoven that found its way into the periodical *Cäcilia* in 1842,[4] which I summarize: a certain X. brought along for Beethoven's inspection a string-quintet arrangement that he had made of the C-Minor Piano Trio; probably he wanted to find out what the composer thought of it. Beethoven evidently found a great deal wrong with it, but the undertaking was sufficiently attractive to lead him to make his own transcription, which involved many changes. In this way a new score came into being which was quite different from X.'s; and on the cover the composer, in high good humor, wrote the inscription that has already been quoted.

(c) The identity of X., "Herr Gutwillen," is revealed in a letter from Beethoven to the publisher Steiner. This letter, now in the Beethovenhaus in Bonn,[5] is undated but must have been written in the middle of August, 1817:

> Here is the quintet *for the L[ieutenan]t G[enera]l's office.* I shall soon know what conditions to lay down for this work. Herr Kaufmann must not be told anything about it, because the day after tomorrow I shall write him a letter which will put an end to the whole affair. For Herr

---

[3] The figure was originally 4, i.e. "4-part quintet."

[4] *Cäcilia*, XXI (1842), 59–60. The anecdote is unsigned; it may have been contributed by the editor S. W. Dehn.

[5] SBH 424; Anderson no. 801.

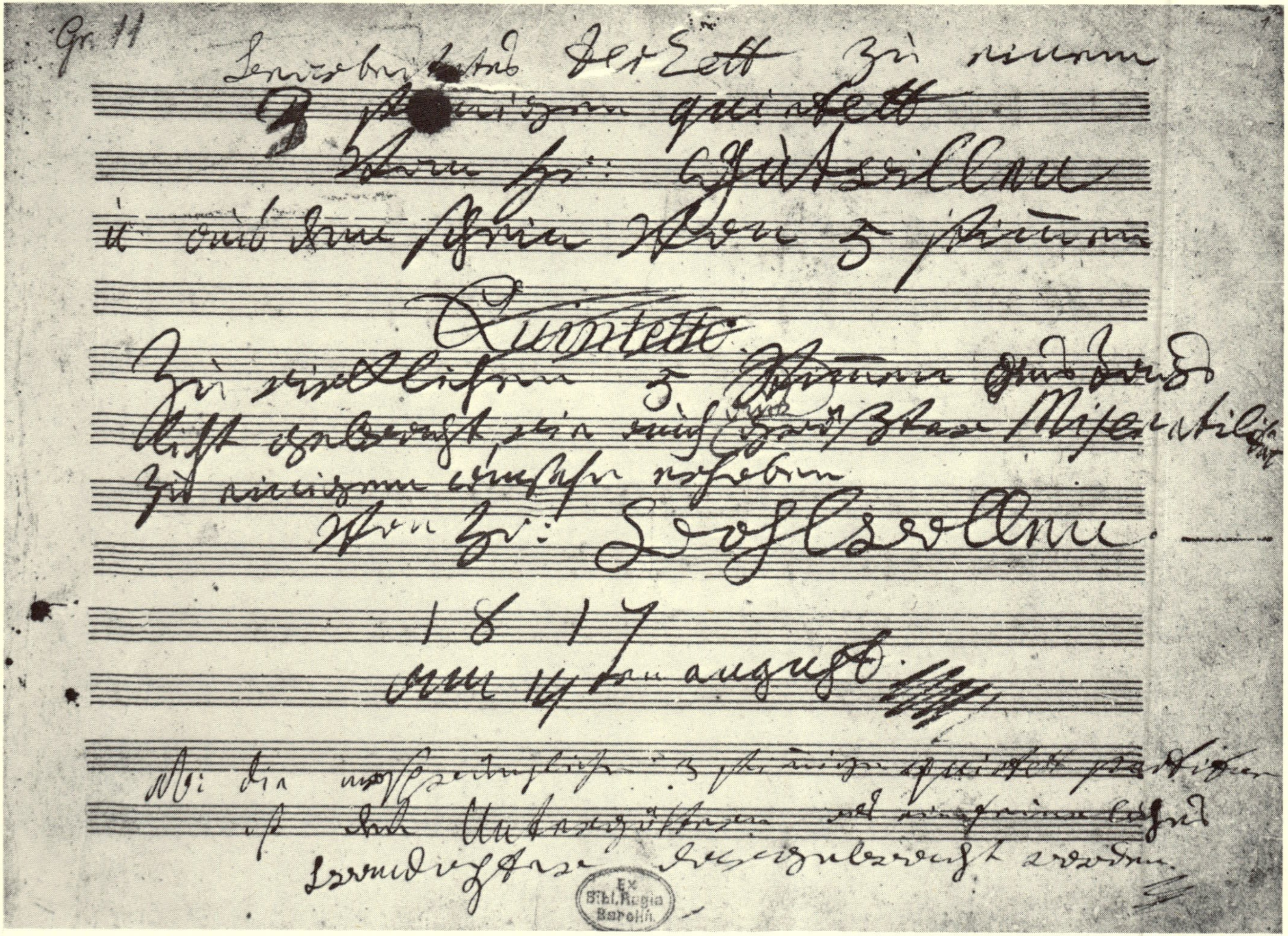

Plate XI ❧ Grasnick 11 (StPK, Berlin), title page (folio 1r).

K[aufmann] *only provided me with the occasion to undertake this complete revision.*[6]

By putting the three sources together one can form a fairly coherent picture of Herr Kaufmann visiting Beethoven with his own quintet arrangement of the trio; of Beethoven's dissatisfaction with it,[7] perhaps expressed initially only in an attempt to improve it, but later driving him to prepare his own quite distinct version; and finally, it is at least hinted, of the sacrificial burning of Herr Kaufmann's hapless score. But does this picture correspond to the facts? The crucial document here is the *Abschrift* already referred to, a score that evidently preserves more than one layer of work.

This *Abschrift* was written by two good copyists on twelve-staff paper that is uniform throughout;[8] there are two systems on each page, each with a blank staff under it (see plates XII–XIV). The major portion of the score (folios 1–24, comprising the first three movements and measures 1–119 of the finale) was copied by Wenzel Schlemmer, Beethoven's chief and preferred copyist for many years before his death in August, 1823. The rest (folios 25–35, with the remainder of the finale from measure 120), is in the hand of the copyist who was evidently Schlemmer's chief assistant and who is, in fact, represented in considerably more of the surviving *Abschriften* than Schlemmer himself.[9] The third hand found throughout the score is, of course, Beethoven's. Working at first in pencil, often in a somewhat tentative manner, and later inking over at least some of his definitive corrections or changes, he has left his mark on every page of the music, as well as taken command of the title page (as we have seen) and filled fourteen blank staffs at the end of the score with a penciled draft of a corrigenda list.

Thus the score of the quintet appears to take its place beside the

---

[6] I am assuming that "Kaufmann" (which also means "merchant") is a proper name here. Its owner has not been identified. For instances of the same name (or word) in the conversation books cf. *Konversationshefte*, ed. Georg Schünemann, I (Berlin, 1941), 156 (Dec., 1819), 337 (March, 1820), and Schünemann's notes to these passages.

[7] Hess goes a good deal further: "faced with the obviously clumsy work of this obliging gentleman, Beethoven may well have broken out into Homeric laughter."

[8] Its watermark (on the left half of the sheet, quadrants 1 and 2) is a crowned shield bearing a fleur-de-lis with the name C & I HONIG underneath. The letters GK in the bottom-right-hand corner of the sheet (in quadrant 4) suggest that the paper was made by the Kiesling brothers ("Gebrüder Kiesling").

[9] Cf. Alan Tyson, "Notes on Five of Beethoven's Copyists," *Journal of the American Musicological Society*, XXIII (1970), 439–71, where the second copyist is listed as "Copyist B." It is suggested there that in his later years Schlemmer may have left more and more of the work to be done by Copyist B.

large number of *überprüfte Abschriften* listed by Kinsky-Halm: scores prepared by copyists directly from Beethoven's autograph scores and checked by the composer. These, rather than the messy autographs them-selves, were normally regarded as embodying the definitive text of the work in manuscript form, and the composer usually corrected each one carefully before submitting it to a publisher as the *Stichvorlage* for an edition. Further scrutiny of the *Abschrift* would normally take place when the proofs of the engraved parts were compared and checked against it, and new corrections or revisions (e.g. added dynamics) would be inserted. It is not surprising, therefore, that by the time a work came to be published the *Abschrift* that had provided the text often contained a considerable number of corrections by the composer; such corrections, we have already said, are on every page of the quintet score. And yet—there is something wrong with classifying Grasnick 11 as an ordinary *überprüfte Abschrift*. The changes here are of a much more radical nature; and the suspicion arises that Beethoven could have had little to do with the text that Schlemmer and his assistant copied, and that his responsibility is limited to the changes that he subsequently made in it.

There is, in the first place, a striking difference between the quality of many of Beethoven's own entries and that of the rest of the score. The most consistent feature of what stood on the page before Beethoven's pencil and pen set to work on it is the literalness of the transcription. A little reflection will show what, at the lowest level of artistry, is required to turn a piano trio into a string quintet. Since two of the parts, a violin and a cello, are common to both ensembles, the problem might seem to a pedestrian arranger to consist in distributing the piano's part among the remaining three instruments—another violin and the two violas. In prac-tice something a little more subtle is often required, especially in passages where the piano's bass line is significant and needs a cello to do justice to it. But a common formula in the present arrangement (as Munter, for instance, observed) was for the first violin to be assigned the notes of the piano's right hand, and for the second violin to take over the trio's violin part. For an extended example of this treatment one need look no further than the first fifty or so measures of the quintet. This blameless but un-inspired scoring is rendered more opaque by double-stopping in the violas, and it is noteworthy that the imaginative touches and the devia-tions from literalness on the first page (plate XII)—the use of the violas' and the cello's C-string sonority in measures 1–2 and 4–5 (cello in mea-sure 1 only), the whole of the cello part in measures 8–10 and 14, and its pizzicatos, beginning in measures 11 and 15—all come from Beethoven's additions; it is easy to see that they were not in the original score.

In most of the other *überprüfte Abschriften,* moreover, it is noticeable that the changes introduced by Beethoven's revising hand are mainly confined to the elimination of errors, or the addition of minutiae already implied in the score (phrasing, dynamics, marks of expression); only occasionally do they contribute a further creative idea. The alterations in the quintet score, on the other hand, are substantial and run through the whole work; they are especially conspicuous in the second (variation) movement, where in several places the voice-leading has been considerably revised and enriched (e.g. the second movement, measures 24–27, 47, 51–53, 65–78, 85–88, 105–08, 113–19). Plate XIII shows the extent of the changes in the first half of variation 3 (the second movement, measures 65–72). While no reminder is needed of Beethoven's zeal for constantly improving his compositions prior to their publication, it must still be said that revisions of so fundamental a nature—and at this stage—are quite untypical of him and are restricted to those painful cases, such as that of the oratorio *Christus am Oelberge*, where an exceptionally long span of time intervened between the realization of his ideas on paper and their later publication.[10] There is no reason to suppose that Op. 104 falls into that category.

The view is thus forced on us that the *Abschrift* consists of two quite separate creative layers: a somewhat literal transcription of the piano trio for string quintet, for which Beethoven bears no responsibility, and an imaginative attempt to improve and vitalize it, which is wholly his. The author of the former can only be Herr Kaufmann, alias Herr Gutwillen, alias Herr X. Perhaps his original score was messy or hard to read, or perhaps there was no room in it for making any changes; it seems likely at all events that it was Beethoven himself who arranged to have it clearly copied out by his favorite copyist, before setting to work in an effort to raise it to respectability—i.e. to turn it into a genuine string quintet, with five real parts instead of a mere semblance of five parts, a "three-part quintet." One of the evident aims of Beethoven's changes was the enrichment of the part writing, especially (as has been said) in the slow movement. And when that task had been completed it may have struck him as a prudent move to make a burnt offering of Herr Kaufmann's original manuscript.[11]

---

[10] The 1814 revision of the opera *Leonore*, first produced in 1805 (and again, in a drastically cut version, in 1806), may be reckoned as another instance of this. Many of the changes there were for extramusical reasons. Beethoven disliked rewriting music that he had once regarded as finished; cf. his letter to Treitschke of April, 1814 (SBH 450; Anderson no. 479).

[11] Beethoven's letter to Steiner (quoted above) gives the impression that he was anxious to dismiss any claims by Herr Kaufmann to have contributed to the finished quintet.

Plate XII ❧ Grasnick 11 (StPK, Berlin), folio 1ᵛ
(measures 1–17 of the first movement of Op. 104).

Plate XIII ❧ *Grasnick 11 (StPK, Berlin), folio 15r*
(measures 65–72 of the second movement of Op. 104).

In the Berlin *Abschrift* itself there is no real difficulty in distinguishing Herr Kaufmann's underlying arrangement from the changes and additions that Beethoven imposed on it. But since no printed edition distinguishes the two layers, no one who does not have access to Grasnick 11 can at present be certain whether some detail that his eyes or ears have noted in Op. 104 comes from Beethoven, or whether it is due to Kaufmann. The publication of a critical score, indicating the separate contributions of the two men, must be regarded as a priority of Beethoven scholarship, since matters of some aesthetic importance are involved here. An appropriate place of publication would be, perhaps, in an Appendix to the critical notes of the new *Gesamtausgabe*.

We are bound to view certain passages in a somewhat different way if we realize that Beethoven may have had no part in them.[12] There are, for instance, several places where Kaufmann strayed beyond the notes that Beethoven provided in the piano trio and added melodic strands of his own. Since Beethoven did not eliminate these counterpoints but allowed them to stand and ultimately to be published in a work bearing his name, he may be said to have approved them; but they are likely to be an embarrassment to us—not, I think, because the licence that Kaufmann took in such passages is unpardonable (on the principle that "quod licet Jovi non licet bovi"), but because we are simply not prepared to extend to the work of an unknown arranger the same interest in the smallest details of craftsmanship that is known to bring its reward in the case of genius. Beethoven himself put his finger on the central problem in his letter of July 13, 1802, to Breitkopf & Härtel; [13] discussing the difficulties of arranging his piano sonatas for strings, he observed:

> . . . Not only would whole passages have to be entirely omitted or altered, but some would have to—be added; and there one finds the nasty stumbling-block, to *overcome* which one must either *be the composer* himself, or at any rate possess the same *skill and inventiveness*.

---

[12] Although it will be clear by now that I do not believe Beethoven to have been responsible in the first place for what Schlemmer and his assistant copied, two other possibilities, which cut across the distinction drawn here between the two layers, deserve to be weighed carefully. The first of these is that Kaufmann, in making his version, may have been following some suggestions given to him by Beethoven. This idea, it should be noted, finds no support in the anecdote. The second possibility is that Beethoven had already corrected some passages in Kaufmann's score before having it copied by Schlemmer & Co.; they *might* include one or another of the changes discussed in this section (despite their awkwardness). Those apart, the literalness of the transcription suggests that Beethoven could have contributed little or nothing at this early stage.

[13] Anderson no. 59; the German text in Thayer-Deiters-Riemann II (1910), 328.

A few examples will show the nature of the problem that we must face here.

(a) In a number of places in the first movement the first-violin part does not correspond to anything in the trio. These passages include: measures 69–75, 272–74 (first two notes), 315–21, and 323–27 (first note). It may be assumed that the first-violin part in all these measures was freely composed by Kaufmann, and that the same applies to similar counterpoints in the lower strings: e.g. viola 2, measures 61–75; violin 2, measures 268–70. The passages are harmless though rather insipid imitations, thrown into an uncalled-for prominence whenever the first or second violin is playing above the other instruments.

(b) In the finale there are a good many places, particularly in the development, where the lower strings are given figures that are not in the trio: e.g. measures 184–85 (violin 2, cello), 190–91 (violas 1 and 2, changed here by Beethoven to viola 2 and cello), 200–01 (viola 2), 206–10 (viola 1). I assume that all these additions—like the descending scales in measures 411, 413, and 415 of the coda—are by Kaufmann. Some, such as the second viola's sixths in double-stopping in measures 200–01, are clumsy.

(c) A third example of workmanship that seems to be due to Kaufmann rather than to Beethoven is the treatment of the return to the recapitulation in the finale, measures 230–37—a passage singled out for mention by both Thayer and Munter. In the original version for trio the strings were silent in these eight measures, while the piano had a straightforward descending chromatic scale in the first four, and an ascending one in the last four measures. In the quintet arrangement the descending chromatic scale (an infrequent feature of violin writing of the period) is eliminated; instead, the first violin holds an f''' for three measures while the lower strings enter one by one with the figure of the main theme's first measure, and when all are playing (measure 234) the first violin begins its chromatic ascent from its lowest note. This is certainly an imaginative piece of rescoring;[14] perhaps its most awkward feature (which needs careful rehearsal) is the diminuendo (taken over from the trio) from fortissimo to pianissimo as more and more instruments enter.

Whatever *we* may think of these embellishments by Kaufmann which depart from the original trio version, it is conspicuous that Beethoven not only left them untouched but on occasion copied them or built on them.

---

[14] The most "advanced" feature of the passage, however, is the anticipation of tonic harmony by the middle of measure 236 (a $^6_4$ chord), characteristic of Beethoven in 1817 but surprising in Kaufmann. See n. 12.

In the first movement, for instance, the measures 264–66 (first note) of the first-viola part are an addition by Beethoven, evidently modeled on a Kaufmann counterpoint in the parallel passage, measures 61–63 of the second-viola part. At the recapitulation in the same movement a figure that Kaufmann gives to the first viola in measure 219 is just saved from being ridiculous by Beethoven's addition of the same motif to the second violin in the next measure. In the finale, too, Beethoven several times adds an upbeat before a figure from the second subject that is also used extensively in the development (measures 76, 162, 191); this appears to be modeled on Kaufmann's addition of an upbeat in measure 201. A less direct imitation of Kaufmann, nonetheless unmistakable, is Beethoven's filling in of the lower strings in measures, 101–06 and 328–33 of the finale; for these passages surely owe something to Kaufmann's treatment of the lower strings at the point of recapitulation in the same movement (measures 231–37, already discussed).

In such places, then, Beethoven made use of Kaufmann's invention. But what is also striking is that he abstained from changing several passages that were banal, or technically incompetent, or incorrect. Some of Kaufmann's banalities have already been mentioned; to these one might add the cello upbeat in measure 223 of the first movement, or the facile imitations by the second violin in measures 251–57 of the finale. Technically unsatisfactory passages include long stretches of double-stopping in the finale (e.g. measures 151–61 of viola 1, measures 206–11 of violin 2), and there are places, such as measures 155–58 in the same movement, where the cello doubles the second violin at the lower octave producing a $\frac{6}{4}$ chord. By passing all these passages without modification, Beethoven ensured that they survived into the final (published) version of the quintet.

The impression is left that Beethoven's revision of Kaufmann's work was a somewhat uncritical affair. Even his own additions, whose intrinsic merit is usually not in doubt, seem to have been inserted with a good deal of haste and some degree of carelessness. A few of his interventions are hard to justify, some even hard to understand. What, for instance, is the meaning of the single A♯ that he added to the cello part in measure 143 of the first movement? Is it not likely that he intended the cello to double the first violin and first viola in measure 142 as well as 143? But if so, he did not make his meaning clear. Again, what are we to make of the first violin's single B♭ in measure 112? (It is in the last measure of a page in Grasnick 11, always an accident-prone position from the point of view of textual accuracy.) Surely this, too, is a survival of some revision that he did not see through—possibly one aimed at improving the fusty filling-in part that Kaufmann gave to the first violin in measures 113–17 and that has survived till today.

There are a number of passages in Beethoven's works that confront editors (and the performers that depend on them) with an insoluble problem. These are the ones in which carelessness on the part of the composer has resulted in a state of affairs that cannot be right in itself and yet cannot be satisfactorily resolved by emendation, since he has provided either too little or—what is equally awkward—too much information, usually of an irreconcilable kind. In the former cases the editor is obliged to bridge the gap by composing a missing portion, without much confidence that it is exactly what Beethoven would have composed; in the latter cases he must flout some of Beethoven's expressed intentions in order to give weight to other wishes of the composer that cannot be reconciled with them. There is an excellent instance of the latter type of problem in the quintet.

It arises in measures 84–87 of the first movement. One of Beethoven's bolder devices for "improving" a passage was the addition of a high cello part where previously (i.e. in Kaufmann's score) the cello had had a rest. (An example of this is on the very first page, in measures 8–10; but we can find a more striking instance in measures 144–51 of the first movement; none of this cello part was originally in the score.) In Kaufmann's score measures 76–89 and the parallel ones 279–92 follow the piano trio very literally. The basis of the adaptation is clear: the trio's violin part was transferred to the second violin of the quintet, while the piano's right-hand part was given to the first violin and its left hand distributed among the violas. The cello, having nothing to say, was silent. Beethoven decided to give it a high tonic pedal—e♭′ in measures 80–89, and a c″ in measures 283–92, at first sustained, but giving place to a series of eighth notes on the third beat of each measure; and he wrote the necessary e♭′s and c″s in the blank cello stave. So far so good. But unfortunately the score contains a small copying error in the first-violin part in one of those passages: the second note in measures 84 and 85 is in each case wrongly preceded by a natural sign, since those notes must be a♭′s (plate XIV). Even Schlemmer nods; in copying he simply anticipated the two subsequent measures (measures 86–87) where a♮′s are, indeed, required. But Schlemmer's error had a most unfortunate consequence, since it persuaded Beethoven—whom we must imagine to be working vertically as much as horizontally in his revising—to cross out the e♭′ eighth notes in measures 85 and 87 and to replace them (via a *Vi-de* sign) by g♭′ eighth notes. The crucial difficulty is in measure 85; for here the g♭′ is compatible with the first violin's a♮′s—the *wrong* note—but not with the a♭′, which is correct and which Schlemmer *should* have written. All the

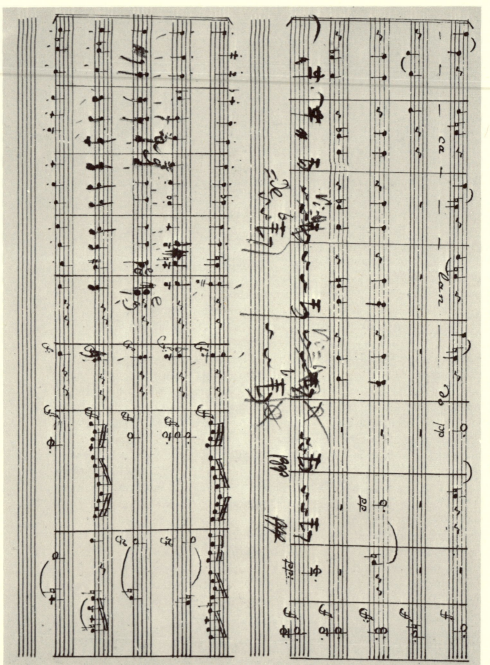

Plate XIV ℘ Grasnick 11 (StPK, Berlin), folio 4r
(*measures 83–99 of the first movement of Op. 104*).

scores and sets of parts that I have examined, including the new critical edition published by the Beethovenhaus,[15] have resolved the "impossible" dilemma by keeping naturals before the a's in measures 84 and 85, and printing g♭'s in measures 85 and 87; but I believe that a strong case can be made out for printing a♭'s in measures 84 and 85 and for returning to Beethoven's earlier idea and retaining e♭'s in measures 85 and 87. This results in measures 76–89 and 279–92 being truly parallel—perhaps no bad thing, seeing that they were parallel in the original piano trio.

The text of the quintet continued to give Beethoven trouble even after the work had been sent for publication. It appeared in Vienna in February, 1819, published not by Steiner (to whom he had first offered it) but by Artaria, who issued it without an opus number and with a title page that referred to the two violas as "Alt-Violen." Clearly the plates of this edition were revised more than once, and to judge from surviving copies corrections were introduced into the plates from time to time as they were spotted.[16] At some stage the wording "Alt-Violen" was changed to "Bratschen" on the title page; a little later an opus number, "104," was added.

Beethoven also tried to arrange for the work to be published in England; in March, 1818, he asked Ferdinand Ries, who had settled in London, to find a publisher for it, and on January 30, 1819, he wrote in some urgency in a further letter to Ries:

> You will have now received the quintet which I arranged myself and the sonata [Op. 106]. Do see to it that both works, and especially the quintet, shall be engraved immediately.[17]

Five weeks later he sent Ries an extended list of corrigenda, "mistakes which perhaps have been made in the quintet," the basis for which is the draft list at the end of Grasnick 11.[18]

The quintet was published in England by Elizabeth Lavenu, almost

---

[15] *Beethoven, Werke: VI, 2: Streichquintette,* ed. Johannes Herzog (Bonn, 1968).

[16] It is important to bear in mind that copies with identical title pages may have slightly different musical texts. There are, for instance, at least four different "states" of the first violin part, only three of which are reflected in variants of the title page.

[17] SBH 346; Anderson no. 935.

[18] Anderson no. 938 (her list has a few minor inaccuracies). The draft list in Grasnick 11 includes a couple of further corrections to the first-viola part that were omitted, doubtless by an oversight on Beethoven's part, from the letter: in movement 1, m. 113, the last note should be B♭, not F, and in m. 261, the last note should have a natural before it. The error that Beethoven discovered in the second-viola part in movement 2, m. 68 (or var. 4, m. 4), seems to have been the omission of the natural sign before the

certainly in 1819. Ries, who refers in his *Notizen* [19] to his part in further-
ing the authentic English editions of Opp. 106, 110, 111, 119, and the
abortive edition of Op. 120, never mentions the quintet. The authenticity
of Lavenu's edition has, therefore, for long been in doubt; [20] but I think
that it is now possible to show that it is authentic and is textually independent of the Viennese edition of Artaria. It is true that it contains many
errors and that it has not profited from the corrigenda sent to Ries on
March 8, 1819; [21] but a careful study of its readings wherever they differ
from those of the Artaria edition, especially in comparison to what is to
be found in Grasnick 11, forces one to conclude that Lavenu's edition is
based on the score or (more likely) set of parts that Beethoven sent to
Ries in London at the end of 1818.[22] Additional proof that the London
edition of Op. 104 is authentic comes from a document of the year 1820,
now in the Beethovenhaus.[23] This is a certificate listing all the works by
Beethoven that were the property of Artaria & Co.; it was signed by Beethoven on April 4, 1820. It is significant, therefore, that under the entry
for Op. 104 Beethoven felt obliged to add the following note:

> NB: dieses Quintett ist mit Vorwissen u. Genehmigung des H. Artaria
> u. Comp. auch nach London verkauft worden, indes nur für England.

> [N.B.: this quintet was also sold to London, with the foreknowledge
> and permission of Messrs. Artaria & Co., but with rights only for
> England.]

It seems to have been Beethoven's good fortune to find publishers
both in Vienna and in London for a quintet which, in the strictest sense,
he did not wholly write. We shall not, therefore, expect to find in Op. 104
a mature example of Beethoven's art of transcription. Future interest is

---

second note; but unfortunately he also
omitted the natural sign in quoting the
measure both in the draft list and in the
letter! This error, like the other two just
mentioned, is found in the first issue of
Artaria's edition; but all three passages
have been corrected in later issues.

[19] F. G. Wegeler and Ferdinand Ries,
*Biographische Notizen über Ludwig van
Beethoven* (Koblenz, 1838), pp. 107–08,
123–24.

[20] Alan Tyson, *The Authentic English
Editions of Beethoven* (London, 1963),
pp. 108–09.

[21] The letter containing the list was
received in London (as is shown by the
post-office stamp on the cover) on March
27. This suggests that the quintet was
published in London before the end of
March.

[22] Many examples could be given, but
two must suffice. In Lavenu's edition the
cello has staccato marks in movement 1,
m. 18, and octaves (i.e. including the
open C-string) in movement 4, m. 25;
both of these details are in Grasnick 11,
but neither is in Artaria's edition.

[23] SBH 10; Anderson, Appendix G
(11), which gives Beethoven's certificate
at the end of the list, but not the list
itself.

likely to be concentrated on the aspect of the work that is exposed by the two layers of the Grasnick 11 score: the swift, brilliant, but also somewhat careless transformation of a pedestrian transcription into something to which Beethoven could set his name and which he himself described as the process of raising it "from the most abject misery to some degree of respectability."

The Artaria Collection
of Beethoven Manuscripts:
A New Source*

Douglas Johnson

❉ EVERY SCHOLAR who has studied the manuscript or printed sources for Beethoven's works has encountered the Artaria family and firm. The Artarias opened a shop in Vienna in the late 1770s and established themselves quickly as the favored publishers of Haydn and Mozart and many of their contemporaries. For a time after Beethoven moved to Vienna in 1792, the firm had almost exclusive access to his compositions. As early as July, 1793, they published the Variations on "Se vuol ballare" for Piano and Violin (WoO 40), a piece Beethoven had finished shortly after his arrival. These were followed in the next five years by a series of works which included his Op. 1 to Op. 8, some songs, and a few sets of dances and variations without opus numbers. Beethoven may have been on particularly good terms with Tranquillo Mollo, a partner in the Artaria firm from 1793 to 1798, and with young Domenico Artaria III, son of another partner, for when these two left to establish an independent shop in Mollo's name (1798), they took Beethoven's favor with them. From 1798 to 1802 a few works were awarded to the Artarias, but most of the important ones (Opp. 11, 14–18, 23–24) went to Mollo. This sudden deflation of the Artaria monopoly, helped along by several other new competitors, was partially halted in 1802, when Mollo and Domenico Artaria III bought out the last of the remaining Artaria partners and ran the two shops jointly. But at the same time a more serious problem developed with

---

* The writer wishes to express special thanks to Dr. Karl-Heinz Köhler, Grita Herre, Eveline Bartlitz, and the staff of the DStB, and to Dr. Rudolf Elvers and the staff of the StPK for graciously making large numbers of manuscripts available for study, and to Dr. Johann A. Schannetzsky of Berlin for help and advice in the preparation of the text of the present article.

Beethoven himself: a dispute leading ultimately to a lawsuit over an Artaria edition of the String Quintet, Op. 29. During the years 1803–05, while the feud was brewing, Artaria's (and Mollo's) access to the flow of new works nearly dried up.[1] Domenico III eventually parted company with Mollo, in 1804, but he seems never to have regained the full measure of Beethoven's confidence. Even in later years, when time had softened the hard feelings, Beethoven gave only a few important works (the piano score of Op. 72 in 1814, Op. 106 in 1819) exclusively to Artaria.[2]

After Beethoven's death in 1827, Domenico Artaria was among the men selected by officials to prepare the composer's musical *Nachlass* for auction. There is evidence that the job of preparing an auction catalogue was in turn largely delegated to Anton Gräffer, a long-time employee of Artaria and an experienced cataloguer, who also acted as auctioneer at the sale itself on November 5, 1827. Artaria and fellow publisher Tobias Haslinger did most of the buying at that auction. Domenico bought about eighty, or nearly half, of the first 188 catalogue entries—those devoted to manuscripts in Beethoven's hand. Haslinger bought about forty.[3] And whereas Haslinger (and Spina, representing the Diabelli firm) bid highly for some of the unpublished autographs, Artaria confined his spending to the cheaper items, accumulating a large number of the sketches and fragments and many autographs of already published works. It is this collection of Beethoven's autograph manuscripts, largely acquired by Artaria at the *Nachlass* auction, that will concern us in the following inquiry.

What had motivated Domenico's greedy bidding? Evidently not an irrepressible urge to possess the autographs of Beethoven's best-loved works, for by the time of his own death fifteen years later he had parted with the *Spring Sonata*, the Fifth and Sixth Symphonies, and fragments of the *Missa solemnis* and *Fidelio*. Nor was Domenico much interested in

---

[1] At least one important work, Op. 48, was published by Artaria-Mollo, but may have been acquired before the dispute over Op. 29 arose. For the complicated story of Beethoven's relations with the Artarias and Mollo during the period 1798–1804, see Alexander Weinmann, *Artaria & Comp. Vollständiges Verlagsverzeichnis* (Vienna, 1952) and his *Verlagsverzeichnis Tranquillo Mollo* (Vienna, 1964), and Donald MacArdle, "Beethoven, Artaria, and the C major Quintet," *The Musical Quarterly*, XXIV (1948), 567–74.

[2] The piano reduction of Op. 72

was prepared by Moscheles. See Kinsky-Halm under Op. 69 for a suggestion that Artaria had a working agreement with Breitkopf & Härtel to issue certain works in Vienna.

[3] The totals differ very slightly because of conflicting attributions in surviving copies of the *Nachlass* auction catalogue. For a discussion of all the events surrounding the *Nachlass* auction, see Georg Kinsky, "Zur Versteigerung von Beethovens musikalischem Nachlass," *Neues Beethoven-Jahrbuch*, VI (1935), 66–86.

publishing new works. He dropped out of the bidding for most of the attractive items, leaving them to Diabelli or Haslinger. Within five years of the auction, he had published only the three piano quartets of 1785 (WoO 36) and the *Gratulationsmenuett* (WoO 3), together with the Wind Octet, Op. 103, which the firm had issued in its string-quintet form as Op. 4 back in 1796. Many of the other publishable items he had bought—songs with piano or orchestral accompaniments and a variety of pieces for piano—never appeared. Perhaps it is best, then, to credit Domenico with intending exactly what we know him to have done. Taking advantage of the local nature of the auction, he bought manuscripts cheaply and resold them, mostly to foreign collectors, when the occasion later presented itself.

August Artaria, Domenico's son, became a partner in 1833 and ran the business for another half century after his father's death in 1842. He shared Domenico's willingness to part with Beethoven manuscripts, and by the middle of the century a large number of autograph scores had left the collection. Father and son were, if anything, even more profligate with the sketchbooks. Domenico had purchased the lion's share of these at the *Nachlass* auction, paying very little for them. Their value must have been considered slight; several were given away to friends. Many others were sold. And a favorite practice was to extract a folio or two as a token of esteem for a new or passing acquaintance.

In the later years of August's tenure, the exodus of Beethoven manuscripts slowed. Visitors like Thayer and Nottebohm, who came to examine the collection, doubtless contributed to a growing awareness of its importance and value. Near the end of his long life, August Artaria issued two catalogues of the collection. The first was prepared by Guido Adler in 1890, evidently making use of notes left by Nottebohm.[4] Three years later another catalogue was published, this one under August's own name.[5] It provided a different numerical classification of the Beethoven collection and included the rest of the firm's manuscript holdings (principally a collection of Haydn autographs) as well.

August Artaria died that same year (1893). His sons sold the Vienna business, which had ceased publishing music in the 1850s, to a local competitor. Together with the smaller Haydn collection, the Beethoven manuscripts were sold in 1897 to Erich Prieger of Bonn, who sold them in turn to the Berlin Königliche Bibliothek (later the Preussische Staatsbiblio-

---

[4] See "Adler" in the list of Abbreviations on p. xiii. The full title includes the remark "Auf Grundlage einer Aufnahme Gustav Nottebohm's neuerlich durchgesehen von Prof. Dr. Guido Adler."

[5] See "Artaria" in the list of Abbreviations on p. xiii.

thek) in 1901. Today these collections are divided between the Deutsche Staatsbibliothek (DStB) and the Stiftung Preussischer Kulturbesitz (StPK), in different sectors of Berlin. For their safety during the last war, a large number of manuscripts were removed from Berlin to various smaller towns. Most have since been returned, although a single collection has now become two. What August's sons and Prieger had sought to avoid, a division of the Artaria Collection, was thus accomplished by the war. And regrettably, a considerable number of manuscripts, including some of the most valuable, have disappeared and must for the moment be considered lost.

The collection of Beethoven manuscripts which came to Berlin in 1901 had been systematically (though not always accurately) described in the catalogues of 1890 and 1893, prepared by Guido Adler and August Artaria respectively, and the library simply retained the numerical classification of the latter. Naturally, therefore, the name Artaria has retained its association with those manuscripts appearing in August Artaria's 1893 catalogue, in large part corresponding to the collection left at August's death. This collection, however, was a mere torso of that assembled by Domenico Artaria at the *Nachlass* auction of 1827. Depletion of manuscripts at the hands of both Domenico and August, especially in the early years following the auction, had shrunk it to a fraction (perhaps less than half) of its original size.

If all this traffic were well documented, it would pose few problems for interested scholars. But the early history of the Artaria Collection has had to be inferred from rather imprecise sources. The first and most important of these is the *Nachlass* auction catalogue. A master copy of this catalogue was apparently prepared by Artaria's employee, Anton Gräffer, and several copies were made from it.[6] The Viennese collector Aloys Fuchs made a copy and inscribed the cover as follows:

Vollständiges Verzeichniß: des am 5. November 1827 zu Wien am Kohlmarkt No. 1149 öffentlich versteigerten musik. Nachlaßes des Tonsetzers Ludwig van Beethoven mit genauer Angabe der Schätzungs- u. Verkaufspreise mit Nachweisung des Käufers von

---

[6] Gräffer's master copy is probably that in the Vienna city archives. Facsimiles of several sides can be seen in Robert Bory, *Ludwig van Beethoven: His Life and his Work in Pictures* (Zurich–New York, 1960), pp. 222–23. Included is the final page, with the signatures of Artaria, Haslinger, Czerny, Sauer, Hotschevar, and other officials involved in the preparation of the auction. Published transcripts of the *Nachlass* catalogue are found in Thayer's *Verzeichnis* and in Theodor v. Frimmel's *Beethoven-Studien*, II (Munich, 1906). Although both are supposed to be based on the copy in the Vienna city archives (according to Kinsky), they do not reproduce exactly the entries facsimiled by Bory.

jedem Stücke. Von dem Original-Protokoll des Herrn Schätzmeisters und Ausruffers Anton Gräffer copirt von Aloys Fuchs.[7]

Kinsky drew heavily upon Fuchs's private copy, with its comprehensive list of buyers, for his valuable discussion of the *Nachlass* auction.[8] Another copy of the catalogue, apparently unknown to Kinsky, was copied by Gräffer for Jacob Hotschevar, who became guardian of Beethoven's nephew Karl after the composer's death.[9] This copy has another complete list of buyers, noted by Hotschevar at the auction, and the list differs in a few instances from that published by Kinsky (from Fuchs). These lists would seem to make it easy to tell who bought what at the auction, but in fact their usefulness is lessened by the imprecision of the catalogue entries themselves. Even the autographs of published works are sometimes ambiguously described; entries mentioning the type of work while omitting key and/or opus number are common. Although such terseness has proved frustrating to later scholars, however, it doubtless caused no problem at the auction. Precise descriptions of already well-known works would have been superfluous there, since the buyers were present anyway, and the unpublished pieces, fragments, and sketches were either not susceptible to brief, explicit description or could be covered by entries like "Lied" or "Klavierstück," which (like the sketches themselves) have proved problematical only to those for whom they were not intended.

Despite its ambiguities, the auction catalogue has remained the most valuable guide to the Artaria Collection in its early years. Some further information can be deduced from the dedicatory inscriptions or guarantees of authenticity which were frequently added to manuscripts when they were sold or given away. When such inscriptions exist, they usually provide precise dates and, in the case of gifts, the names of recipients as well. Still other references can be found in the works of nineteenth-century scholars, of whom Thayer and Nottebohm were the most important, who saw the manuscripts in Artaria's possession or elsewhere. Piecing these scattered references and the random inscriptions together, we have been able to reconstruct some portions of the long history of the Artaria Collection. The central problem preventing a more complete reconstruction has remained that of equating the vague entries of the *Nachlass* auction catalogue with the more explicit ones of the 1890 and 1893 catalogues.

---

[7] Fuchs's copy of the catalogue is in the collection of Dr. Georg Floersheim, Basel.

[8] Kinsky, "Zur Versteigerung von Beethovens musikalischem Nachlass."

Fuchs's cover inscription is taken from Kinsky's account.

[9] Hotschevar's copy of the catalogue is now in the Beethovenhaus, Bonn.

There is considerable significance, therefore, in the discovery that a handwritten catalogue in the Deutsche Staatsbibliothek, with the signature Mus. MS. Beethoven Autograph 47a, can be identified with the Artaria Collection of Beethoven manuscripts as it existed at some time between 1838 and 1844. The library's own earliest entry for this catalogue identifies it as "Ein geschriebenes Verzeichnis Beethoven'scher Werke in Autographen u. Copien, anscheinend aus Fischhof's Besitz." This seems to indicate that the catalogue entered the library in 1859, along with other Beethoveniana from the *Nachlass* of the Viennese professor Joseph Fischhof (1804–57). Fischhof also owned a sketchbook miscellany, now StPK Autograph 28, which he probably obtained from the Artarias, and he could have picked up the catalogue from them as well, perhaps when it had been superseded by another. Although it contains no direct reference to Artaria and there is nothing in its provenance to connect it with the firm, there can be no doubt about the catalogue's origins, for an overwhelming correlation exists between its entries, those of the 1890 and 1893 catalogues, and Domenico Artaria's purchases at the 1827 auction.

In its present state, the catalogue comprises eight handwritten sides. Halfway down the last side begins a section devoted to copies, and this evidently continued onto additional sheets, now lost. But the first seven and a half pages, devoted to manuscripts in Beethoven's hand, are intact. The evidence for dating the catalogue between 1838 and 1844 derives from its content. An autograph of the first movement of Op. 111, sold in 1844, is included; the autograph of the *Pastoral Symphony*, sold in 1838, is not. A more specific date cannot be documented, although a general stocktaking at about the time of Domenico's death in 1842 might be suggested as a plausible reason for compiling such a catalogue.[10]

Autograph 47a was written by Anton Gräffer. The handwriting matches a known sample from Gräffer, a signed statement witnessing Beethoven's signature on a thematic catalogue of those of his works which belonged to Artaria in 1820.[11] The hand also matches that of both the master copy of the *Nachlass* auction catalogue and the extra copy that Gräffer prepared for Jacob Hotschevar. Gräffer himself is an interesting figure. A biographical sketch in the *Oesterreichische National-Encyclopädie*, VI (Vienna, 1837), of which his brother was an editor, portrays him as a Jack-of-all-trades who at one time or another composed for the piano, violin, and guitar, performed on and wrote a method for the guitar, did some engraving, and wrote a number of essays and articles on

---

[10] The possibility cannot be completely excluded that the catalogue was compiled at Fischhof's request.

[11] This thematic catalogue, with Gräffer's signature as witness, is in the Beethovenhaus, Bonn (SBH 10).

various artistic topics. And though he held a permit for a shop of his own, he worked from about 1815 for Artaria. Besides Autograph 47a and the *Nachlass* auction catalogue, Gräffer apparently also compiled the catalogue of Beethoven's published works which was issued by Artaria with the first edition of Op. 106 in 1819 and reissued in 1837 in an updated second edition.[12]

Gräffer wrote his original entries in the Autograph 47a catalogue in a neat hand in ink. Information was entered in five columns, headed "Paquet," "Compositionen," "Blätter," "Tonart," and "Anmerkungen" (see plate XV). The first of these may have referred to bundles or boxes in the shop; a preliminary attempt at classification is evident, although it has not been systematically pursued. In listing the compositions themselves, Gräffer was more explicit than he had been in the *Nachlass* catalogue, supplying opus numbers and keys for nearly all the published pieces. Most of the songs, including the unpublished ones, were entered with text incipits. It was only for a few of the fragments and obscure pieces that he seems to have reverted to his original *Nachlass* catalogue descriptions (e.g. "Skizze eines Clavierconcertes," "Mehrere Lieder"). A note of explanation is required concerning the column headed "Blätter." In counting the folios in each manuscript, Gräffer omitted all those with *both* sides blank. This accounts for most of the discrepancies between these entries and those in Kinsky-Halm, and, as we shall see, it also provides some valuable evidence concerning the early state of the sketchbooks.

At first the column of "Anmerkungen" was used primarily for noting the presence of autograph inscriptions and for specifying whether or not the lesser-known works had been published. The sketches and fragments posed special problems of legibility and identification; the first time through Gräffer entered most of them without remarks. Later, perhaps after consulting with someone, he returned to the catalogue and made a few additional comments, in a more hurried hand and with somewhat lighter ink.[13] Then, finally, Gräffer abandoned his pen and began an extensive series of comments in pencil (see plates XVI and XVII).[14]

---

[12] The remark "2te Auflage v. J. 1837" was written by Aloys Fuchs on his copy of the catalogue, which is now in the DStB. Kinsky (Kinsky-Halm) suggests an earlier date for this second edition, based on the published works it included. In Kastner and Frimmel, *Bibliotheca Beethoveniana*, 2nd ed. (Leipzig, 1927), the updated catalogue is listed under the year 1828. But I have found no new evidence to contradict the date assigned to the catalogue by Fuchs.

[13] One entire entry, no. 6 in the appended transcript, was also squeezed in later in this lighter ink (see pl. XV).

[14] The apparent point of transition from pen to pencil occurs remarkably within a single entry on p. 7 (see entry 92 and pl. XVII).

47a **Beethoven.**

Paquet	Compositionen	Blätter	Tonart	Anmerkungen.
I	Quintett für 2 Violinen 2 Bratschen und Violoncelle Op 29. Partitur	43	C	Original
	Terzett für 2 Oboen und englisch Horn oder für 2 Violinen und Viola Op 29. Partitur	16	C	
	Sonate für Pianoforte und Violoncelle. Op 69. Partitur	9	A	
	Trio für Pianoforte, Violin und Violoncelle Op 70. N1. Partitur	34	D	
	Trio für Pianoforte, Violin und Violoncelle Op 70. N2. Partitur	41	Es	
	Variations für 2 Oboen u. engl. Horn	7	C	
II	Entr' actes zu Egmont Op 84. Partitur	81		
	Oratorium: Christus am Oehlberg. Op 85. Partitur	44		
	Ein Theil des Gloria der ersten Messe Op 86. Partitur	21		
III	Sonate für Pianoforte und Violoncelle Op 102. Livraison 2	13	D	eigenhändig. August 1815.
	Sonate für Pianoforte allein Op 110.	29	As	eigenhändig. am 25 December 1821.
	Adagio ma non troppo aus dieser Sonate Op 110.	8	As	
	Sonate für Pianoforte allein Op 111.	20	Es	eigenhändig. im 13 Jäner 1822.
	Maestoso, erstes Stück obiger Sonate Op 111.	9	Es	eigenhändig 13 Jäner 1822.

Plate XV ☙ Autograph 47a (DStB, Berlin), page 1.

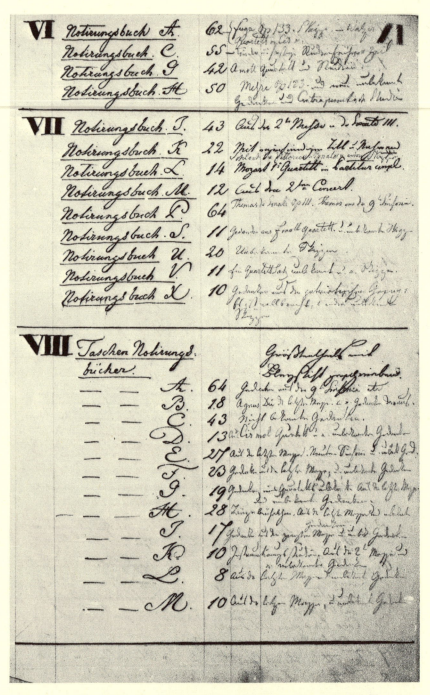

Plate XVI ✌ Autograph 47a (DStB, Berlin), page 3.

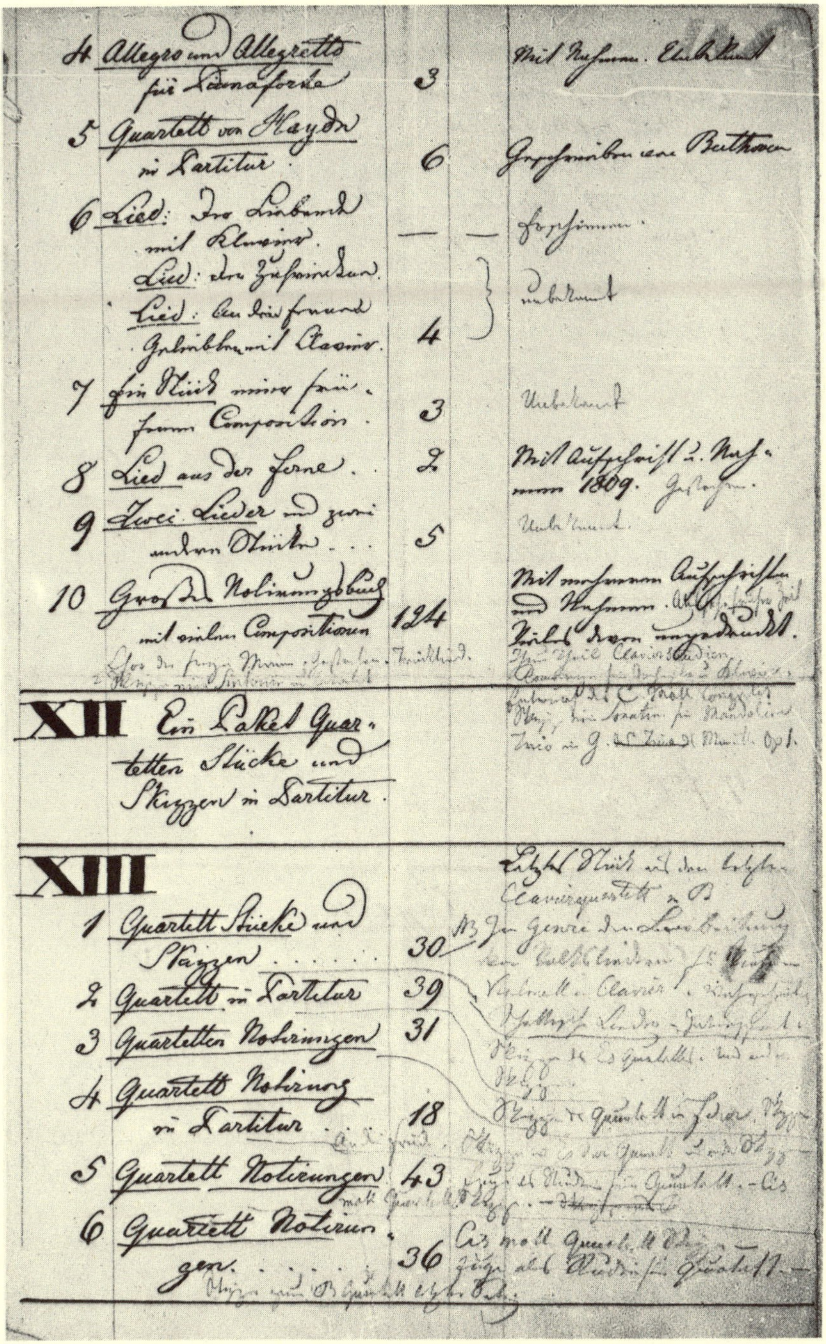

Plate XVII ❦ *Autograph 47a (DStB, Berlin), page 7.*

The bulk of these identify the content of the sketchbooks, although a few other entries received additional remarks as well. Similar brief identifications, in pencil and in Gräffer's hand, are found in several of the sketchbooks themselves; these may have been memoranda for the catalogue entries. When he put his pen aside, Gräffer surrendered neatness as well, and his penciled comments are jotted in a very casual hand, making frequent use of abbreviations and in places ignoring the boundaries of the "Anmerkungen" column. In fact these last comments appear just different enough from the earlier entries in ink that one is initially tempted to suggest a second cataloguer. Careful examination, however, shows the hand to be Gräffer's throughout.

Autograph 47a fills out our picture of the Artaria Collection as it existed ten to fifteen years after the *Nachlass* auction, supplying us with a list of manuscripts not previously associated with the collection and providing some clues as to when others might have been sold or given away. By comparing its entries with the list of items bought by Domenico Artaria at the *Nachlass* auction and with the catalogues of 1890 and 1893, we are able to suggest which manuscripts had left the collection before Autograph 47a was written, which ones left later, and which were acquired after the auction, either before or after Autograph 47a was compiled. Excluding all the materials vaguely described as sketches and fragments in the *Nachlass* catalogue, those of Artaria's *Nachlass* auction purchases which are not accounted for in Autograph 47a are listed in an appendix to the annotated transcript of Autograph 47a which follows (see pages 234–36). Manuscripts which left the collection after Autograph 47a was written are discussed as they occur in the transcription of the catalogue itself (consult the index on pages 237–42 for references to particular works). The final group, manuscripts acquired after the *Nachlass* auction, is easily lost in the clatter of the outgoing traffic. The only major acquisition which followed Autograph 47a was the score (minus the overture) of the music to *König Stephan,* Op. 117 (Adler 48; Artaria 162; StPK Artaria 162). This autograph was obtained from Haslinger, probably before 1852, when Artaria dealt a copy of the same score to Otto Jahn. Haslinger had also owned the copy of an early Sonata for Flute and Piano, Kinsky-Halm Anh. 4, which later turns up in the Artaria Collection (Adler 35; Artaria 130; DStB Artaria 130). Other manuscripts appearing in the Adler and Artaria catalogues but missing from Autograph 47a are the *Punschlied,* WoO 111 (Adler 61; Artaria 171; DStB Artaria 171), on a single folio and perhaps included in one of the vaguely described bundles in Autograph 47a, and two folios, DStB Artaria 176 (Adler 37; Artaria 176), from the autograph of Op. 73.

Much of the information provided by Autograph 47a concerns surviving autographs and is self-explanatory. Rather more interesting is information which can be deduced from the catalogue indirectly, in particular from the entries for the sketchbooks. These have been more difficult to work with than autographs because (among other, obvious reasons) their original state cannot be reconstructed by reference to completed scores. In cases where the folios of sketchbooks were rearranged or simply removed—and there is ample evidence that this occurred frequently—we must rely on historical and actual physical evidence, as well as sketch content, to achieve plausible reconstructions. Autograph 47a provides several clues as to how the Artarias handled the sketches in their collection, and these merit some elaboration here.

The first two sections of the *Nachlass* auction catalogue were headed: "I. Beethovens eigenhändige Notirungen und Notirbücher" and "II. Brauchbare Skizzen, Fragmente und zum Theil unvollständige Werke noch ungedruckt und eigenhändig geschrieben." Together the two sections comprised seventy entries. Domenico bought thirty-eight of these. There is no way of estimating satisfactorily how many bundles of sketch folios and compositional fragments were actually involved, since many of the auction-catalogue entries are plural and the distinction between "Notirungen" and "Notirbuch," for example, is not clear. There can also be little doubt that the inclusion among the notebooks listed in Autograph 47a of autograph fragments, studies, and copies (as well as compositional sketches in the usual sense) was carried over from the *Nachlass* catalogue entries. If anything, one assumes that Autograph 47a must have refined somewhat the *Nachlass* catalogue classification and that some of the Autograph 47a entries that have no explicit counterpart in the *Nachlass* catalogue had in fact been buried anonymously there among the "Notirungen." Beethoven's copies from Mozart's K. 387 and Bach's Inventions (Autograph 47a, numbers 29 and 80), for example, appear with the general designation "Notirungsbuch" or "Notirungen" in Autograph 47a and were probably so described in the *Nachlass* catalogue. Several other Autograph 47a entries for which no *Nachlass* catalogue equivalents can be found may have been rescued from a similar oblivion.

From Autograph 47a we can reconstruct the initial classification of the notebooks Domenico had bought. First a general distinction was made between books in large, oblong format and those in small, upright or oblong format—the type Beethoven liked to carry about with him in his later years. Each group was then arranged in a lettered sequence, comprising A through at least X (no J) of the large format and A through at least M (no J) of the pocket sketchbooks. What remained of these two groups when Autograph 47a was written can be seen on page 3 of the catalogue (plate XVI). Several sketchbooks and bundles of folios, all apparently in the larger format, were omitted from the two lists, however, and are found scattered on the later pages of the catalogue. It appears that, except for the distinction between large and small format, the sketchbooks had been stored in more or less the order in which they were bought at the *Nachlass* auction (had they retained lot numbers?). Hence the books left out of the alphabetical lists included those bundles of quartet sketches (on page 7) which were probably among the last lots of sketches in the *Nachlass* auction catalogue.[15]

The Artarias provided each of the large-format sketchbooks in the alphabetical list with a cover of heavy gray paper, folded once so as to enclose the folios front and back. The front cover was then given an inscription comprising (a) "Notirungsbuch" or "Notirungen," (b) a letter, and (c) a number indicating the number of used folios in the book (see plate XVIIIa). In most cases, perhaps all, the letter of the sketchbook was then inscribed carefully on the recto of the first folio. One must be cautious for the present in considering these letters, however, because in a few instances where a manuscript *appears* to be preserved intact as Artaria owned it, the first folio letter is missing.[16]

This initial classification must have been made before 1835, for in that year part of Notirungsbuch K (including the lettered first folio) left the collection. In order to estimate how many other sketchbooks had left before Autograph 47a was written, we need only fill in the alphabetical gaps on page 3 of the catalogue. Sketchbooks B, D, E, F, N, O, Q, R, T, and W (possibly Y and Z) are missing from the list of full-size books. It can be no coincidence, then, that eight sketchbooks which entered the Berlin Königliche Bibliothek in 1862 from the collection of Ludwig Landsberg, those now identified as Landsberg 5, 6, 7, 8, 9, 10, 11, and 12 (SV 59–66), are accompanied by early Artaria covers with the letters B, D, E, F, O, Q, T, and W.[17] Landsberg apparently bought the eight

---

[15] *Nachlass* lots 52, 54, 57, and 64, all bought by Artaria, specify "Quartett Skizzen."

[16] A similar alphabetical classification was provided for some of the Haydn autographs in the Artaria Collection. StPK Haydn Aut. 48 and 44, the Symphony no. 94 (*Surprise*) and the Concertante of 1792, have title pages respectively inscribed I and N. Both were sold by Artaria in 1834. Haydn scholars should be alert to such letters on other Haydn manuscripts; where they appear, they indicate previous ownership by Artaria.

[17] Landsberg 5, 11, 6, 7, 8, 9, 10, and 12 respectively. Landsberg 6 and 11 (E and D) have been missing since World War II, but their descriptions (letter plus number of folios) in old card-catalogue entries are clearly taken from the original Artaria covers. A film of Landsberg 6 survives in the DStB. The book is identified in the film as "Skizzenbuch E 90," but the cover was not photographed. The manuscript as photographed has ninety-one folios, all used, but there is no folio inscribed with an *E*.

Plate XVIII 🦗 (*a*) *Cover of Landsberg 7 (StPK, Berlin)*—
Notirungsbuch F in the first Artaria classification.

(*b*) *Cover of Artaria 201 (StPK, Berlin)*—
Skizzenbuch E in the second Artaria classification.

sketchbooks between 1827 and the time of Autograph 47a and simply retained the accompanying covers.

Of the other large-format sketchbooks, only N and R are missing from the Autograph 47a list, although some of those which are listed cannot be conclusively identified. A cover inscribed "Notirungen/N/4∅ 11" survives (see entry 92 in the transcript of Autograph 47a), indicating the original size of the bundle and the subsequent removal of twenty-nine folios. In addition to N and R and those sold to Landsberg, the following sketchbooks left the Artaria Collection before Autograph 47a was written:

(a) part of Notirungsbuch K was inscribed to "M.M. J. Artôt et L'huillier" by August Artaria on May 19, 1835 (see catalogue entry 28).

(b) a large sketchbook for *Leonore* (now StPK Mendelssohn 15 = SV 67) was sold to Heinrich Beer, inscribed only "Artaria und Compag/ Wien 14 Juny 1834." The book seems not to have been included in the alphabetical list.

(c) the miscellany of early sketches StPK Autograph 28 (fifty-six folios = SV 31), obtained in the *Nachlass* of Joseph Fischhof, had probably been separated from the 124-folio miscellany listed on page 7 of Autograph 47a (later sold to Johann Kafka). Gräffer quoted from a sketch on folio 24ᵛ of StPK Autograph 28 in a little book, *Über Tonkunst, Sprache und Schrift. Fragment,* published in 1830. Although Autograph 28 cannot be conclusively associated with Artaria, the similarities in content and paper types to the 124 folios of early sketches retained by Artaria make it probable that the two miscellanies together had formed a single large portfolio bought at the *Nachlass* auction. Fischhof apparently acquired his miscellany before 1835, when he inscribed a folio of early sketches to A. Thomas (Paris Bibliothèque Nationale MS. 83 = SV 235).

After Autograph 47a was written, August Artaria continued to sell sketchbooks. Books A, C, G, L, S, U, and X, plus the remainder of K and probably V, had all left before 1890, when Adler's catalogue appeared. Two of the unlettered large-format books (entries 69 and 90 in Autograph 47a) were also sold, to Johann Kafka, who later sold them to the British Museum.[18] And one more book, now partially dismembered, can also be traced to the Artaria Collection at the time of Autograph 47a. This book was described by Thayer as a "Notirbuch Beethovens, 56 Seiten stark (im Besitz des Hrn. Gustav Petter in Wien)," and he refers to it in his *Verzeichnis* entries for Opp. 18, 22, 23, 24, 67, and 80. The core

---

[18] Another miscellany in the British Museum, Add. MS. 29997, was also obtained from Kafka, and it seems likely that Kafka got it from Artaria, although it cannot be identified with any of the Aut. 47a entries.

of the book, with sketches for Opp. 17, 18, 22, and 23, is now StPK Autograph 19e, folios 75–94 (SV 29). Identifications in Gräffer's hand are found on nearly all of these folios. Several other folios, now scattered, also have Gräffer's penciled identifications and sketches for the works mentioned by Thayer, and hence appear to have belonged with the Autograph 19e folios at one time. These include SV 56, 180, 308, 357, 359, and 378. A bundle of about thirty folios, then, should have been part of Artaria's collection when Autograph 47a was written, but such a bundle cannot be identified with any of the catalogue's entries (see further discussion of quartet sketches on pages 196–98).

That the Artarias did substantial surgery on the books in their possession can be inferred from discrepancies between the number of folios indicated on the early covers, the number indicated in Autograph 47a, and the number present in surviving manuscripts. It may also be observed in the displacement of lettered pages, each of which must be presumed to have been a 1^r at the time of the original classification. The sketchbooks bought by Ludwig Landsberg, some of which do not conform to their cover descriptions, had probably already been altered by Artaria. Certainly by the time of Autograph 47a several books were no longer in the state in which Domenico Artaria bought them. The extent of these changes can be seen in my notes to the appended transcript of Autograph 47a and from the table on pages 190–91.

By the time the Autograph 47a catalogue was compiled, then, a large number of the large-format sketchbooks had been sold and several of those remaining had been altered. Thus it is not surprising that the early covers, which no longer made a continuous sequence for purposes of classification and which in many cases were no longer accurate, were later considered dispensable. Sometime after 1847 (when books A and G were sold) and before the sale of two unlettered books to Johann Kafka (before 1875), August Artaria made a second alphabetical classification of the few large-format sketchbooks that remained. Since Thayer's *Verzeichnis* of 1865 refers to several books by their earlier letters, the date of this new classification can probably be further narrowed to the period 1865–75.[19] When it occurred, the old covers were removed and some were turned inside out and used again, with new inscriptions. And simultaneously with the new alphabetical classification of the sketchbooks, a variety of other manuscripts, including some loose sketches and some fragments, were given similar covers (usually the old sketchbook covers

---

[19] Although he had visited Vienna as early as 1851 before taking up residence there in 1860–64, Thayer's study of the sketchbooks was probably concentrated in the later period.

FIRST ARTARIA CLASSIFICATION: NOTIRUNGSBUCH	PRESENT LOCATION OF MANUSCRIPT	PRESENT NO. OF FOLIOS *	FOLIO WITH INSCRIBED LETTER
A	StPK Autograph 24	62	*ibid.*, fol. 1ʳ
B	DStB Landsberg 5	56	*ibid.*, fol. 1ʳ
C	William Scheide, Princeton, N.J.	56 **	*ibid.*, fol. 55ʳ
D	formerly PrStB Landsberg 11	50?	?
E	formerly PrStB Landsberg 6	91	?
F	StPK Landsberg 7	93 (2)	?
G	Beethovenhaus, Bonn, SBH 680	40	*ibid.*, fol. 1ʳ
H	StPK Artaria 195	50	*ibid.*, fol. 1ʳ
I	StPK Artaria 197	44	*ibid.*, fol. 9ʳ
K	Beethovenhaus, Bonn, SBH 625, 637, 638, 648, 655, 664	41 (2)	*ibid.*, SBH 664. fol. 1ʳ
L	Beethovenhaus, Bonn, SBH 602 (1 folio) Pierpont Morgan Library, New York (1 folio)	2	?
M	DStB Artaria 183	12	?
N	?	?	?
O	DStB Landsberg 8	55	*ibid.*, fol. 16ʳ
P	StPK Artaria 201	64	?
Q	DStB Landsberg 9	36 (1)	?
R	?	?	?
S	DStB Grasnick 20a	11	DStB Landsberg 12, fol. 22ʳ
T	StPK Landsberg 10	87	*ibid.*, fol. 33ʳ
U	DStB Grasnick 20b	24 (3) †	*ibid.*, fol. 1ʳ
V	?	?	?
W	DStB Landsberg 12	38 (1)	*ibid.*, fol. 1ʳ
X	? StPK Autograph 19e, fols. 64–74	11 (1)	?

* No. of totally blank folios in parentheses.   ** Part of one folio has been ripped away.
† Parts of two folios have been ripped away.

re-used) and classified numerically. The new inscriptions comprised either (a) "Skizzenbuch"/letter/a number plus "Blätter" (see plate XVIIIb); or (b) a number/a brief description of the content. The following manuscripts have retained their covers from this second classification:

Skizzenbuch/B/55 Blätter—William Scheide, Princeton, N.J. (SV 364) —Notirungsbuch C in the earlier classification.

PRESENT LOCATION OF FIRST ARTARIA COVER	FOLIOS NOTED ON FIRST ARTARIA COVER ††	POSITION IN SECOND ARTARIA CLASSIFICATION	FIRST ARTARIA CLASSIFICATION: NOTIRUNGSBUCH
?	?	—	A
ibid.	61	—	B
Beethovenhaus, Bonn SBH 648	55	Skizzenbuch B	C
?	50?	—	D
?	90?	—	E
ibid.	91	—	F
?	?	—	G
?	?	Skizzenbuch C	H
British Museum Add. MS. 29801, fols. 39–162	43	Skizzenbuch D	I
DStB Artaria 200	39 (→ 22)	no. 4 (SBH 625, 637, 638, 648, 655)	K
DStB Artaria 160	29 or 20 (→ 14)	?	L
formerly DStB Artaria 183	?	?	M
DStB Artaria 187	40 (→ 11)	?	N
ibid.	36	—	O
DStB Artaria 180	64	Skizzenbuch E	P
ibid.	38	—	Q
?	?	?	R
DStB Grasnick 20a	39 (→ 11)	—	S
ibid.	78	—	T
ibid.	20	—	U
?	?	?	V
ibid.	30	—	W
?	?	?	X

†† Emended no. of folios shown in parentheses.

Skizzenbuch/C/50 Blätter—StPK Artaria 195—Notirungsbuch H in the earlier classification.

Skizzenbuch/D/43 Blätter—StPK Artaria 197—Notirungsbuch I in the earlier classification.

Skizzenbuch/E/64 Blätter—StPK Artaria 201—Notirungsbuch P in the earlier classification.

Skizzenbuch/F, later emended to Skizzenbuch/B [20]—British Museum
  Add. MS. 29801, ff. 2–37—not included in the earlier classification
  (number 69 in Autograph 47a).

2./Klavier-Konzert/nicht vollendet—DStB Artaria 184—number 79 in
  Autograph 47a.
3./Skizzenblätter/aus früher Zeit—cover now on DStB Artaria 180—? in
  Autograph 47a (see the discussion on pages 193–96).
4./Skizzen/zu Christus am Oelberge; Wellington's Sieg/Meeresstille und
  glückliche Fahrt zur/Sonate op. 102 N° 2 etc. etc./25 Blätter—cover
  now on SBH 648—part of Notirungsbuch K in the earlier classification.
6./Skizzenblätter/zur 2. Messe/Op. 123—cover now on DStB Artaria
  200—? in Autograph 47a (see the discussion on pages 193–96).
7./Skizzen zu Volksliedern—DStB Artaria 187—probably number 92 in
  Autograph 47a.

Between 1890 and 1893 August Artaria compiled his own catalogue,
with its single numerical list of the entire collection. While doing so, he
had his own new numbers added above the inscriptions on the covers of
all the manuscripts which remained from the above list (see plate
XVIIIb). In some cases the number of folios was also added below.
These additions have combined with various other remarks and cancella-
tions (some from before 1893, others later) to obscure the nature of
some of the original inscriptions. One further point of confusion is the
duplication of several letters which resulted from the earlier and later
alphabetical classifications of the Artaria sketchbooks. This duplication
has been adopted without comment, for example, in Hans Schmidt's
"Verzeichnis der Skizzen Beethovens," where the letter *D* is associated
with both Artaria 197 and Landsberg 11 and the letter *E* with Artaria
201 and Landsberg 6.[21] The reasons for these duplicated letters should
be clear from the above discussion.

The lettered covers and folios that have survived greatly simplify
identification of Artaria's large-format sketchbooks. And even where folios
have been removed or rearranged, the sketch content is generally varied
enough to allow us to make use of Gräffer's brief identifications in Auto-

[20] There have been several additions
to this cover inscription, and it is difficult
to tell how much was originally there.
See no. 69 in the appended transcript of
Aut. 47a.

[21] Schmidt also includes the number

of folios listed on the original covers
(where they survive) as though the number were part of a signature; e.g. Landsberg 7 is referred to as Notirungsbuch
F 91, etc.

graph 47a. When we turn to the pocket sketchbooks and the sketches for the late quartets, however, we lose all these advantages.

Despite the alphabetical classification on page 3 of Autograph 47a, there is no evidence that lettered covers were provided for the smaller books, nor were the letters inscribed on the manuscripts themselves. Moreover, the various bundles of sketches for the late quartets, listed on page 7 of the catalogue, were never included in the alphabetical classification at all.

Perhaps even more problematic is the considerable overlap of content in the pocket sketchbooks and among the late quartet sketches. Beethoven's use of the small books, for sketching away from home, was concentrated in the years after 1814–15, if the evidence of the surviving manuscripts is to be trusted.[22] Work on the *Missa solemnis,* Op. 123, consumed an especially large number of pocket sketchbooks, and Domenico Artaria seems to have bought a disproportionate number of these. This drastically reduces the usefulness of Gräffer's identifications in Autograph 47a. Of the eleven Taschen Notirungsbücher B through M (A is significantly different in size and content), nine are associated with the Mass, and the content of one other goes unidentified. The presence of the Latin text in the Op. 123 sketches doubtless made them susceptible to quick identification, perhaps to the exclusion of other, more extensive sketches in the books.

The quartet sketches on page 7 of the catalogue are more clearly distinguished from one another in Gräffer's notes, despite a certain inevitable duplication of content in these sketches as well. Had the various bundles survived intact from the time of Autograph 47a, one suspects they would be relatively easy to identify. Such is unfortunately not the case, for although most of these sketches, like those for Op. 123, remained in the Artaria Collection, the folios have been combined in new bundles which do not match those described in the catalogue.

The single positive factor in this otherwise discouraging situation is that most of the late sketches bought by Domenico Artaria did remain in

---

[22] Systematic use of pocket sketchbooks apparently goes back only to 1814–15, when Beethoven used such a book (SV 70) for work on the sonatas of Op. 102 and the unfinished piano concerto, Hess 15. This book, formerly in the Mendelssohn Collection of the PrStB, has been missing since World War II (it was described by Nottebohm, N II, pp. 304–20). It was preceded by the ten tiny folios of DStB Art. 205, bundle 2, with sketches for Op. 113 (1811–see p. 194). The other surviving pocket sketchbooks are devoted to the works of Beethoven's last ten years. He seems not to have used these small books in earlier years, although some individual folios survive which have been folded to pocket size, apparently for use away from home.

the collection. It would be interesting to postulate that this reflected a high-minded interest on the part of father and son in retaining sketches for certain of the late works, but this would be pure fantasy. We must suppose rather that among the friends and collectors to whom the Artarias gave and sold manuscripts there was a preference for sketches for the earlier, better-known works. Then, too, the sketches from the early and middle periods were mostly in manageable bundles of relatively uniform and legible folios. The tattered and ugly little pocket sketchbooks did not make very attractive gifts, certainly, and few among the prospective buyers could have been expected to know the late quartets or to be able to read the sketches for them.[23] When Ludwig Landsberg came to buy a batch of sketchbooks for his collection, he went away with seven from the period 1800–12 and one book of sketches mostly for the Ninth Symphony. Other buyers showed a similar preference. In fact, of the 700-plus sketch folios which remained in the collection when August Artaria died in 1893, the earliest are those for the Mass in D and the piano sonatas, Opp. 109–111.[24] Although the pocket sketchbooks and the bundles of sketches for the late quartets must have been reassembled since Autograph 47a, therefore, we may suggest with some confidence that the folios remaining in the collection when August Artaria died do correspond in large part to those described in the Autograph 47a entries.

The small-format sketches which came to Berlin had been brought together into the following three (now two) packages:

1. DStB Artaria 205 (SV 17). This manuscript now comprises seven pocket-size, individually bound bundles. These are apparently the seven bundles described in the catalogues of 1890 and 1893:
   Adler 76—"7 kleine Skizzenhefte—104 Bl.—Mit Entwürfen zu den 'Ruinen von Athen', zur 'Weihe des Hauses', zur 9. Symphonie, zur Missa Solennis, zu den Quartetten Op. 127, 131, 132, 135, u.a.m."
   Artaria 205—"7 kleinere Hefte: Taschen-Skizzenhefte, mit Bleistift geschrieben in 109 halben Blättern . . ." (same identifications).
   The present state of Artaria 205 is as follows:
   Bundle 1 (15 folios): sketches for Opp. 124, 125.
   Bundle 2 (10 folios): sketches for Op. 113.
   Bundle 3 (18 folios): sketches for Opp. 131, 135.

---

[23] Most of the sketches for the Ninth Symphony were sold, however, doubtless owing to the fame of the piece. These included Notirungsbuch K, fols. 1–19, Notirungsbuch O (= Landsberg 8), and Taschen Notirungsbuch A.

[24] This excludes exercises and pedagogical notes, such as those of Art. 153 (see entries 67–68).

Bundle 4 (22 folios): sketches for Opp. 127, 125.[25]
Bundle 5 (24 folios): sketches for Op. 125.
Bundle 6 (19 folios): sketches for Op. 123.[26]
Bundle 7 (8 folios): sketches for Op. 132.

This arrangement is not the original one, however, for there is an earlier, continuous foliation (now nearly illegible in places) in which the bundles occur in a different sequence and from which at least ten folios are missing. Identifications by Gräffer are found on the first folios of the present bundles 1—"Skizzen zur Weihe des Hauses"—and 4—"Skizze zum Quartett Es (Gallizin) 1st, 2^{t} ?, 3tes Stück/zuletzt Schluß zum Lied an die Freude (Sinf.)." The former inscription, now nearly rubbed out, was probably suggested by Beethoven's own inscription "die Weihe des Hauses," written clearly at the top of folio 8^{v}, for there are only a few brief sketches for the overture, the rest of the book being devoted to Op. 125. Strangely, neither the inscription on bundle 1 nor that on bundle 4 seems to match any of the identifications in the Autograph 47a list of Taschen Notirungsbücher.[27]

2. DStB Artaria 180 and 200 (SV 13). These two bundles are now stored in a single package in the library, although their separate covers remain.[28] Together they comprise fifty-seven loose, full-size folios (Artaria 180 has fifty-one folios; Artaria 200 has six folios).[29] Of these, five were used by Beethoven in their full format. The other fifty-two folios were folded once vertically and used in a pocket-size upright format, but have since been straightened out. Although groups of these could have been folded together and used in small gatherings, only eight have stitch holes along their folds.[30]

---

[25] This bundle comprises two separate gatherings of eleven folios each. The first has sketches for Op. 127; the second has sketches for both Op. 127 and Op. 125.

[26] This bundle comprises three separate gatherings of 13, 2, and 4 folios, all with sketches for Op. 123.

[27] There is a correspondence between the inscription on bundle 4 and the identification of sketches in entry 95 of Aut. 47a. The latter refers to sketches in score, however, and the correspondence with the inscription on the pocket-size book, Art. 205, bundle 4 (which has no sketches in score), is probably coincidental.

[28] The covers were those originally designed for Notirungsbuch K (now on Art. 200) and Notirungsbuch P (now on Art. 180). Both were turned inside out when they were used the second time.

[29] One other loose folio now stored with this bundle does not, in fact, belong, but was added by a Berlin librarian, whose note on the folio indicates that it was earlier filed with Art. 178 (a copy of Op. 84, with which the folio also does not belong).

[30] This suggests that the term "sketchbook" does not really apply to most of the pocket-size sketches; rather they appear to have been generally used in small unsewn gatherings.

The Adler and Artaria catalogue entries for these manuscripts are thoroughly confusing:

Adler 77—"Skizzenblätter, zum Theil zusammen geheftet und zusammengehörend—Skizzen zum 'Christus am Oelberg', 'Wellington's Sieg', 'Meeresstille u. glückliche Fahrt', zur Sonate Op. 102 Nr. 2, u.a.m." (no number of folios given).

Adler 78—"Lose Skizzenblätter zur Missa Solennis (Op. 123)—62 Bl."

Artaria 180—"Lose Skizzenblätter, enthaltend Entwürfe zu: Christus am Oelberg, Wellington's Sieg, Meeresstille und glückliche Fahrt u.a.m.; viele davon mit Bleistift, andere mit Tinte geschrieben—50 Bl."

Artaria 200—"Skizzen zur 2. Messe, Op. 123. Lose Blätter. Autograph. —6 Bl."

Between 1890 and 1893, the sketches listed in Adler 77 had apparently been sold.[31] Most of the Adler 78 folios were put in the former Adler 77 cover, leaving behind six folios of Op. 123 sketches in Adler 78, which became Artaria 200. The others became Artaria 180, which August Artaria wrongly identified with the former content of Adler 77, doubtless because of the cover inscription. Along the way, five folios are unaccounted for (Artaria 180 + Artaria 200 = 57 folios; Adler 78 = 62 folios).

Together Artaria 205, 180, and 200 comprise about 220 pocket-size folios. This compares reasonably with the 216 folios of Taschen Notirungsbücher B through M of Autograph 47a. It seems futile to attempt further to account for the differences, since there are discrepancies even between the present state of the manuscripts and the descriptions in the Adler and Artaria catalogues.

The situation with the late-quartet sketches is equally ambiguous. For the surviving Artaria bundles do not match those described in Autograph 47a, page 7 (see plate XVII). And the total number of folios involved is further confused by the Autograph 47a entry for Paquet XII (entry 91), "Ein Paket Quartetten Stücke und Skizzen in Partitur," which lists no number of folios. Two other assumptions—that only *late*-quartet sketches are involved and that all the folios are full-size—are actually not supported by any very solid evidence. The list may have included the bundle of sketches for Op. 18, discussed on pages 188–89, which cannot be fitted among the lettered sketchbooks. And Gräffer's identifications of sketches for Op. 127 on the fourth bundle of pocket-size folios in Artaria

---

[31] All or most of these turned up in the Bodmer Collection, now in the Beethovenhaus, Bonn (see discussion of Notirungsbuch K on pp. 209–11).

205 (see page 195), which matches nothing in the list of Taschen Noti-rungsbücher, suggest the possibility that these small folios might also be-long in the list on page 7. More likely, however, the small books had been systematically separated from the larger ones and were listed and stored together.

In any case, no special effort was made to keep all the late quartet sketches in the collection together. Notirungsbuch A, Notirungsbuch G, and Taschen Notirungsbuch D included them; and Notirungsbuch V and Taschen Notirungsbuch G, both with unidentified quartet sketches, could also have been late. By the time the collection came to Berlin, however, the remaining quartet sketches in large format (all late) had not been in the alphabetical lists, and it is likely that these do correspond substantially to the sketches listed on page 7 of the catalogue, although the folios had since been reassembled into completely different bundles. The present conformations are listed below for comparison with the list in Autograph 47a. Except for the number of folios indicated, they receive similar brief descriptions in the Adler and Artaria catalogues.

Artaria 206 (49 folios) = Adler 80 (52 folios) = SV 18 (56 folios with 102 written sides). This bundle has been missing since World War II. Sketches for Op. 127.

Artaria 209 (24 folios) = Adler 85 (24 folios) = SV 19. Now in StPK. 24 bound folios with sketches for Op. 130, finale.

Artaria 210 (165 folios) = Adler 81 (152 folios) =SV 20. Now in StPK. 169 loose folios; halves of two have been ripped off; 14 are completely blank. Sketches for Op. 131.

Artaria 211 = Adler 21 = SV 21. This manuscript has been missing since World War II. It comprised the autograph of most of Op. 131 plus sketches for two movements and handwritten parts to the first move-ment. It is not clear how many sketch folios were involved.

Artaria 213 (22 folios) = Adler 82 (21 folios) = SV 22. Now in StPK. 22 bound folios with sketches for Op. 132.[32]

Artaria 214 (5 folios) = Adler 83 (10 folios) = SV 23 (6 folios with 12 written sides). This bundle has been missing since World War II. Sketches for Op. 133.

Artaria 216 (79 folios) = Adler 84 (80 folios) = SV 24. Now in StPK. 80 bound folios with sketches for Op. 135 and WoO 196.

---

[32] Art. 213, in fact, consists of two bundles, bound separately. The first con-tains nineteen oversize folios with twenty-three staffs to a page; the second has three normal-size sixteen-staff folios, which were for a time enclosed with Art. 210. These last three folios, with sketches for both Op. 132 and Op. 130, never formed an integral unit with the first bundle.

Although there is rough agreement between the 1890 and 1893 catalogues concerning these sketches and the bundles seem not to have been drastically rearranged since 1893, these descriptions cannot be made to coincide with the entries in Autograph 47a. Even the total number of folios involved is difficult to compare. Autograph 47a, entries 93–97, comprise only 167 folios. The manuscripts Artaria 206, 209, 210, 213, 214, 216, and the sketch folios included in Artaria 211 together comprise about 360 to 370 folios; the total varies from one catalogue to another. This leaves a rather large group of folios (about 200) to accommodate the package of "Quartetten Stücke und Skizzen," indicated as Paquet XII of Autograph 47a (entry 91).

In concluding this survey of the sketches that passed through the Artaria Collection, we should emphasize once more the two general points which have emerged. First, the Artarias disposed of nearly all of their early- and middle-period sketches. These were on full-size folios. A large number were included in an early alphabetical classification of the sketchbooks, made sometime before Autograph 47a. As a part of this classification, the books were provided with lettered covers and the first folio of each (or most) was inscribed with a matching letter. Sometime after Autograph 47a, when most of the sketchbooks in the first list had already left the collection, a second classification, part alphabetical and part numerical, was made of the sketches that remained. The old covers were turned inside out and sometimes exchanged, and new inscriptions were added. The nature of deletions from and changes in the internal arrangement of sketchbooks from the Artaria Collection can often be inferred from the inscribed covers and folios, where they survive, and from other descriptive information provided by the entries of Autograph 47a.

Second, most of the late sketches bought by Domenico Artaria remained in the collection. Some of these, mostly for Op. 123, were in pocket sketchbooks, and although these books were also classified alphabetically, the letters were not inscribed on the manuscripts and no special lettered covers survive. Sketches for other late works, most notably the quartets, are found on a large number of full-size leaves in the collection, but these were omitted from the alphabetical lists. The Autograph 47a entries for both the pocket sketchbooks and the bundles of late-quartet sketches do not correspond to the manuscripts as they are presently constituted, and there seems to be no satisfactory way to relate the surviving sketches in the Artaria Collection to their counterparts in Autograph 47a.

Because the sketches were handled with little regard for the integrity of their initial state, the entries for them in Autograph 47a are perhaps the most valuable in the catalogue. At the same time, we should reaffirm the importance of the catalogue as a guide to the Artaria Collection as a whole at an early stage of its history. New information concerning the state and provenance of all the manuscripts described in Autograph 47a can be found in my notes to the entries in the appended survey of the catalogue, and it is there that the reader is referred to for further discussion of the individual manuscripts.

In the following annotated transcript of Autograph 47a, the text of the catalogue appears in italics. Gräffer's original entries in ink are separated from his later additions in pencil by a double solidus (//). The actual format of the catalogue may be visualized by referring to plates XV–XVII. To facilitate cross reference, I have supplied a single continuous numeration of all the catalogue's entries. Despite a few peculiarities and inconsistencies of spelling, which have been reproduced in the present transcription, the catalogue presents no serious problems of legibility. For clarity, in the absence of the original columns I have added "dur" or "moll" to the letter indicating tonality and "Bl." to the number of folios. Gräffer was also careless about punctuation, and I have introduced an occasional comma or period to separate items originally distinguished by their columnar arrangement. Remarks about the present number of folios occur only where a possible conflict with Gräffer's count exists. Descriptions quoted from the *Nachlass* auction catalogue are taken from Gräffer's copy for Jacob Hotschevar. Unless otherwise indicated, all the *Nachlass* lots referred to were bought by Domenico Artaria. See also the list of abbreviations at the beginning of this volume.

---

page 1 [see plate XV]

Beethoven.
Original.

Paquet I

1. *Quintett für 2 Violinen, 2 Bratschen und Violoncelle Op. 29 Partitur —43 Bl.—C dur—Eigenhändig darauf bemerkt Quintetto von Beethoven 1801.* (The entire entry is canceled, but *gilt* is written to one side.)

    Nachlass 110, "Quintett für Violin"; formerly PrStB Mendelssohn 5, but missing since World War II. The score belonged to Paul Mendelssohn (Thayer, *Verzeichnis*), Joseph Joachim, and Ernst von Mendelssohn-Bartholdy. Kinsky (Kinsky-Halm) suggests that it may have passed from Artaria to Heinrich Beer, a younger brother of Meyerbeer, before entering the Mendelssohn Collection, since several other manuscripts owned by Paul Mendelssohn had first belonged to Beer.

2. *Terzett für 2 Oboen und englisch Horn oder für 2 Violinen und Viola Op. 29 Partitur—16 Bl.—C dur—Mit eigenhändigen Nahmen auf dem copirten Titelblatt. Wovon 4 Blätter copirt sind.*

   Adler 25; Artaria 151; DStB Artaria 151.

   This trio, Op. 87, was not sold in the *Nachlass* auction because it had already been promised to Artaria. The opus number 29 was associated with the work throughout its early publication history and is still given in Artaria's 1893 catalogue, with the remark "Dasselbe Werk ist auch unter der Bezeichnung als Op. 87 erschienen." The autograph is complete on twelve folios, one of which is blank and two of which are used for sketching and revisions to the autograph. The four folios in a copyist's hand begin an extra copy of the score, encompassing most of the first movement. See also entry 6 below.

3. *Sonate für Pianoforte und Violoncelle Op. 69* [33] *Partitur—9 Bl.—A dur—Mit eigenhändigen Nahmen. Erstes Stück.*

   Nachlass 91 or 138, "Sonate für Pianoforte und Violoncell"; the other is Op. 102, no. 2 (see entry 10 below). The suggestion in Kinsky-Halm that the two separated *Nachlass* entries refer to the two sonatas of Op. 102 (no. 1 having later been sold) is probably an error. Artaria still owned the manuscript in 1868.[34] Later it belonged to Heinrich Steger and to the Wittgenstein family of Vienna; it was obtained from the latter by the present owner, Felix Salzer. Its fragmentary state predates Autograph 47a and probably extends back to the *Nachlass*.[35]

4. *Trio für Pianoforte, Violin und Violoncelle Op. 70 N. 1 Partitur—34 Bl.—D dur.*

   Adler 32.

---

[33] The number is emended from 59, which was the opus number assigned to the work in its earliest editions. It was Beethoven himself who suggested the wrong opus numbers for this work and the Fifth and Sixth Symphonies, in a letter to Breitkopf & Härtel of March 4, 1809 (Anderson 199).

[34] According to Gustav Nottebohm, *Thematisches Verzeichnis der im Druck erschienenen Werke von Ludwig van Beethoven*, 2nd ed. (Leipzig, 1868).

[35] For a fuller discussion of this manuscript, see Lewis Lockwood, "The Autograph of the First Movement of Beethoven's Sonata for Violoncello and Pianoforte, Opus 69," *The Music Forum*, II (1970), 1–109.

Nachlass 73, "2 Clavier-Trio bei Breitkopf sammt Abschrift"; [36] this autograph was sold between 1890 and 1893 to Max Friedlaender and is now in the Pierpont Morgan Library, New York. Actually thirty-eight folios, but in one place adjacent pages have been stitched together, two other folios are completely blank except for one brief sketch, and the first folio of the second movement is entirely in a copyist's hand.[37]

5. *Trio für Pianoforte, Violin und Violoncelle Op. 70 N. 2 Partitur—41 Bl.—Es dur.*

   Adler 33; Artaria 175; StPK Artaria 175.

   Nachlass 73 (see entry 4 above). Actually forty-two folios, one of which is in a copyist's hand.

6. *Variations für 2 Oboen u. engl. Horn—7 Bl.—C dur—Variat. aus Dn Juan La ci darem Original ungestochen.*

   Adler 26; Artaria 149; StPK Artaria 149.

   This autograph of WoO 28 did not appear explicitly in the *Nachlass* auction catalogue. It is my opinion that the work was originally associated with Op. 87, perhaps as a finale or merely as a companion piece for a specific performance occasion.[38] Hence the possibility exists that the manuscript was enclosed with the autograph of Op. 87 (see above), which was among the works promised to Artaria by the composer. The entire entry has been squeezed in later, perhaps because the piece had been found in the back of Op. 87.

---

[36] See Kinsky-Halm for a reference to a copy (now lost) of the piano part to Op. 70, no. 1. The copy, which must have been purchased by Artaria with the autograph, may have been included on later pages of Aut. 47a, now missing, or could have left the collection before the catalogue was written.

[37] It occurs as no. 73 in the *Catalogue of the Mary Flagler Cary Music Collection. The Pierpont Morgan Library* (New York, 1970). For a detailed description of this autograph, see Alan Tyson, "Stages in the Composition of Beetho-

ven's Piano Trio Op. 70, No. 1," *Proceedings of the Royal Musical Association*, XCVII (1970–71), 18–19.

[38] In support of this opinion I would point out that the autographs of both WoO 28 and Op. 87 employ a paper type otherwise extremely rare among early Beethoven manuscripts (I know of only one other folio) and that the WoO 28 autograph has no title other than "Thema Andante." The two works may well have been performed together at a concert on Dec. 23, 1797, but both were probably composed earlier.

Paquet II

7. *Entr'actes zu Egmont Op. 84 Partitur—81 Bl.*

    Adler 3; Artaria 177; StPK Artaria 177.

    Nachlass 137, "Entr'Actes zu Egmont." Actually eighty-four folios, three of which are blank. The manuscript comprises numbers 1–6; if Artaria ever owned the overture and numbers 7–9, he had parted with them before Autograph 47a was written.

8. *Oratorium: Christus am Oehlberg Op. 85 Partitur—44 Bl.—Complet, jedoch nur 44 Blätter eigenhändig.*

    Adler 46; Artaria 179; StPK Artaria 179.

    Nachlass 103, "Christus am Oelberg. Partitur."

9. *Ein Theil des Gloria der ersten Messe Op. 86 Partitur—21 Bl.*

    Nachlass 104, "Gloria aus der 1^t Messe. Partitur." Subsequently owned (with the Kyrie, *Nachlass* 87, bought by Karl Holz) by Aloys Fuchs and others (see Kinsky-Halm); both the Kyrie and this Gloria fragment (measures 1–205) are now in the Beethovenhaus, Bonn—SBH 559. Artaria also bought the Agnus Dei, *Nachlass* 132, but had parted with it before Autograph 47a was written, and it is now lost.

Paquet III

10. *Sonate für Pianoforte und Violoncelle Op. 102 Livraison 2—15 Bl. —D dur—Eigenhändig: August 1815.*

    Adler 34; Artaria 192; StPK Artaria 192.

    Nachlass 91 or 138 (see entry 3 above). The sonata Op. 102, no. 1 (StPK Autograph 18), was owned in the 1860s by Otto Jahn (Thayer, *Verzeichnis*). Although it is possible that *Nachlass* 91 and 138 were the two sonatas of Op. 102 and that Op. 69 did not appear in the auction (as per Kinsky-Halm), it seems more likely that Op. 102, no. 1, made its way to Jahn without passing through the Artaria Collection.

11. *Sonate für Pianoforte allein Op. 110—29 Bl.—As dur—Eigenhändig: Nahme und: am 25 December 1821.*

    Adler 38; Artaria 196; StPK Artaria 196.

    Probably *Nachlass* 135, "Zwei Sonaten für Pianof." (with Op. 111?), or *Nachlass* 101, "Sonate für Pianoforte." [39]

---

[39] *Nachlass* 101 was bought by Artaria, according to Hotschevar's copy of the auction catalogue; Fuchs entered no buyer in his copy. An unidentified piano

12. *Adagio ma non troppo aus dieser Sonate Op. 110—8 Bl.—As dur.*

Beethovenhaus, Bonn—SBH 564. Formerly owned by H. C. Bodmer and G. B. Davy. Ownership by Artaria not previously known. The movement receives no separate entry in the *Nachlass* auction catalogue; it was probably included with the autograph of Op. 110 (see previous entry).

13. *Sonate für Pianoforte allein Op. 111—20 Bl.—Es dur[!]—Eigenhändig: am 13 Jäner 1822.*

Adler 39; Artaria 198; DStB Artaria 198.
Probably *Nachlass* 135 or 101 (see entry 11 above).

14. *Maestoso, erstes Stück obiger Sonate Op. 111—9 Bl.—Es dur[!]— Eigenhändig: 13 Jäner 1822.*

Beethovenhaus, Bonn—SBH 565. The manuscript was inscribed by August Artaria to Joseph Fischhof on October 11, 1844, and this date provides a *terminus ante quem* for Autograph 47a (see Kinsky-Halm for subsequent owners).[40] Together with the autograph of the last movement listed on page 6 of Autograph 47a (entry 81—now lost), the present manuscript apparently made a complete autograph of the sonata which preceded the one listed above (entry 13). In the *Nachlass* auction catalogue, the two autographs of Op. 111 were probably entered together, perhaps with those of Op. 110 (see entry 11 above).

page 2

15. *Fest Ouverture für Orchester Op. 124. In Partitur—45 Bl.—C dur— Mit eigenhändiger Nahmensschrift und Anmerkung der Aufführung.*

Adler 2; Artaria 203.
Nachlass 109, "Festouverture in Partitur." The score was presented to the Stadtbibliothek, Vienna, in 1897 by Carl August Artaria (one of August's sons) and hence did not come to Berlin with the rest of the collection.[41]

---

sonata was also among the works promised to Artaria before the auction.

[40] The first page of this autograph, inscribed "Herrn Prof. Fischhof zum freundlichen Angedenken von/August Artaria/Wien, den 11 October 1844," is illustrated in *Ludwig van Beethoven*, ed. Joseph Schmidt-Görg and Hans Schmidt (London, 1970), p. 185, and in the Appendix to Hubert Unverricht, *Die Eigenschriften und die Originalausgaben von Werken Beethovens in ihrer Bedeutung für die moderne Textkritik* (Kassel, 1960). On pp. 28 ff., Unverricht discusses the chronology of the two autographs of Op. 111.

[41] According to Franz Grasberger, "Beethoven-Handschriften in Wien," *Öst-*

16. *Aus der Sinfonie: An die Freude Op. 125 Partitur—D moll*[42]*—*
     Presto 4tes Stück—23 Bl.; fünftes Stück—10 Bl.; Andante maestoso
     und Allegro energico, 7tes und 8tes Stück—15 Bl.; Allegro ma non
     tanto und Prestissimo, 9tes und 10tes Stück—19 Bl.; Part des Con-
     trefagottes—2 Bl.

    Adler 1; Artaria 204; DStB Artaria 204 and StPK Artaria 204.

    Probably *Nachlass* 113, "Sinfonie in Partitur." This is the
autograph of most of the finale. A section from the middle of the
movement, the "Allegro assai vivace alla Marcia" (the tenor solo,
"Froh, wie seine Sonnen fliegen," and the following chorus through
bar 594), is missing.[43] Most of this section, together with the first
three movements, belonged to Schindler, who sold his score to the
Berlin Königliche Bibliothek in 1846 (this was formerly PrStB Autograph 2, which has been missing since World War II). Artaria
204 was divided following the war. The first two fragments listed
in the Autograph 47a entry (twenty-three and ten folios) and the
first nine folios of the third fragment are now DStB Artaria 204.
The remaining six folios of the third fragment, the nineteen folios
of the fourth, and the contrabassoon part are now StPK Artaria
204.[44]

    Paquet IV

17. *Aus der Messe Op. 123—D dur—Das Credo Partitur—57 Bl.; Das*
     Sanctus Partitur—34 Bl.; Das Agnus Dei Partitur—49 Bl.—Mit B's
     Siegel versehen.[45]

    Adler 45; Artaria 202; StPK Artaria 202.

    Nachlass 126, "Letzte Messe in Partitur." Domenico Artaria
had sold the Kyrie (now StPK Autograph 1) in 1828 to Georg
Pölchau of Berlin. If Artaria owned the Gloria (now lost) as well,
it had left the collection before Autograph 47a was written.

---

erreichische   Musikzeitschrift,   XXVI
(1971), 41–45.

  [42] The key is entered as *Dm* in Aut.
47a.

  [43] GA ser. 1, IX, 211–33; bar 595
then begins: "Seid umschlungen, Mil-
lionen." Another folio (bars 650–54 with
the text "Über Sternen muss er wohnen"
= *ibid.*, 239, bars 3–7) is also missing.

  [44] The remainder of fragment 3 is

actually eight folios, two of which are
blank. Fragment 4 is seventeen folios
plus two more, supplying a revision (incomplete) of bars 815–26. The contrabassoon part is four folios, two of which
are blank.

  [45] This remark stands opposite the
Agnus Dei entry and applies to that
movement only.

Paquet V

18. *Ruinen von Athen Partitur Op. 113—56 Bl.—Ungestochen, aber nicht vollständig.—Davon noch einzeln: Andante poco sostenuto N. 2 Partitur* (Kinsky-Halm 1)—*6 Bl.; Marcia alla Turca N. 5 Partitur* (Kinsky-Halm 4)—*7 Bl.; Allegro con fuoco Finale N. 10 Partitur* (Kinsky-Halm 8)—*18 Bl.*

Adler 47; Artaria 159; now filed as part of DStB Autograph 16, which also includes the autographs of the overture and Kinsky-Halm 2, 3, 6, and 7.

Nachlass 164, "Ruinen von Athen. Partitur, unvollständig." This entry is puzzling. It seems to imply that Artaria owned an autograph fragment of Op. 113 totaling fifty-six folios, plus the three pieces listed individually. It was these three pieces, together with the duet, "Ohne Verschulden" (Kinsky-Halm 2—nine folios), which comprised Artaria 159, the manuscript described in the 1890 and 1893 catalogues and now in the DStB. If Artaria did own a fifty-six-folio fragment in addition to the three individual pieces, this fragment apparently included the duet, Kinsky-Halm 2, and other pieces totaling forty-seven folios. One possible combination would be Kinsky-Halm 7 (thirty folios, twenty-nine of which are used), which belonged to F. A. Grasnick and could have been obtained from Artaria, plus Kinsky-Halm 6 (eighteen folios). The latter was obtained by the library with the overture and Kinsky-Halm 3 from Carl Haslinger, however, and probably never belonged to Artaria.

19. *a. Fuge von Haendel—2 Bl.—B dur—Eigenhändig von Beethoven.*

DStB Grasnick 13—Beethoven's copy of the fugue from the overture to *Solomon*. The manuscript is inscribed "Die Echtheit von Beethoven's Handschrift bestätigen Artaria & Co., Wien, den 29. Oktober 1849," when it was presumably sold to Grasnick. This copy does not appear explicitly in the *Nachlass* auction catalogue.

20. *b. Drei Quartetten für Pianoforte, Violin, Viola und Bass in Partitur —49 Bl.—Im 13ᵗ Jahre componirt 785. Nachgelassen. Mit eigenhänd. Titl und Nahmensaufschrift.*

Adler 31; Artaria 126; StPK Artaria 126.

Nachlass 166, poorly described as "Drey Originalsätze eines Quartetts für Pfte, 2 Violinen und Violonclle." These are the autographs of WoO 36.

21. *c. Parthie harmonique für 2 Oboe, 2 Clarinette, 2 Horn, 2 Fagotti*

Partitur—18 Bl.—Es dur—Mit eigenhändigem Titl und Nahmen.//
Hat als Grundlage zu sein Original Quintett Op. 4 gedient

    Adler 23; Artaria 132; StPK Artaria 132.

    The Octet does not appear in the *Nachlass* auction catalogue. I suggest that *Nachlass* 139, the "Quintett in Es," was in fact the Octet. The Op. 4 autograph, like those of Beethoven's other works published before 1800, probably disappeared in the process of publication. It would have been natural in 1827, then, to equate the unpublished Op. 103 autograph with the already published quintet version, Op. 4. This would also eliminate the difficulty (encountered in Kinsky-Halm) in accounting for an Op. 4 autograph that disappeared from Artaria's collection shortly after 1827 and an Op. 103 autograph that suddenly appeared in its place.[46] Artaria 132 actually comprises nineteen folios, all used.

22.   *d. Introduction Partitur—7 Bl.—Mit eigenhändiger Aufschrift und Bemerkungen.* (Entire entry canceled.)

    Adler 6; Artaria 152; DStB Artaria 152.

    This work, the introduction to act 2 of *Tarpeja*, WoO 2b, does not appear explicitly in the *Nachlass* auction catalogue.[47] The manuscript was for several years in Haslinger's possession, probably from about the time of Autograph 47a (hence the canceled entry) until sometime after Thayer's *Verzeichnis* (1865), which places the score "bei C. Haslinger." But by 1890 it had re-entered Artaria's collection. Haslinger may have bought or borrowed the manuscript at about the time he was publishing the companion piece, WoO 2a, in 1840; this date falls within the time span suggested for Autograph 47a (1838–44).

page 3 [see plate XVI]

Paquet VI

23.   *Notirungsbuch A—62 Bl.//Fuge Op. 133 Skizze. Walzer. Quartett in Cis m.*

---

[46] It should be noted, however, that a copy of Op. 4, now DStB Art. 134, was owned by Artaria. This copy probably appeared on pages missing from the end of Aut. 47a.

[47] This autograph probably remained unidentified because it lacks any identifying inscription. Since its tempo indication begins "Alla marcia . . . ," the score may have been included with the various marches listed on p. 6 of Aut. 47a as *Nachlass* 178, "Märsche für Orchester ungewiß ob schon bekannt."

StPK Autograph 24—sixty-two folios.

The cover carries Artaria's seal and the inscription "Autographe de Louis van Beethoven. Livre d'esquisses, contenant les idées pour la grande fugue, pour les valses, et pour différents quatuors. L'authenticité est guarantié par les soussignés Artaria & Co. à Vienne 1847." August Artaria evidently sold this book and Notirungsbuch G (see entry 25) together in 1847, when both received new covers, similar inscriptions, and Artaria's seal. The present book entered the Berlin Königliche Bibliothek in 1880 as a gift from Franz Kullak; intermediate owners are not known. An A has been inscribed in the upper right corner of folio 1^r.

24. *Notirungsbuch C—55 Bl.//Lieder u. sonstige Studien früherer Zeit.*

Now in the library of William Scheide of Princeton, N.J. (= SV 364). The book formerly belonged to Eugen v. Miller (of Vienna), G. B. Davy, and Louis Koch, but Artaria's ownership was unknown. It actually comprises fifty-six folios, although most of one is torn away. A C is inscribed in the upper-right-hand corner of folio 55^r; the last two folios appear to have been folded back at one time in such a way that folio 55 was the first folio in the book and hence received the inscribed letter. The original cover is now used, inside out, as a cover for SBH 648 (= SV 140) in the Beethovenhaus, Bonn—sketches formerly owned by Artaria (see entry 28, Notirungsbuch K). It was inscribed "Notirungsbuch/C/55." When the second alphabetical classification of Artaria's sketchbooks was made, the present book was moved up from C to B, and the later cover, with the inscription Skizzenbuch/B/55 Blätter, still accompanies the book.[48] A further remark, "Skizzen zu den Sonaten Op. 102 No. 2, zum Liederkreis Op. 98 etc. etc.," has been added in pencil. Since the sketches are from 1815, Gräffer's description ("früherer Zeit") is a bit puzzling. The reference may have been relative to the bulk of sketches remaining in the collection, or specifically to the previous entry, for Notirungsbuch A.[49]

25. *Notirungsbuch G—42 Bl.//A moll Quartett und Studien.*

This sketchbook is now in the Beethovenhaus, Bonn (SBH 680 = SV 104). It was owned in this century by Cecile de Roda of Madrid and his heirs, but intermediate owners between Artaria and

---

[48] Another sketchbook (see entry 69), originally F in this classification, was later moved up to B. The present book may therefore have been sold by Artaria before entry 69 (i.e. before 1875).

[49] Gräffer may not have been familiar with some of the works sketched in the book; it begins with extensive sketches for an unfinished piano concerto, Hess 15.

de Roda are not known. August Artaria probably sold the book together with Notirungsbuch A (see entry 23 above) in 1847, providing the present cover, with the company seal and the inscription "Autographe de Louis van Beethoven. Livre d'esquisses, contenant des motifs du Quatuor en La Mineur et autres études. L'authenticité en est guarantié par Artaria & Co. à Vienne 1847." The book now has forty folios, with sketches for Opp. 132, 130, and 133. Thus two folios have been removed since Autograph 47a was written. The letter *G* is inscribed in the upper-right-hand corner of folio 1ʳ. There are identifications written on many folios, but none of them appears to be by Gräffer.

26. *Notirungsbuch H—50 Bl.//Messe Op. 123—und neu unbekannt Gedanken und Contrapunktische Studien.*

Adler 72; Artaria 195; StPK Artaria 195—fifty folios.

The snippet of a cover has been preserved, with an inscription dating from Artaria's second alphabetical classification: "Skizzenbuch/C/50 Blätter"; the later Artaria number, 195, has been added above. The original letter *H* has been inscribed in the upper-right-hand corner of folio 1ʳ. There are two references to this book in Thayer's *Verzeichnis*. In the entry for Op. 109, he remarks: "Skizzen zu dem 'Prestissimo' und 'Andante con Var.', zwischen Entwürfen des 'Et resurrexit' und des 'Benedictus' der Messe in D, sind in einem Notirbuch, im Besitz von Artaria u. Co., vorhanden." Then in the entry for Op. 123, Thayer quotes explicitly from two autograph inscriptions (on folios 1ʳ and 4ʳ), but identifies the book as Notirungsbuch F. There is no satisfactory explanation for this; it may merely have been an error.

Paquet VII

27. *Notirungsbuch I—43 Bl.—Aus der 2ᵗᵉ Messe u. d. Sonate 111.*

Adler 73; Artaria 197; StPK Artaria 197—forty-four folios.

A snippet from one of the later Artaria covers carries the inscription "Skizzenbuch/D/43 Blätter," with the Artaria number, 197, added above. The cover from the original classification, inscribed "Notirungsbuch/I/43," was removed and used for the sketch miscellany, British Museum Add. MS. 29801, folios 39–162 (see entry 90 in Autograph 47a), which passed from Artaria to Johann Kafka (probably directly, between about 1870 and 1875) and then to the British Museum. The earlier cover also has Gräffer's penciled remark "Aus der 2ᵗᵉⁿ Messe/Aus der C mol Sonate Op.

111 C"(?), omitting mention of the many sketches for Op. 110. This inscription probably antedates the similar description in ink in the Autograph 47a entry.

The folios of this sketchbook are a mixture of different paper types and have been reassembled by Artaria. Folio 9^r, the first page of a certain paper type, has the letter I inscribed in the upper-left-hand corner and was almost certainly folio 1 of an earlier arrangement. The "43 Bl." of the Autograph 47a entry may have been an error, retained on the later cover as well. I suspect that the error stemmed from the omission of the present folio 28, which is nearly blank (there are a few verso sketches), although it is also possible that one folio was added later.

Thayer makes detailed references to Notirungsbuch I (which he identifies as such) in his *Verzeichnis* entry for Op. 123, quoting sketches and inscriptions on folios 1^v, 4^v, and 11^v. Since he gives the present page numbers (8 and 22) for the latter two sides, the book had obviously been reassembled before he saw it.

28. *Notirungsbuch K—22 Bl.—Mit eigenhändigen Titl u. Nahmen.// Schlacht v. Vittoria Signale u. andere Skizzen.*

This sketchbook has been badly dismembered, but its history can be partially reconstructed from the several surviving sources. The original Artaria cover is now found, inside out, as the cover of DStB Artaria 200. It was first inscribed "Notirungsbuch/K/39"; the "39" has subsequently been canceled and "22" written alongside. Hence the book at one time comprised thirty-nine (used) folios. In 1835, nineteen of these were removed and given by August Artaria to two French friends. This segment of the book is now in the Beethovenhaus, Bonn (SBH 664 = SV 107), obtained in the collection of H. C. Bodmer.[50] The first folio is inscribed with a K. Its present cover was added when these folios were separated from the rest of Notirungsbuch K; it is inscribed "Esquisses Autographes de Louis Van Beethoven. En signe d'amitié à M.M. J. Artôt et L'huillier. Vienne, le 19 Mai 1835 par Auguste Artaria."

Left behind were the folios entered in Autograph 47a. Thayer refers to them in his *Verzeichnis* entry for Op. 91: "Ein Notirbuch, im Besitz von Artaria u. Co., ist diesem Werke gewidmet: man liesst darin von B's Hand 'Wellington's Victory Vittoria, bloss God save the king, aber eine grosse Siegs-Ouverture auf Wellington.'" When

---

[50] Published in facsimile by W. Engelmann, *Beethovens eigenhändiges Skizzenbuch zur 9. Symphonie* (Leipzig, 1913).

August Artaria made a second classification of his sketches, these folios left over from Notirungsbuch K were relegated to the numerical list of fragments and loose folios. The cover which had belonged to Notirungsbuch C in the earlier classification was turned inside out and used for this bundle, receiving the new inscription: "4./Skizzen/zu Christus am Oelberge, Wellington's Sieg/Meeresstille und glückliche Fahrt, zur/Sonate Op. 102 No. 2. etc. etc./25 Blätter."

This package of sketch folios remained in Artaria's collection until 1890, when its cover suggested the following entry in Adler's catalogue (entry 77): "Skizzenblätter, zum Theil zusammengeheftet und zusammengehörend—Skizzen zum 'Christus am Oelberge', 'Wellington's Sieg', 'Meeresstille u. glückliche Fahrt', zur Sonate Op. 102, Nr. 2, u.a.m." (number of folios not given). Although Adler's description is lifted more or less intact for entry 180 in August Artaria's catalogue of 1893, this was apparently an error (see discussion, pages 195–96). The folios of Adler 77 were evidently sold between 1890 and 1893 to an unknown buyer, and they eventually turned up in the collection of H. C. Bodmer, which is now in the Beethovenhaus. The sketches in question are now in five separate bundles:

SBH 655: 8 folios, numbered 1–8—Op. 112
SBH 637: 4 folios, numbered 9–12—Op. 85 [51]
SBH 625: 2 folios, numbered 13–14—Op. 72 (1814), Hess 317
SBH 638: 3 folios, numbered 15–17—Op. 91
SBH 648: 8 folios, numbered 18–25—Op. 102, no. 2

The inscription quoted by Thayer occurs on the first folio of SBH 638; the cover from Artaria's second classification now encloses only SBH 648. Since two folios of SBH 648 are entirely blank and one folio of SBH 638 is entirely in a foreign hand (the trumpet calls which prompted Gräffer's "Signale"), these five bundles probably comprised the "22 Blätter" listed by Gräffer in Autograph 47a $(25 - 3 = 22)$. If the nineteen folios of SBH 664—the ones removed in 1835—are restored, however, the total size of the original Notirungsbuch K $(22 + 19 = 41)$ would have been two more than that indicated on the early cover (39). This suggests that either

---

[51] As Alan Tyson has pointed out ("The 1803 Version of Beethoven's *Christus am Oelberge*," *The Musical Quarterly*, LVI [1970], 551–84), the Op. 85 sketches in SBH 637 (and two more folios from the Bodmer Collection, SBH 635 and 636) were removed at some time from the "Wielhorsky" Sketchbook (SV 343), now in Moscow. This could imply that the latter book had also been in Artaria's collection before Aut. 47a was written.

the two folios of SBH 625 or those of SBH 638 were added to the package between the time of the first cover and that of Autograph 47a.

The separation of the first nineteen folios of Notirungsbuch K was not arbitrary, for these are similar in their physical characteristics and content, and date from about eight to ten years later than the other folios of the book. These other folios had not formed part of a single integral sketchbook,[52] but were at some time brought together and added to the first nineteen folios—perhaps by Beethoven himself, perhaps during the preparation of the *Nachlass*, or perhaps by the Artarias before the original cover was provided.

29. *Notirungsbuch L—14 Bl.—Mozart 1ᵉ Quartett in Partitur compl.*

A copy in Beethoven's hand of the first of Mozart's quartets dedicated to Haydn, K. 387. The score has been partially disassembled since Autograph 47a was written. The next-to-the-last folio (finale, bars 177–245) has been in the Beethovenhaus, Bonn (SBH 602), since 1957. And the very last folio is in the Pierpont Morgan Library, New York.[53] The present location of the remainder of the score is unknown.

Artaria's original cover for the manuscript has been re-used (inside out) to enclose part of DStB Artaria 160, copies of some movements of Op. 113. It was first inscribed "Notirungsbuch/L/29" (or "20"?); the number of folios was subsequently canceled (and obscured), and "14" was added alongside. This indicates that some other manuscript (sketches?) had been enclosed with the K. 387 copy and was removed before Autograph 47a was written. It may also explain how the copy got into the list of notebooks in Autograph 47a and why it received no explicit entry in the *Nachlass* auction catalogue (as did, for example, Beethoven's copy of Haydn's Op. 20, no. 1).

30. *Notirungsbuch M—12 Bl.—Aus dem 2ᵗᵉⁿ Concert.*

Adler 86; Artaria 183; DStB Artaria 183—twelve folios.

This is a fragment in score, comprising most of the tutti exposition of a concerto movement, probably for two solo instruments and apparently left incomplete.[54] Sketches for the piece occur in the

---

[52] The sketches are not contemporary, nor is the paper of the various folios uniform, although the latter fact does not preclude the possibility that the folios were used together.

[53] No. 74 in the *Catalogue of the*

Mary Flagler Cary Music Collection, where the key is incorrectly given as A major.

[54] The final page ends several bars into the solo entry following the tutti exposition. Pages are missing at the begin-

"Kessler" Sketchbook of 1801–02 (SV 263). The association of this manuscript with the "2ᵗᵉⁿ Concert" is a mystery and was perhaps simply an error.

Artaria 183 has been given a new cover, but there is evidence that a cover bearing the inscription "Notirungsbuch M" was once associated with the manuscript. Among the unpublished notes of Erich Hertzmann, preserved in the Columbia University Music Library, is a reference to Artaria 183 with the remark that the cover, inside out, bore the canceled inscription "Notirungsbuch M." [55] In the *Nachlass* auction catalogue, this fragment was apparently included among the "Notirbücher" and "Notirungen," and it was only later (prior to the Adler and Artaria catalogues) that it was decided not to include the manuscript among the sketchbooks. Artaria 184, a similar working autograph (see entry 79), seems to have arbitrarily escaped similar classification in the auction catalogue, appearing rather in the second section (the "Brauchbare Skizzen, Fragmente," etc.) as "Skizze eines Klavierconcerts."

31. *Notirungsbuch P—64 Bl.//Themas d. Sonate Op. 111. Themas aus d. 9ᵗᵉ Sinfonie.*

Adler 74; Artaria 201; StPK Artaria 201—sixty-four folios.

A snippet from a late Artaria cover carries the inscription "Skizzenbuch/E/64 Blätter," with the number 201 added above. Artaria's original cover, inscribed "Notirungsbuch/P/64," was removed and used again (inside out) to enclose the present DStB Artaria 180. Gräffer's identifications of sketches for Op. 111 occur on folios 2ᵛ, 9ʳ, and 24ᵛ of this sketchbook.[56] Thayer's *Verzeichnis* entry for Op. 123 has explicit references to inscriptions on folios 38, 39, and 40 of this book, which he specifically identifies as Notirungsbuch P. The absence of an inscribed *P* on any of the folios is puzzling, since the original cover indicates the book had sixty-four folios when the first alphabetical classification was made.

32. *Notirungsbuch S—11 Bl.//Gedanken aus f moll Quartett. u. unbekannte Skizzen.*

DStB Grasnick 20a—eleven folios.

Like Notirungsbuch K, this sketch miscellany seems to have

---

ning of the score, however, and other folios may have followed. Richard Kramer discovered the sketches for this concerto, and he kindly informed me of them.

[55] Since Hertzmann does not mention the number of folios listed on the cover

he saw, it is possible that a folio inscribed with an *M* has been removed from the beginning of the score.

[56] Another identification ("Op. 111") on fol. 8ᵛ may also be in Gräffer's hand.

undergone some surgery at Artaria's hands. The earliest Artaria cover still accompanies the manuscript and bears the inscription "Notirungen/S/39." The "39" has been emended to "11." Hence we must assume that twenty-eight folios were removed between the time of the original inscription and that of Autograph 47a. At least some of these missing folios are now included in the sketchbook Landsberg 12 (DStB), for there is an identifying S inscribed in the upper-right-hand corner of folio 22ʳ of the latter book. To complicate matters slightly, folios 22–23 of Landsberg 12 appear to have belonged originally to the sketchbook Mendelssohn 15 (StPK).[57] Even if this is true, the inscribed S on folio 22 indicates that this folio and probably others were at least temporarily (at the time Artaria provided the Grasnick 20a cover) included in Notirungsbuch S. The present content of Grasnick 20a includes sketches for Op. 95; indeed, it seems likely that the miscellany as it exists today corresponds to the book described in Autograph 47a. It is not known if there were intermediate owners between Artaria and Grasnick.

33. *Notirungsbuch U—20 Bl.//Unbekannte Skizzen.*

DStB Grasnick 20b—twenty-four folios.

The earliest Artaria cover still encloses this miscellany, with the inscription "Notirungen/U/20." The "20" appears to have been emended from "30," indicating a probable loss of folios between the time of the original cover inscription and that of the Autograph 47a entry. Of the present twenty-four folios, three are blank and two have been ripped vertically to half size and were perhaps counted as a single folio (this would reduce the twenty-four to the twenty noted by Gräffer). The letter U is inscribed in the upper-right-hand corner of folio 1ʳ. It is not known if there were intermediate owners between Artaria and Grasnick.

34. *Notirungsbuch V—11 Bl.//Ein Quartett Satz unbekannt u. a. Skizzen.*

Unidentified manuscripts. The remark seems to indicate that a complete movement in quartet score was involved. A copy by Beethoven of a piece unknown to Gräffer is also a possibility. Or perhaps these were merely sketches in full quartet score. The last

---

[57] These folios do, in fact, match those of Mendelssohn 15 in their physical characteristics and content. Nottebohm (N II, p. 409) first noted that folios were missing from Mendelssohn 15. The original sequence of folios appears to have been: Mendelssohn 15, fol. 12; Landsberg 12, fols. 22–23; Mendelssohn 15, fol. 13; Mendelssohn 15, fols. 1–11, 14 ff.

could have included the sketches for Op. 18, discussed on pages
188–89, or sketches for Op. 131 in British Museum Add. MS. 29997,
a miscellany owned by Johann Kafka and perhaps obtained by him
from Artaria (see footnote 18). (For a discussion of the quartet
sketches that remained in the Artaria Collection, see pages 196–98.)

35. *Notirungsbuch X—10 Bl.//Gedanken aus de(m) patriotischen
    Gesang: Es ist vollbracht, u. andere unbekannte Skizzen.*

  Probably StPK Autograph 19e, folios 64–74—eleven folios,
one of which is blank. There is no inscribed *X* on any of these
folios, however. Autograph 19e now comprises three segments:
folios 64–74, 75–94, and 95–98. That the first of these formed a
separate entity is indicated by the entry for "Es ist vollbracht"
(WoO 97) in Thayer's *Verzeichnis,* which includes the comment:
"Ein Notirbuch im Besitz des Herrn G. Petter in Wien enthält:
1. Entwürfe zu den Chören in 'Glorreiche Augenblicke'; 2. Skizzen
zu einem P.-F. Quartett; 3. Sinfonie (8 Takte); 4. Skizzen zu: 'Es ist
vollbracht'" (i.e. the present content of Autograph 19e, folios 64–
74). It was evidently the subsequent owner, R. Wagener of Mar-
purg, who combined these folios with the various other manuscripts
that now comprise Autograph 19e. The entire collection came from
Wagener through a bookdealer to the library in 1874. No intermediate owners of folios 64–74 are known between Artaria and
Petter.

*Paquet VIII—Taschen Notirungsbücher—Größtentheils mit Bley-
stift geschrieben.*

36. *A—64 Bl.//Gedanken aus der 9ᵗᵉ Sinfonie etc.*

  Adler 75—sixty-four folios.

  This sketchbook does not appear in Artaria's 1893 catalogue; it
was apparently sold between 1890 and 1893 and has since disappeared. Nevertheless, we can safely identify the book from Adler's
entry: "Taschen-Skizzenbuch—64 Bl.—Skizzen zur Sonate Op. 106,
zur 9. Symphonie u.a.m." Nottebohm devoted a full essay to this
book (N II, pp. 349–55), placing it in Artaria's collection and
quoting an inscription inside the front cover: "Poldrini/1817/Mit
inniger Empfindung, doch entschlossen, wohl/accentuirt u. sprech-
end vorgetr." Carlo Boldrini, who presumably owned the book at
one time, had joined the Artaria firm in 1807 and left about 1824.
His name is also written as "Poldrini" by Beethoven in a letter of
1820 (Anderson no. 1040). As Nottebohm points out, 1817 refers to

the year in which the book was used and the last comment, added later, was taken from the inscription published with the song *Resignation,* WoO 149, which was sketched in this book.

37. *B—18 Bl.//Agnus Dei d. letzten Messe u. a. Gedanken daraus.*

Perhaps DStB Grasnick 5—nineteen full-size folios folded once into a single large gathering of thirty-eight pocket-size folios, two of which are blank. But this creates the confusing possibility that Gräffer sometimes recorded the number of half-size folios (as used) and at others the number of full-size folios folded to make the smaller ones. The content of Grasnick 5, clear sketches for the Agnus Dei of Op. 123, matches the Autograph 47a description. It is not known where Grasnick obtained the book.

38. *C—43 Bl.//Nicht bekannte Gedanken.* (See below, after entry 47.)

39. *D—13 Bl.//Aus Cis mol Quartett u. a. unbekannte Gedanken.* (See below.)

40. *E—27 Bl.//Aus der letzten Messe. Neunten Sinfonie u. unbek. Ged.* (See below.)

41. *F—23 Bl.//Gedanken aus der letzten Messe; u. unbekannte Gedanken.* (See below.)

42. *G—19 Bl.//Gedanken eines Quartetts unbekannt. Aus der letzten Messe und unbekannte Gedanken.* (See below.)

43. *H—28 Bl.//Tänzebüchelchen. Aus der letzten Messe und unbekannte Gedanken.*

One suspects that this book, so distinctively described, included the present DStB Artaria 205, bundle 2, which comprises ten tiny folios (13.5 cm. × 7.5 cm.). These contain some sketches for Op. 113 and hence probably date from 1811. On several of the folios Beethoven has written neatly the names of various dances (Fandango, Gavotte, etc.). Possibly these folios were combined with others from a later period (Op. 123) to form the twenty-eight folios of the book listed here.

44. *I—17 Bl.//Gedanken aus der zweyten Messe u. unbek. Gedanken.* (See below.)

45. *K—10 Bl.//Instrumentierungsstudien. Aus der 2te Messe und a. unbekannte Gedanken.* (See below.)

46. *L—8 Bl.//Aus der letzten Messe und unbekannte Gedanken.* (See below.)

47. *M—10 Bl.//Aus der letzten Messe, u. unbekannte Gedanken.*

Except for the first in this list of pocket-size sketchbooks, none can be conclusively identified. The problems of relating these books to manuscripts still in the Artaria Collection are discussed on pages 194–96.

In his *Verzeichnis* entry for Op. 123, Thayer makes detailed references to three of Artaria's full-size sketchbooks (H, I, and P),[58] then remarks that "Notirungsbücher J, K, L, M, u.a.m. gehören auch meistens zur Messe." The latter are almost certainly the last four in the Autograph 47a list of pocket-size sketchbooks.

page 4

Paquet IX—Gesangstücke—NB. Die Nummern 1 bis mdns.[59] 11 ist der Text wahrscheinlich von Metastasio. Die Pianofortebegleitung scheint von einem andern Compos. da die Originale ohne dieselbe sind.[60]

48. *1. Duetto, Terzetto e Quartetto ital. Fra tutte. Partitur—4 Bl.— Ungestochen. Original. nebst Copie mit Pianofortebegleitung.* (WoO 99, nos. 3 a–c; Hess 208–10.)

49. *2. Duetto für Sopran und Tenor und Terzetto für Sopran, Alt und Tenor: Ma tu tremi. Partitur—2 Bl.—Ungestochen. Original. nebst Copie mit Pianofortebegleitung.* (WoO 99, nos. 1 and 6; Hess 211–12.)

50. *3. Quartett für Sopran, Alt, Tenor und Bass: Quella cetra. Partitur —1 Bl.—Ungestochen. Original. nebst Copie mit Pianofortebegleitung.* (WoO 99, no. 10a; Hess 213.)

51. *4. Duetto für Sopran und Bass: Nel mirarvi.*
     Duetto für 2 Soprane: Sù questi colla.
     Quartetto für Sopran, Alt, Tenor u. Bass: Nel mirarvi.
     Terzetto für Sopran, Tenor und Bass: Quanto è bella la campagna.
     Terzetto für Sopran, Tenor und Bass: O core.
     Quartetto für Sopran, Alt, Tenor und Bass: La pastorella.
     Terzettino für 2 Sopran, u. Bass: Se lontan ben.

---

[58] Notirungsbuch H is identified as Notirungsbuch F, however (see discussion, p. 208.

[59] Presumably an abbreviation of "mindestens."

[60] This note was entered as a second thought, in the available space opposite entry 51. At the same time, Gräffer revised his earlier comments, in most cases canceling "nebst" or "und" and adding periods after "Original," to clarify the fact that only the copies have accompaniments.

Terzettino für Sopran und Bass u. Tenor: L'onda—6 Bl. (all of entry 51.)—*Diese acht Gesangstücke sind ungestochen.* ~~und das Original so wie~~ *Die Copie mit Pianofortebegleitung.*

The songs of entry 51 are actually copies in Beethoven's hand of settings by two of Salieri's pupils, C. Doblhoff and A. Cornet. Although this was pointed out by Nottebohm in 1873, it was not noted in the later Adler and Artaria catalogues.

52. *5. Terzett für Sopran, Tenor, und Bass: Chi mai di questo—2 Bl.— Ungestochen. Original.* ~~und~~ *Copie mit Pianofbegleit.* (WoO 99, no. 2; Hess 214.)

53. *6. Duetto für Sopran u. Tenor: Scrivo.* (WoO 99, no. 11; Hess 215.) *Terzetto für Sopran, Alt,* ~~und~~ *Bass: Per te d'amico.* (WoO 99, no. 9; Hess 216.)
Coro für Sopran, Alt, Tenor u. Bass: Nei campi e nelle. (WoO 99, no. 7a; Hess 217.)—*4 Bl.* (all of entry 53)—*Ungestochen. Original.* ~~und~~ *Copie mit Pianofortebegleitung.*

54. *7. Terzett u. kleines Quartett—2 Bl.—Ungestochen.* (WoO 99, nos. 10b and c; Hess 218–19.)

55. *8. Terzett und Duett—2 Bl.—Ungestochen.* (WoO 99 nos. 5b and 1; Hess 227 and 211.)

page 5

56. *9. Quartett für Sopran, Alt, Tenor und Bass: Nei campi e nelle selve. Partitur—2 Bl.—Ungestochen. Original.* ~~und~~ *Copie mit Pianofortebegleitung.* (WoO 99, no. 7b; Hess 220.)

The first nine entries of Paquet IX comprise the nine bundles of the present package of manuscripts, DStB Artaria 166. This package also includes the copies mentioned in the Autograph 47a entries. August Artaria's catalogue of 1893 (number 166) reproduces the nine separate entries of Autograph 47a with one minor error (eight folios instead of four for bundle 1) and one addition (the fragmentary end of a song, *Venne contento,* which begins bundle 4). In Adler's 1890 catalogue, the nine bundles are given separate entries (numbers 63–71).

This group of manuscripts, written out as part of Beethoven's studies with Salieri in setting Italian texts, was surely *Nachlass* 151, "Italienische Gesänge, wahrscheinlich unbekannt," although this package may have included others of the following settings of Italian texts as well.

57.   *10. Arie mit Pianofortebegleitung: Dimmi ben mio—4 Bl.—Unge-*
stochen, Original und Copie.

   Adler 60.

   This manuscript does not appear in August Artaria's catalogue.
It was sold to Charles Malherbe between 1890 and 1893 and is now
in the Bibliothèque Nationale, Paris (MS. 38). The copy mentioned by Gräffer has disappeared. The piece may have been *Nachlass* 58, "Italienische Ariette," as Kinsky suggests, although that
entry occurs in the section devoted to sketches and fragments. Or
it may have been included with the other "Italienische Gesänge"
under *Nachlass* 151. Apparently unknown to Gräffer, the song had
been published as Op. 82, no. 1, by Breitkopf & Härtel in 1811 and
many times subsequently.

58.   *11. Arie für Sopran mit Quartettbegleitung: No non turbarti. Partitur—13 Bl.—Ungestochen. Original und Copie.*

   Adler 53; Artaria 165; DStB Artaria 165.

   This recitative and aria, WoO 92a, may have been *Nachlass*
188, "Lied mit 5 stimiger Begleitung, vollständig," bought by Domenico Artaria, although the autograph score has an accompaniment
in four parts only.[61] Artaria 165 includes both autograph and copy;
the autograph comprises sixteen folios, three of which are blank.

59.   *12. Arie mit Pianofortebegl. In questa tomba oscura—2 Bl.—Original und Copie. Worte von Carpani.*

   Two autographs of this song, WoO 133, survive, each occupy-
ing two folios. One is in the Memorial Library of Music, Stanford University; the other is in the R. O. Lehman Collection, on
deposit at the Pierpont Morgan Library, New York.[62] Kinsky (Kinsky-Halm) assumes that the Stanford autograph, which is accompanied by a copy of the poem in Carpani's hand, is the one owned
by Artaria, and he provides a list of all the subsequent owners. But
Gräffer's remark "Worte von Carpani" in the present entry might
also have been suggested by an inscription from the poet to Tranquillo Mollo, Domenico Artaria's former partner and the first publisher of the song, on the first page of the Lehman autograph.
Whichever of the two autographs in fact belonged to Artaria, it
left the collection sometime between 1868, when Nottebohm's *Ver-*

---

[61] *Nachlass* 188 does not correspond
satisfactorily to any other of Beethoven's
songs.
   [62] The Stanford autograph appears as
no. 39 in Nathan van Patten, *Catalogue*
of the Memorial Library of Music (Stanford, Calif., 1950). The Lehman autograph formerly belonged to Julius Lichtenberger of Heidelberg.

zeichnis still placed it there, and 1890, when Adler's catalogue appeared without it. The copy remained with Artaria, appearing as number 170 in the 1893 catalogue; it is now DStB Artaria 170. Like *Dimmi ben mio* (see entry 57 above), this work was not explicitly named in the *Nachlass* auction catalogue. It, too, could have been the "Italienische Ariette" (*Nachlass* 58) or one of the "Italienische Gesänge" (*Nachlass* 151), or it may have been acquired by Artaria (from Mollo?) before 1827.

60. *13. Canon 4 stimig. Partitur—2 Bl.—Aus* ~~Graun's Tod Jesu~~ *Haendel's Messiah.*

Beethovenhaus, Bonn, SBH 601—four folios, only two of which are used. This manuscript was given ca. 1885–90 by August Artaria to Max Friedlaender, from whom the Beethovenhaus obtained it in 1927.[63] It contains copies in Beethoven's hand of two works, a four-voice canon and a setting of the chorale *Du, dessen Augen flossen,* from Kirnberger's *Die Kunst des reinen Satzes in der Musik.* The chorale tune was well known from its use in Graun's *Tod Jesu* (hence Gräffer's original remark), which Beethoven had once examined with Carl Czerny's father, making comparisons with *Messiah.*[64] It is interesting to speculate that someone acquainted with Czerny's then unpublished account of the event (or Czerny himself) suggested the incorrect emendation in the Autograph 47a entry. Together with the chorus *Wir bauen und sterben* (see next entry), the manuscript was probably *Nachlass* 155 "Canon und vierstimiges Lied."

61. *14. Vierstimmiges Lied: Dir* (sic) *bauen u. sterben . . . —1 Bl.— Ohne Begleitung und unbekannt.*

Adler 62.

Now Beethovenhaus, Bonn, SBH 587—two folios, one of which is blank. The manuscript was obtained from August Artaria by Max Friedlaender between 1890 and 1893 and hence does not appear in the 1893 catalogue. It was later in the collection of H. C. Bodmer. This work, WoO 96, no. 1, together with the previous entry, probably comprised *Nachlass* 155 "Canon und vierstimiges Lied."

---

[63] It is discussed by Joseph Schmidt-Görg, *Unbekannte Manuskripte zu Beethovens Weltlicher und Geistlicher Gesangsmusik,* Veröffentlichungen des Beethovenhauses in Bonn, V (Bonn, 1928).

[64] The account in Czerny's own hand is found in DStB Mus. MS. Theorie Czerny 2; it is reprinted in Schmidt-Görg, *op. cit.,* and in Friedrich Kerst, *Die Erinnerungen an Beethoven,* I (Stuttgart, 1913), 56–57.

62.   *15. Lied: Mit Mädl sich vertragen. Mit Begleitung von 2 Oboen, 2 Horn, 2 Violinen, Viola und Bass. Partitur—9 Bl.—Mit Beethovens Aufschrift und eigenen Nahmen. Nicht gestochen.*

Adler 50; Artaria 172; StPK Artaria 172.

This work, WoO 90, does not appear explicitly in the *Nachlass* auction catalogue. DStB Artaria 172 is a copy of the song, also from Artaria's collection.

63.   *16. Lieder: Es blüht eine Blume—Scheinen bekannt.*[65]
Merkenstein
Nord oder Süd. . . . Erschienen. Componirt 1817.
~~*Kann der Winter morden*~~
Klage: Eichengrün—Ungestochen.
5 Bl. (Refers to all four songs).

The autographs of the first three songs, WoO 96, no. 2, WoO 144 or Op. 100, and WoO 148 respectively, have been lost. Thayer noted that the autograph of WoO 148, "früher im Besitz von Artaria u. Co., war mit obigem Datum (1817) versehen." The entry "Kann der Winter morden" was an error; this is merely the latter portion of *Nord oder Süd* and hence was subsequently canceled.

Two slightly different autographs of *Klage*, WoO 113, survive. Both are in the Gesellschaft der Musikfreunde in Vienna, with the signatures A 9 and A 66 (each occupies two folios). Since there is no text or title in the A 66 autograph, it is likely that A 9, which is texted and has an identifying title (in a foreign hand), was the manuscript owned by Artaria.

These four songs are not explicitly named in the *Nachlass* auction catalogue. They were probably purchased in a single package, as they occur here, and at least the first three may have subsequently disappeared together.

64.   *17. Mehrere Lieder—10 Bl.—Skizzen. französisch. Romanze und Quartett? a. Don Juan?.*

Unidentified pieces. This entry probably corresponds to *Nachlass* 156, "Mehrere Lieder, scheinen bekannt." [66] No similar entry occurs in the Adler and Artaria catalogues; the folios had apparently left the collection by 1890. Gräffer's description suggests that two folios in the Bodmer Collection, SBH 605, with Beethoven's

---

[65] This initial remark probably referred to all the songs. The two subsequent remarks were added in lighter ink.

[66] In Thayer's transcript of the *Nachlass* catalogue, entry 156 reads "Mehrere Lieder, scheinen unbekannt." I suspect that this is the intended reading and that the "bekannt" in Hotschevar's copy of the catalogue was a slip by Gräffer.

copies of music from Salieri's *Les Danaides*, originally belonged to this group.[67] Beethoven also copied extensively from Mozart's *Don Giovanni*. Four folios survive with sections of the act 1 finale (Paris, Bibl. Nat. MS. 42 and W. 6, 7—one folio each; DStB MS. 15,151/20 —two folios). Another twelve folios, now in the Moldenhauer Archive (United States), contain the trio and the sextet from act 2. Finally, four folios (?) containing the male trio from the first scene and the quartet (no. 9) were at one time in the collection of Max Friedlaender.[68] The Paris and DStB folios and those owned by Friedlaender might well have originated with Artaria; the Moldenhauer manuscript is too large to have formed part of the bundle described in Autograph 47a.

65.   *18. Schottische Lieder. Mit Begleitung von Pianof., 2 Violin, Viola u. Bass Partitur.—42 Bl.—Ohne Text auch. Schon bekannt.* (Entire entry canceled, but reinstated by a *gilt* in the margin.)

   Adler 55; Artaria 190; StPK Artaria 190.

   Nachlass 76, "Manuscript für Pianoforte und andere Instrumente, wahrscheinlich Schottische Lieder." The manuscript contains eight songs from WoO 153, all twelve songs of WoO 154, and numbers 1 and 2 of the untexted pieces listed in Kinsky-Halm under WoO 158. All the songs are apparently Irish rather than Scottish. The cancellation of the Autograph 47a entry may indicate that this manuscript, like the autographs of Op. 29 and WoO 2b, temporarily left the Artaria Collection and was later returned to it.

Paquet X

66.   *1. Menuette* [69] *für Orchester Partitur.—11 Bl.*

   Probably Adler 7; Artaria 142; StPK Artaria 142—eleven folios. Artaria 142, the autograph of the *Gratulationsmenuett*, WoO 3,

---

[67] Identification of this music was provided to me by Alan Tyson and Winton Dean. The text incipits, unidentified, are given by Max Unger, *Eine Schweizer Beethovensammlung. Katalog* (Zurich, 1939), entry Mh 44, and by Hans Schmidt (SBH 605).

[68] Kinsky describes the Moldenhauer folios (and mentions the Friedlaender folios) in his *Katalog der Musikautographen-Sammlung Louis Koch* (Stuttgart, 1953), entry 53, and in "Die Beethoven-Handschriften der Sammlung

Louis Koch," *Neues Beethoven-Jahrbuch,* V (1935), 50. The DStB folios are inscribed "appartient à Charles Gounod"; it seems likely that they were separated from the folios now in Paris by Gounod (or another Parisian owner). Surprisingly, Max Unger could not identify this music in his "Die Beethovenhandschriften der Pariser Konservatoriumsbibliothek," *Neues Beethoven-Jahrbuch,* VI (1935), 100 and 114.

[69] Possibly "Menuetti."

may correspond to *Nachlass* 181, "Menuette für Orchestre nebst Abschrift"; if so, the accompanying copy has since been lost.[70] The absence of Beethoven's own title in the Autograph 47a entry is inconclusive; Artaria had published WoO 3 in 1832 without mentioning it.[71]

67. *2. Scolastische Notirungen—22 Bl.*

68. *3. Scolastische Notirungen—24 Bl.*

Probably Adler 88; Artaria 153; DStB Artaria 153.

Artaria 153 is a bundle of loose folios containing a few sketches and a variety of studies prepared by Beethoven for one (or more) of his pupils. This bundle once comprised at least fifty folios, six of which are now missing and six more of which are blank. The six missing folios are surely those of DStB Autograph 63 (same paper types and content as Artaria 153), whose numbered sides 9–19 correspond to the pages missing from Artaria 153.[72] Presumably, then, if the suggested concordance is correct, at least two more folios have been removed (52 original — 6 blank = 46 of Autograph 47a). The two extra folios are probably DStB Grasnick 27, with content and paper related to Artaria 153 and Autograph 63 (Grasnick 27 includes two additional blank folios). Adler's entry lists forty-six folios, possibly accepting the tally first indicated in Autograph 47a; Artaria's 1893 catalogue lists forty-eight folios.

69. *4. Notirungsbuch—35 Bl.//Skize zu Ruinen u. König Stephan.*

This sketchbook is now British Museum Add. MS. 29801, folios 2–37 (one is blank), which was purchased from Johann Kafka in 1875, together with folios 39–162, the miscellany of early sketches which occurs as the "Grosses Notirungsbuch" on page 7 of Autograph 47a (entry 90). Presumably Kafka purchased these two

---

[70] One copy of this work was given to the Archduke Rudolph in 1823 (Kinsky-Halm). Copies without autographs of the minuets, WoO 7 and WoO 12, and the German dances, WoO 8 and WoO 13, were also part of the Artaria Collection which came to Berlin in 1901. These copies would presumably have been listed on pages now missing from the end of Aut. 47a.

[71] The first edition was entitled simply "Allegretto pour l'Orchestre," and the work is similarly entered as "Allegretto für Orchester" among the "Nach-

gelassene Werke" in the updated catalogue of Beethoven's works which was issued in 1837 (see n. 12).

[72] Kinsky's report that an autograph of *O care selve*, WoO 119, was included among the missing folios goes back to an unknown source and is probably an error (he wrongly cites Mandyczewski's notes to the GA ser. 25 suppl. vol.). The actual WoO 119 autograph described by Kinsky and Mandyczewski is almost certainly that in the "Kafka" Sketchbook (British Museum Add. MS. 29801, f. 62v).

sketchbooks from Artaria sometime between about 1870 and 1875.[73] Both had been omitted from Artaria's first alphabetical list of large-format sketchbooks. When the second alphabetical classification was made, the present book was included and a cover was provided. This cover now carries the inscription "No. 16/Beethoven/Skizzenbuch/B/Skizzen zu den 'Ruinen von Athen'/zu 'König Stephan' u.a.m./40 [canceled word] Blätter zusamen." The letter was originally "F" and the number of folios originally "35," but both of these were subsequently emended. The original inscription may have been merely "Skizzenbuch/F/35" (see discussion, pages 189–92). A note by Gräffer on the first folio, "Skizze zu Ruinen von Athen u. König Stephan," was apparently a memorandum for his Autograph 47a comment (and perhaps suggested the later cover inscription as well).

page 6

70. 5. *Kleinigkeiten für Pianoforte. 6 Stücke vollstaendig—12 Bl.—Mit eigenhändiger Aufschrift 1822. ~~Scheinen unbekannt~~.//Erschienen ~~bekannt~~ Bagatellen.*

Adler 42; Artaria 199; StPK Artaria 199.

Nachlass 176, "Kleinigkeiten unbekannt und vollständig für Clavier." This is the autograph of Op. 119, nos. 1–6. The inclusion of the manuscript among the entries for unpublished works in the *Nachlass* auction catalogue may explain the erroneous initial remark in Autograph 47a.

71. 6. *Fragment eines Sextettes—6 Bl.—Unbekannt.*

Adler 24; Artaria 185; DStB Artaria 185.

Nachlass 69, "Sextett." This piece is actually a wind-quintet fragment, Hess 19, probably for oboe, three horns, and bassoon, including the end of a first movement, an adagio, and the beginning of a minuet.[74] An empty staff has been left between the oboe part and the horns, and the entry of a key signature at one point indicates that this was to have been a clarinet part. Most likely, however, a sextet was not intended; the empty clarinet staff was prob-

---

[73] For a discussion of the provenance of the two books, see Joseph Kerman, Preface to vol. I of *Beethoven: Autograph Miscellany from circa 1786–1799. British Museum Additional Manuscript 29801,* ff. 39–162 (*the 'Kafka Sketchbook'*), 2 vols. (London, 1970).

[74] The piece has been published in this form by Willy Hess, ed., *Beethoven: Supplemente zur Gesamtausgabe,* VII.

ably to have been a performance alternative to the oboe part.[75] The fragmentary state of the autograph dates back at least to the time of Autograph 47a and almost certainly to the *Nachlass* auction, when the piece was included among the sketches and fragments.

72. *7. Allegro und Menuetto für Oboe u. Flöte—2 Bl.—Mit Aufschrift und Nahmen, und 1797.//Unbekannt.*

Adler 27; Artaria 135; DStB Artaria 135.

This is the autograph of WoO 26, a duet for two flutes. The inscribed date, actually 1792, was wrongly read (or copied) as 1797 as late as the 1893 Artaria catalogue, although Thayer had given it correctly in his *Verzeichnis* of 1865. The piece does not appear explicitly in the *Nachlass* auction catalogue. The description "Oboe u. Flöte" in Autograph 47a is difficult to explain. But on the autograph itself the indication "Flauto 1mo" was sloppily written and corrected, and a passing glance might have read "Hautbois" from the resultant mess.

73. *8. Kriegslied 7 stimmig in Partitur. Walzer mit Trio, 11 stimig in Partitur. Deutscher Tanz mit Coda in Partitur. Marsch 10 stimmig in Partitur. Deutscher Gesang und Jagdlied. 6 stimmig—14 Bl.// Aus früher Jugend. Unbekannt.*

Adler 5; Artaria 129; DStB Artaria 129.

This is the autograph of the so-called *Ritterballet*, WoO 1, which receives no explicit entry in the *Nachlass* auction catalogue. Gräffer has made a few errors. The autograph is in two separate gatherings, and he has mistakenly entered the dances of the second gathering first (doubtless as he found them). At the same time he has misplaced the indication "Walzer," which actually belongs to the following *Deutscher Tanz* (eight parts), but which appears here in place of the *Trinklied* (eleven parts). And in the first part of the score, which begins with the *Marsch*, he has omitted the *Minnelied* which follows the *Jagdlied* in the autograph.

74. *9. Marsch für Orchester in Partitur—8 Bl.—Mit Aufschrift und Nahmen und 1809.//für die böhmische Landwehr 1809.* (See below.)

---

[75] A similar example occurs in a copyist's score of the Trio for two Oboes and English Horn, Op. 87, a fragment of which is included with the autograph as DStB Art. 151. In this score, possible performance by two violins and viola is suggested, and the English horn part is duplicated in alto clef for viola throughout on a fourth staff.

75. *10. Zapfenstreich für ~~Orchester~~//Militärmusik* (pencil)*//Partitur—4 Bl.—Mit Aufschrift und Nahmen.* (ink)*//Nicht gestochen.* (See below.)

Entries 74 and 75 are joined by a *Zusam̃en.*

76. *11. Marsch für ~~Orchester~~//Militärmusik* (pencil)*//Partitur—2 Bl.* (ink)*//~~Nicht Beethovens Handschrift~~. Original und Copie.*

Entries 74–76 belong together. Entry 74 is an autograph of the March in F, WoO 18 (Adler 14; Artaria 144; StPK Artaria 144—four folios). The other four folios, completing the eight listed in Autograph 47a, were probably StPK Artaria 146 (Adler 16; Artaria 146). The latter manuscript is a trio in F minor (two folios) plus a sketch to it (two more folios), evidently belonging to WoO 19, another F-major march. Both this trio and one autograph of WoO 19 have inscriptions referring to "Zapfenstreich No. 3." But no manuscript of the march itself was owned by Artaria; hence the probability that the trio, despite its inscription, had been tucked in with the autograph of WoO 18 (Artaria 144).

The *Zapfenstreich für Militärmusik* (entry 75) is nothing more than a later copy by Beethoven of WoO 18, with the inscription "Zapfenstreich No. 1." This manuscript is StPK Artaria 145 (Adler 15; Artaria 145), the six folios of which also include entry 76, a trio in B♭ apparently belonging to this march, together with a copy thereof as indicated in the catalogue. Hence entries 75 and 76 together probably represent Beethoven's real intentions concerning the March, WoO 18, and its trio (written later than the march?[76]), whereas entry 74 includes an earlier score of WoO 18 with a trio apparently intended for WoO 19.[77]

These various marches, together with the march listed as entry 77 below (and possibly WoO 2b as well), probably comprised *Nachlass* 178 "Märsche für Orchester ungewiß ob schon bekannt."

77. *12. Grosser Marsch zur grossen Wachtparade, für Militärmusik in Partitur.—14 Bl.—Mit Aufschrift und Nahmen. 1816. Nebst Copie.*

Adler 17; Artaria 147 (and 148?[78]); DStB Artaria 147.

---

[76] Letters from Beethoven to C. F. Peters indicating that new trios were to be written for some of the marches are quoted in Kinsky-Halm under WoO 24. See particularly the letter of September 13, 1822 (Anderson no. 1100).

[77] For a discussion of the various au-

tographs of WoO 18 and 19, see Willy Hess, "Beethovens Zapfenstreiche in F-Dur," *Beethoven-Jahrbuch,* I (1953/54), 103–07, and Hess's notes to *Supplemente zur Gesamtausgabe,* IV.

[78] Artaria 148, "Marcia von Beethoven in D dur für Orchester und Stim-

This is the autograph (plus a copy) of WoO 24, including ten folios of score and four folios of percussion parts. August Artaria's 1893 catalogue erroneously lists only thirteen folios.

78. *13. Skizze eines Quartettes für Gesang, Violin, Violencelle u. Clavier. Partitur.—7 Bl.—Unbekannt.*

Adler 57; Artaria 188; DStB Artaria 188.

Probably *Nachlass* 165, "Quartettskizze oder für Gesang." [79] Artaria 188 includes Beethoven's folksong settings, WoO 158, nos. 23, 5, 6, 9, and 10, numbered 14–18 and all untexted except for one revision passage of five bars.

79. *14. Skizze eines Clavier-Concerts, Partitur.—27 Bl.—Unbekannt.*

Adler 87; Artaria 184; DStB Artaria 184—thirty folios.

Probably *Nachlass* 65, "Skizze eines Klavierconzertes." A snippet from one of Artaria's later covers is inscribed "2./Klavier-Konzert/nicht vollendet," with the Artaria number, 184, added above. Of the present thirty folios of Artaria 184, only one is blank; this may indicate that folios (2?) were added to the manuscript after Autograph 47a was written. In fact, the sequence of pages has clearly been tampered with, and it is possible that some have been added. [80]

80. *15. Notirungen—5 Bl.//1. Unbekanntes Stück/3 stim̅ige Invention N. 3 v. S. Bach/2 stim̅ige Invention [81] N. 11 v. d==/Skizze zu den Variationen aus Diabelli Tha.*

The copies by Beethoven of the two Bach inventions are now on two folios in the Beethovenhaus, Bonn, SBH 598 (obtained from H. C. Bodmer). The other three folios are unidentified, but may have been dealt off by Artaria in a single packet with the Bach copies.

---

men. Partitur," was apparently an erroneous extra entry for the copy of the score, which had already been mentioned as part of Art. 147. The copy is now part of Art. 147 and there is no Art. 148 in Berlin.

[79] In the transcript of the *Nachlass* catalogue published in Thayer, *Verzeichnis,* entry 165 reads, "Skizze, wahrscheinlich für Quartett oder Gesang," which relates more easily to the Aut.

47a entry.

[80] The rearrangement of folios is not mentioned in the recent discussion of this manuscript by Lewis Lockwood, "Beethoven's Unfinished Piano Concerto of 1815," *The Musical Quarterly,* LVI (1970), 624–46.

[81] The second "stim̅ige Invention" is indicated only by ditto marks in the catalogue entry.

Paquet XI

81. *1. Finale der Sonat Op. 111—8 Bl.*

This manuscript has disappeared. Presumably it belonged with the extra autograph of the first movement listed on page 1 of Autograph 47a (entry 14—still preserved), the two forming a second autograph of Op. 111 which chronologically preceded the complete autograph also entered on page 1 (entry 13).[82] Why the two movements were separated in the catalogue is a mystery but may explain why one is lost and the other survives. With or without this finale, the extra autograph of the first movement was given by Artaria to Joseph Fischhof in 1844.

82. *2. Fuge 2 stimmig—2 Bl.—Verfertigt mit 11 Jahren.*

Adler 43; Artaria 124; StPK Artaria 124.

This work, WoO 31, was purchased together with the concerto, WoO 4 (see next entry), as *Nachlass* 171: "Zwey vollständige Manuscripte vom 11ᵗⁿ und 12ᵗ Jahre des Compositeurs. Eine Fuge und 1 Concert für Pianoforte wahrscheinlich in Abschrift." In Kinsky-Halm this manuscript is described as a copy, but I believe it to be an autograph (with inscriptions partly in a foreign hand).

83. *3. Concert für Pianoforte Clavierstimme—16 Bl.—Mit Aufschrift u. Nahmen. Mit 12 Jahren componirt.*

Adler 30; Artaria 125; StPK Artaria 125.

This is WoO 4, purchased with WoO 31 as *Nachlass* 171 (see previous entry). The manuscript is a copy, with corrections thought to be in Beethoven's hand. There are actually seventeen folios, plus an additional half folio inserted as a revision.

page 7 [see plate XVII]

84. *4. Allegro und Allegretto für Pianoforte—3 Bl.—Mit Nahmen. Unbekannt.*

Unidentified pieces; possibly WoO 33, nos. 4 and 5, now thought to be for musical clock (although these could belong to entry 89 below). The autograph of WoO 33, nos. 4–5, is DStB Artaria 186

---

[82] Kinsky suggested the probable existence of this second autograph of the finale in *Musikhistorisches Museum von* *Wilhelm Heyer in Cöln. Katalog,* IV (Cologne-Leipzig, 1916), 187.

(Adler 44; Artaria 186)—four folios, only three of which are used. The tempo indications of the Autograph 47a entry are given on Artaria 186, and although the pieces are notated in alto and tenor clefs, an attribution to the pianoforte would be easy to understand, given the style of the works and the absence of reasonable alternatives. A more serious problem is Beethoven's signature, which seems to be indicated by Gräffer's remark, but which is missing from Artaria 186.[83] The two pieces may be those of *Nachlass* 157: "Zwey vollständige kleine Stücke früherer Zeit, für Pianoforte."

85. 5. *Quartett von Haydn in Partitur—6 Bl.—Geschrieben von Beethoven.* ʻ

Beethoven's copy of Haydn's Op. 20, no. 1, in E♭. Previously owned by H. C. Bodmer, this manuscript is now in the Beethovenhaus, Bonn, SBH 600—eight folios, two of which are blank. It occurs as *Nachlass* 112: "Quartett von Haydn in Partitur geschrieben von Beethoven."

86. 6. *Lied: Der Liebende mit Klavier//Erschienen.*
Lied: Der Zufriedene
Lied: An die ferne Geliebte mit Klavier—4 Bl. (all three)//*Unbekannt.* (Refers to the last two songs)—the last entry has been corrected by Gräffer in pencil to *An den fernen Geliebten.*

Adler 59; Artaria 173; DStB Artaria 173.

The first of the three songs, WoO 139, had been published by Artaria in 1810. The latter two songs, Op. 75, nos. 6 and 5 respectively, had also been published by Artaria in 1810, in a collection of songs to texts by Reissig, and by Breitkopf & Härtel as part of Op. 75 in the same year. But although Gräffer had included Op. 75 in both editions of his own catalogue of Beethoven's published works, he apparently did not associate the present autographs with the published songs when compiling Autograph 47a. The three songs receive no explicit entry in the *Nachlass* auction catalogue; they may have been included in number 156, "Mehrere Lieder" (see also entry 64).

87. 7. *Ein Stück einer früheren Composition—3 Bl.//Unbekannt.*

This is probably DStB Artaria 131 (Adler 36; Artaria 131— three folios), an autograph fragment of a sonata for violin and

---

[83] Another possibility would be the autographs of WoO 56 (Paris, Bibl. Nat. MS 29—two folios) and WoO 52 (now lost), two pieces for piano owned by Artaria, later by Johann Kafka. The WoO 56 autograph has the indication "Allegretto" (or "Allegrett"), but also lacks Beethoven's signature.

piano, Hess 46. The work has no likely *Nachlass* catalogue entry other than number 136, "Stück einer Sonate für Pianof. und Flöte od. Violin," [84] which was bought by Johann Wolfmayer, a Viennese businessman. August Artaria's 1893 catalogue erroneously lists only two folios.

88. *8. Lied aus der Ferne—2 Bl.—Mit Aufschrift u. Nahmen 1809.// Gestochen.*

There are two autographs bearing the text of the *Lied aus der Ferne,* WoO 137. One, on seven folios, is now in the British Museum (Add. MS. 47852, folios 5–11). It was published with this text in 1810 by Artaria and was presumably the "Andante vivace mit Gesang" in the list of works promised to Artaria before the *Nachlass* auction, although it was no longer in the collection when Autograph 47a was written. The Autograph 47a entry refers in fact to an autograph of WoO 138, *Der Jüngling in der Fremde,* on two folios now in the Library of Congress, Washington. The confusion arose because this latter autograph does have the text of WoO 137 underlaid and the title *Lied aus der Ferne* in Beethoven's hand, although the music had been published (also by Artaria in 1810) with the WoO 138 text. The Library of Congress manuscript has a dedication to Mortier de Fontaine from August Artaria, dated December 7, 1846, and the names of at least two subsequent owners as well (see Kinsky-Halm). It does not appear explicitly in the *Nachlass* auction catalogue; bearing the same text as the autograph of WoO 137, it may have been included with that work and awarded to Artaria before the auction.

89. *9. Zwei Lieder und zwei andere Stücke—5 Bl.//Unbekannt.*

Unknown pieces. They may include the *Punschlied,* WoO 111 (Adler 61; Artaria 171; DStB Artaria 171—one folio), which does not otherwise appear in Autograph 47a.

90. *10. Grosses Notirungsbuch mit vielen Compositionen—124 Bl.—Mit mehreren Aufschriften und Nahmen. Vielen davon ungedruckt.// Aus sehr früher Zeit. Chor der freye Mann; gestochen. Trinklied. 2 Skizze einer Sinfonie unbekannt. Zum Theil Clavierstudien. Romanze für Orchester u. Klavier. Entwurf des C moll Concertes.*

---

[84] Entry 136 in Thayer's transcript of the auction catalogue reads only "Sonate für P.-F. u. Violin." There is in fact no instrumentation given in Art. 131, but the range of the second part goes below that of the flute. The fragment, comprising parts of a first and a last movement, has been published by Willy Hess in his *Supplemente zur Gesamtausgabe,* IX.

*Skizze ein Sonatine für Mandoline. Trio in G. ~~des Trio~~ des Menu-
etts Op. 1.*

This is the miscellany of early sketch folios, British Museum
Add. MS. 29801, folios 39–162, now bound together with the sketchbook described on page five of Autograph 47a (see entry 69).[85] The
two books came to the British Museum in 1875 from Johann Kafka
of Vienna, who had obtained both from Artaria (or an intermediate
owner) sometime after about 1870. The present miscellany is now
wrapped in the cover originally designed for Notirungsbuch I (see
entry 27).

Since Gräffer evidently borrowed descriptions from his *Nachlass* catalogue entries on several other occasions, this book may
well correspond to *Nachlass* 41 "Grosses Notirbuch."

Paquet XII

91. *Ein Paket Quartetten Stücke und Skizzen in Partitur.* (See entry
97 below.)

Paquet XIII

92. *1. Quartett Stücke und Skizzen—30 Bl.—Letztes//Stück aus dem
letzten Clavierquartett in B. NB/Im Genre der Bearbeitung von
Volksliedern für Violine Violoncell u. Clavier. Wahrscheinlich
Schottische Lieder. Interessant.*

The folksong settings described here may be those in DStB
Artaria 187 (Adler 79; Artaria 187—twenty-two folios), which
August Artaria describes in his 1893 catalogue as "Bearbeitung und
Skizzen von verschiedenen Volksliedern." If so, it would mean that
eight folios, presumably including the unidentified "Clavierquartett"
sketches, were separated from the rest of the bundle.

The present cover of Artaria 187 is one originally designed for
Notirungsbuch N (see page 188). It has been turned inside out and
inscribed "7./Skizzen zu Volksliedern." The "7" was later replaced
by the Artaria number, 187, and "22 Blätter" was added below (see
discussion, pages 189–92).

93. *2. Quartett in Partitur—39 Bl.//Skizzen des Es Quartettes und andere Skizzen.* (See below.)

---

[85] This miscellany, the so-called
"Kafka" Sketchbook, has been published
in facsimile and transcription by Kerman,
op. cit.

94. *3. Quartetten Notirungen—31 Bl.//Skizze des Quartett in F dur. Skizzen.* (See below.)

95. *4. Quartett Notirung in Partitur—18 Bl.//An die Freude. Skizzen in Es dur Quartett u. andere Skizzen.* (See below.)

96. *5. Quartett Notirungen—43 Bl.//Fuge als Studien für Quartett. Cis moll Quartett Skizze.—Skizze aus B.* (See below.)

97. *6. Quartett Notirungen—36 Bl.//Cis moll Quartett Skizze—Fuge als Studie für Quartett—Skizze zum B Quartett letzter Satz.*

Despite the ambiguity resulting from the omission of opus numbers, entries 91 and 93–97 presumably refer to sketches for the late quartets (as opposed to Op. 18, no. 1, Op. 59, no. 1, and Op. 74, for example, which are also in keys mentioned by Gräffer). A large number of late-quartet sketches came with the Artaria Collection to Berlin, but the various bundles as presently constituted do not match those described here. The problems of correlating the surviving sketches with the bundles described in Autograph 47a are considered in greater detail on pages 196–98.

Nachlass lots 52, 54, 57, and 64, all bought by Artaria, specify "Quartett Skizzen" and probably correspond, at least in part, to numbers 91–97 of Autograph 47a.

page 8

Paquet XIV

98. *1. Cavatine aus dem Quartett Op. 130 Partitur—5 Bl.*

Adler 20; Artaria 208; StPK Artaria 208.

The autograph includes a sixth folio, inserted to replace folio 4^v and formerly glued to it. This score was not specifically entered in the *Nachlass* auction catalogue, but Artaria bought lots 78, 102, and 127, which are listed there as "Quartettstück" or "Violin Quartettstück" in the section devoted to autographs of published works. See Kinsky-Halm for the present locations of the other movements of Op. 130, apparently never owned by Artaria.

99. *2. Fuge im Quartett Op. 133 Partitur—44 Bl.*

Adler 22; Artaria 215; formerly PrStB Artaria 215, but missing since World War II.

Adler lists forty-four folios, Artaria forty-six. According to Kinsky-Halm, forty-eight folios are present, one of which is blank, two of which are clamped together as one, and two of which are fully in a copyist's hand (which equals forty-four in Beethoven's hand). There is no explicit entry for Op. 133 in the *Nachlass* auction catalogue; numbers 78, 102, and 127 (see the previous entry) probably included this autograph.

100. *3. Violin Quartett Op. 131 Partitur—61 Bl.—Fehlen vom ersten Stück 2 Seiten.*

Adler 21; Artaria 211; formerly PrStB Artaria 211, but missing since World War II (sixty-one folios).

The manuscript actually comprises movements 1, 2, 5, 6, and 7, together with the first four bars of movement 3; hence it is difficult to explain Gräffer's remark. The fourth movement, also formerly in the PrStB, was obtained in the Ernst von Mendelssohn Collection in 1908. If it had belonged to Artaria, it was separated from the remainder of the score before Autograph 47a was written. In the *Nachlass* auction catalogue, only the last movement receives an explicit entry: number 118, "Finale des Quartettes in Cis mol."

101. *4. Adagio und Cantabile aus dem Violinquartett Op. 127. Partitur. —12 Bl.*

Adler 19; Artaria 207; formerly PrStB Artaria 207, but missing since World War II.

Actually thirteen folios, one of which is blank. Not specifically entered in the *Nachlass* auction catalogue, this autograph was probably number 78, 102, or 127 (see entry 98 above). See Kinsky-Halm for the present locations of the other movements, apparently never owned by Artaria.

102. *5. Stück eines Violinquintettes in Partitur—2 Bl.—Unbekannt.*

Probably Adler 18;[86] Artaria 185a; DStB Artaria 185a—two folios.

This fragment is an introduction to a fugue in D minor, Hess 40; the manuscript breaks off four bars into the first fugal entry.[87] Either *Nachlass* 152, "Vollständiger Satz eines Quintetts für Violin," or *Nachlass* 59, "Skizze eines Quintettes noch unbekannt," could refer to this manuscript.

103. *6. Fuge im Quartett für Violin. Partitur—2 Bl.—Unbekannt.*

An unidentified piece. The possibilities include Beethovenhaus, Bonn, SBH 599—two folios from the Bodmer Collection with Beethoven's copies in quartet score of two fugues from Fux's

---

[86] Adler's "12 Bl." is apparently a misprint.

[87] The piece has been published in its present fragmentary form by Willy Hess in his *Beethoven: Supplemente zur Gesamtausgabe*, VI.

Gradus ad Parnassum (not identified as such on the manuscript).

104. *7. Quartett von Mozart in Partitur—7 Bl.—Von Beethoven's Hand-schrift.*

This manuscript, now in the Stiftelsen Musikkulturens främ-jande, Stockholm, is a copy by Beethoven of the andante from Mozart's Quartet in A, K. 464. In 1862 Köchel wrongly identified the movement as the rondo: "Das Rondo dieses Quartetts hat Beet-hoven sich in Partitur geschrieben. Die Handschrift davon besitzt Artaria in Wien." [88]

105. *8. Contrataenze für Orchester Partitur—13 Bl.—Drei davon noch nicht gestochen. Und Copie.*

Adler 12; Artaria 140; StPK Artaria 140.

This is a partial autograph of WoO 14. Of the thirteen folios, the last three are in a copyist's hand, and number 11 of the dances is not included. The copy referred to in the Autograph 47a entry is probably a copy in piano score of nine of the dances that accom-panies the autograph as part of Artaria 140. Of these nine, three were omitted from an 1802 Artaria publication in piano transcrip-tion, and this may account for Gräffer's remark.

The manuscripts of Artaria 140 do not appear explicitly in the *Nachlass* auction catalogue. Possibly Artaria owned them from the time of the first publication of WoO 14 in 1802.[89]

106. *9. Fuge für 2 Claviere von Mozart. Partitur—3 Bl.—Von Beetho-vens Handschrift.*

The first folio of this copy of Mozart's Fugue in C Minor for two pianos, K. 426, is now lost. The middle folio (bars 42–77) was acquired in 1929 by the Beethovenhaus, Bonn (SBH 604). The last folio is in the R. O. Lehman Collection, on deposit at the Pierpont Morgan Library, New York. In 1862 Köchel still placed the entire manuscript with Artaria: "Beethoven hat diese Fuge in Partitur geschrieben. Das Autograph davon besitzt Artaria in Wien." [90] The copy is not mentioned explicitly in the *Nachlass* auction catalogue.

---

[88] Ludwig Ritter von Köchel, *Chron-ologisch-thematisches Verzeichnis sämt-licher Tonwerke Wolfgang Amadé Mo-zarts* (Leipzig, 1862). The error is re-produced in all later editions; it is, of course, possible that Beethoven copied both the andante and the rondo.

[89] WoO 14 was first published under Mollo's name, but between 1802 and 1804 Mollo and his partner Domenico Artaria III were operating the two firms together, and the dances appeared with Artaria's name as early as 1803.

[90] Köchel, *op. cit.*, under K. 426. Schmidt (SBH 604) refers to the manu-script as a copy of K. 546, Mozart's tran-scription of K. 426 for string quartet, but Beethoven's copy is clearly of the two-piano version.

Copien

Paquet XVa

107. *1. Rondo für Pianoforte—G dur—Titel, Nahme und einige Bemer-*
      kungen von B's Hand.
        Adler 41; Artaria 154; StPK Artaria 154.
        This copy of Op. 51, no. 2, does not appear explicitly in the
      Nachlass auction catalogue; it probably served as the *Stichvorlage*
      for Artaria's edition of the work in 1802.

108. *2. Egmont in Partitur—Mit Aufschriften und Anmerkungen von B's*
      Hand.
        Adler 4; Artaria 178; DStB Artaria 178.
        This incomplete copy of Op. 84 does not appear explicitly in
      the *Nachlass* auction catalogue; it may have accompanied the auto-
      graph of part of the score (see entry 7), bought by Artaria as
      Nachlass 137.

109. *3. Wellingtons Sieg für Harmonie, in Partitur—Titl, Nahme und*
      einige Correcturen von Bs Hand.
        Adler 89; Artaria 181; DStB Artaria 181.
        This copy does not appear explicitly in the *Nachlass* auction
      catalogue. In its present state, it includes only the last part of sec-
      tion 2 of the score (from the allegro con brio to the end), but re-
      tains the title page.

(Autograph 47a breaks off at this point, after page 8. In its
original state, however, the catalogue probably had additional
pages, continuing the list of copies.)

APPENDIX

The following is a list of those manuscripts bought by Domenico Artaria
at the *Nachlass* auction that do not appear in Autograph 47a:

Nachlass 80 and 106—"Finale aus d. Pastoralsinfonie in Partitur" and "Andante
   der Pastoralsinfonie Part." The score of the entire symphony is now in

the Beethovenhaus, Bonn (SBH 549); an accompanying leaf is inscribed "J. M. Huijssen v Kattendijke/gekocht bij Artaria te Weenen/Anno 1838." This date is thus the earliest possible for Autograph 47a. How Artaria obtained the other movements is not known.

Nachlass 83—"Abendlied." This autograph of WoO 150 is now in the National-bibliothek, Vienna. It was a gift of Graf Moritz Dietrichstein, probably ca. 1829, when he also presented the autograph of Op. 24 to the library (see below).[91] Dietrichstein probably obtained the WoO 150 autograph from Domenico Artaria shortly after the Nachlass auction.

Nachlass 86—"Sonate für Klavier und Violin." Artaria is not known to have owned any violin-sonata autographs other than the early fragment, Artaria 131. *Nachlass* 86 occurs in the section of the auction catalogue devoted to published works, however. Most likely, the autograph in question was that of Op. 24, which was presented to the Nationalbiblio-thek, Vienna, in 1829 by Graf Moritz Dietrichstein.[92] Dietrichstein also owned the autograph of the *Abendlied*, WoO 150 (see above), and probably obtained the two autographs from Artaria between 1827 and 1829.

Nachlass 96—"Aus Leonore ein Stück in Partitur." This is probably DStB Artaria 157 (Adler 49; Artaria 157), a fragment of the trio "Euch werde Lohn." The manuscript, though listed as an autograph in the catalogues of 1890 and 1893, is in fact a copy and was perhaps entered as such on a later page (now missing) of Autograph 47a.

Nachlass 105—"Fünfte Sinfonie in Partitur." This score is now StPK Mendels-sohn 8. In his *Verzeichnis*, Thayer places it in Paul Mendelssohn's collection. The latter may have obtained the manuscript from Heinrich Beer, who in the early 1830s owned several other important Beethoven autographs (Op. 20, Op. 72 finales) which later appear in Mendels-sohn's collection.

Nachlass 129—"Zwey Finale aus Leonore Part." The autographs of these two finales (1814) are now StPK Mendelssohn 16 and 17. Both are in-scribed "Artaria und Compag./Wien 14 Juny 1834." They were ap-parently sold on that date to Heinrich Beer of Berlin, along with the Overture to *Fidelio* (1814), StPK Mendelssohn 18, and a large sketch-book for the first version of the opera, StPK Mendelssohn 15, which have identical inscriptions.[93] All of these manuscripts passed from Beer to the Paul Mendelssohn family before entering the Berlin library.

---

[91] See Grasberger, *op. cit.*

[92] *Ibid.*

[93] Beer bought some Haydn auto-graphs from Artaria at the same time. The seal and identical inscriptions occur on the autographs of the Symphony no.

94 and the Concertante, now StPK Haydn Aut. 48 and 44, which have retained covers stamped with Beer's name. The Overture to *Fidelio* had been among the works promised to Artaria before the *Nachlass* auction.

The purchase of four important Op. 72 manuscripts by Beer [94] and the purchase of eight sketchbooks by Ludwig Landsberg were the two single largest sales of Beethoven manuscripts made by the Artarias in the years before Autograph 47a was written.

Nachlass 132—"Agnus Dei in Partitur." Apparently the last movement of Op. 86, now lost; Artaria also bought the Gloria (*Nachlass* 104), which he later sold to Aloys Fuchs. In a letter to Schindler in 1851, Fuchs wondered where the other movements were (he owned the Kyrie and the Gloria at the time), but the Agnus Dei must be considered missing already before Autograph 47a.

Nachlass 154—"Italienisches Duett in Partitur." This is StPK Artaria 168 (Adler 52; Artaria 168), the autograph of *Nei giorni tuoi felici,* WoO 93. A copy of the work is now DStB Artaria 168. For some reason the autograph seems to have periodically gone unnoticed beside the copy. Adler's 1890 catalogue includes both, but in 1893 August Artaria mentions only the copy. We may wonder, then, whether Autograph 47a might not have included the work in its list of copies, on pages since lost from the end of the catalogue (see also the trio, "Euch werde Lohn," from Op. 72 above).

Two other *Nachlass* lots—number 81, "Erstes Stück aus der 4tn Sinfonie. Part.," and number 114, "Fuge v. S. Bach in Quartett geschrieben v. Beethoven"—are listed as Artaria purchases in Fuchs's copy of the auction catalogue. Both are attributed to Haslinger, however, in Hotschevar's list of buyers. Haslinger did own the score of Op. 60 (now StPK Mendelssohn 12); he bought the remaining movements as *Nachlass* 97: "Vierte Sinfonie in Partitur." Beethoven's copy in quartet score of the B-minor fugue from the *Well-Tempered Clavier,* Book I, is now in the Gesellschaft der Musikfreunde, Vienna (A 81). Since there is no evidence that Artaria ever owned the manuscript, Hotschevar's attribution to Haslinger is probably correct.[95]

---

[94] Beer may also have been an intermediate owner, between Artaria and the Mendelssohns, of the autographs of Op. 29 and Op. 67.

[95] A copy by Beethoven of the B♭-minor fugue in *quintet* score came with the Grasnick Collection to Berlin (now DStB Gr. 14). *Nachlass* 114 ought to refer to Vienna A 81, but since several other manuscripts owned by Grasnick passed first through Artaria's hands, we might also suggest the possibility of an erroneous entry in the auction catalogue.

Index of Beethoven's Compositions, Sketches, and Letters

COMPOSITIONS

Op. 1: three piano trios, 174
Op. 1, no. 3, in C minor, 158–171
Op. 2: three piano sonatas, 174
Op. 3: string trio, 174
Op. 4: string quintet, 174, 176, 206
Op. 5: two cello sonatas, 174
Op. 6: piano sonata, four hands, 174
Op. 7: piano sonata in E♭, 174
Op. 8: serenade for string trio, 174
Op. 9: three string trios, 21
Op. 10: three piano sonatas
Op. 10, no. 3, in D, 21, 45–51, 53, 57, 64
Op. 11: clarinet trio, 174
Op. 12: three violin sonatas, 139
Op. 13: piano sonata ("Pathétique"), 21, 48
Op. 14: two piano sonatas, 174
Op. 15: piano concerto no. 1, 174
Op. 16: wind quintet, 174
Op. 17: horn sonata, 98, 99, 174, 189
Op. 18: six string quartets, 174, 188, 189, 196, 214
Op. 20: septet, 235
Op. 22: piano sonata in B♭, 188, 189
Op. 23: violin sonata in A minor, 174, 188, 189
Op. 24: violin sonata in F, 174, 175, 188, 235
Op. 27, no. 2: piano sonata in C♯ minor ("Moonlight"), 13, 20
Op. 28: piano sonata in A♭, 20

Op. 29: string quintet, 20, 175, 199, 221, 236
Op. 30: three violin sonatas, 23
Op. 30, no. 2, in C minor, 20
Op. 30, no. 3, in G, 20
Op. 31: three piano sonatas, 23
Op. 32: *An die Hoffnung*, 123, 133
Op. 33: seven bagatelles, 15, 20
Op. 34: piano variations in F, 23
Op. 35: piano variations ("Eroica"), 23
Op. 36: symphony no. 2, 23
Op. 37: piano concerto no. 3, 229
Op. 43: ballet, *Prometheus*, 23
Op. 46: *Adelaide*, 123, 129, 133, 134, 140
Op. 47: violin sonata ("Kreutzer"), 21
Op. 48: six songs by Gellert, 175
Op. 48, no. 6, *Busslied*, 133
Op. 49: two easy piano sonatas
Op. 49, no. 1, in G minor, 21
Op. 51, no. 2: piano rondo, 14, 234
Op. 52: eight songs
Op. 52, no. 1: *Urians Reise um die Welt*, 100
Op. 52, no. 2: *Feuerfarb'*, 99
Op. 52, no. 4: *Maigesang*, 133
Op. 52, no. 8: *Das Blümchen Wunderhold*, 100
Op. 55: symphony no. 3 (*Eroica*), 94, 135
Op. 60: symphony no. 4, 236

Op. 65: *scena, Ah! perfido,* 37
Op. 67: symphony no. 5, 21, 55–65, 175, 188, 200, 235, 236
Op. 68: symphony no. 6 (*Pastoral*), 67, 69, 70, 90, 92, 94, 95, 175, 179, 200, 234, 235
Op. 69: cello sonata in A, 21, 91, 200, 202
Op. 70: two piano trios
    Op. 70, no. 1, in D (*Ghost*), 67, 70, 71, 90, 91, 92, 93, 95, 96, 200, 201
    Op. 70, no. 2, in Eb, 67, 70, 90, 91, 93, 94, 95, 96, 201
Op. 72: *Leonore* (1805, 1806), *Fidelio* (1814), 21, 39, 40, 41, 42, 43, 163, 175, 188, 210, 235, 236
Op. 73: piano concerto no. 5, 138, 184
Op. 75: six songs
    Op. 75, no. 1: *Kennst du das Land,* 135
    Op. 75, no. 2: *Neue Liebe, neues Leben,* 133
    Op. 75, no. 3: *Aus Goethes Faust,* 100, 101
    Op. 75, no. 5: *An den fernen Geliebten,* 99, 129, 228
    Op. 75, no. 6: *Der Zufriedene,* 99, 100, 101, 228
Op. 80: choral fantasy, 188
Op. 82: Italian songs
    Op. 82, no. 1: *Hoffnung* ("Dimmi ben mio"), 218, 219
Op. 83: three songs
    Op. 83, no. 1: *Wonne der Wehmut,* 140
    Op. 83, no. 2: *Sehnsucht,* 128, 129
Op. 84: music for *Egmont,* 135, 195, 202, 234
Op. 85: *Christus am Oelberge,* 21, 24, 26, 27, 37, 38, 39, 40, 86, 96, 163, 192, 196, 202, 210
Op. 86: Mass in C, 202, 236
Op. 87: trio for oboes and cor anglais, 200, 201, 224
Op. 91: battle symphony, 192, 196, 209, 210, 234
Op. 93: symphony no. 8, 139

Op. 94: *An die Hoffnung,* 123, 133, 134, 140
Op. 95: string quartet in F minor, 16, 212, 213
Op. 97: piano trio in Bb (*Archduke*), 101
Op. 98: *An die ferne Geliebte,* 15, 99, 102, 103, 114, 123–157, 207
Op. 100: *Merkenstein,* 220
Op. 101: piano sonata in A, 102, 114, 135, 138
Op. 102: two cello sonatas
    Op. 102, no. 1, in C, 138, 193, 200, 202
    Op. 102, no. 2, in D, 102, 114, 135, 192, 193, 196, 200, 202, 207, 210
Op. 103: wind octet, 176, 205, 206
Op. 104: string quintet, 158–173
Op. 106: piano sonata in Bb, 135, 140, 171, 172, 175, 180, 214
Op. 109: piano sonata in E, 101, 194, 208
Op. 110: piano sonata in Ab, 172, 194, 202, 203, 209
Op. 111: piano sonata in C minor, 172, 179, 194, 202, 203, 208, 209, 212, 227
Op. 112: cantata, *Meeresstille und Glückliche Fahrt,* 192, 196, 210
Op. 113: music for *Die Ruinen von Athen,* 193, 194, 205, 211, 215, 222, 223
Op. 116: terzetto, *Tremate, empi, tremate,* 21, 23
Op. 117: music for *König Stephan,* 184, 222, 223
Op. 119: eleven bagatelles, 172, 223
Op. 120: variations on a theme by Diabelli, 172, 226
Op. 121b: *Opferlied,* 100
Op. 123: Mass in D (*Missa solemnis*), 90, 175, 192, 193, 194, 195, 196, 198, 204, 208, 209, 212, 215, 216
Op. 124: overture to *Die Weihe des Hauses,* 194, 195, 203
Op. 125: symphony no. 9, 95, 99,

154, 194, 195, 204, 209, 212, 214, 215, 231

Op. 127: string quartet in Eb, 194, 195, 196, 197, 230, 231, 232

Op. 130: string quartet in Bb, 140, 197, 208, 231

Op. 131: string quartet in C# minor, 156, 194, 197, 206, 214, 215, 231, 232

Op. 132: string quartet in A minor, 194, 195, 197, 208

Op. 133: *Grosse Fuge*, 156, 197, 206, 208, 231, 232

Op. 135: string quartet in F, 194, 197, 231

Op. 136: cantata, *Der Glorreiche Augenblick*, 214

Op. 138: overture, *Leonore* no. 1, 21

WoO 1: music for a *Ritterballet*, 224

WoO 2a: triumphal march for *Tarpeja*, 206

WoO 2b: entr'acte for *Tarpeja*, 206, 221, 225

WoO 3: minuet for orchestra, 176, 221, 222

WoO 4: piano concerto in Eb, 227

WoO 7: twelve minuets for orchestra, 222

WoO 8: twelve German dances for orchestra, 222

WoO 12: twelve minuets for orchestra, 222

WoO 13: twelve German dances for orchestra, 222

WoO 14: twelve contredances for orchestra, 233

WoO 18: march for wind band, 224, 225

WoO 19: march for wind band, 225

WoO 24: march for wind band, 114, 225, 226

WoO 26: duet for flutes, 224

WoO 28: variations for oboes and cor anglais on *Là ci darem*, 201

WoO 31: organ fugue, 227

WoO 33: five pieces for mechanical clock, 227, 228

WoO 36: three piano quartets, 176, 205

WoO 37: trio for flute, bassoon, and pianoforte, 15

WoO 40: variations for violin and piano on *Se vuol ballare*, 174

WoO 52: bagatelle for piano, 228

WoO 56: bagatelle for piano, 228

WoO 59: bagatelle for piano ("Für Elise"), 95

WoO 87: cantata on the death of Joseph II, 24

WoO 88: cantata on the elevation of Leopold II, 24

WoO 90: aria, *Mit Mädeln sich vertragen*, 220

WoO 92a: scena, *No, non turbarti*, 23, 34, 35, 36, 37, 42, 218

WoO 93: duet, *Nei giorni tuoi felici*, 21, 24, 236

WoO 96: music for *Leonore Prohaska*, 219, 220

WoO 97: song with chorus, *Es ist vollbracht*, 214

WoO 99: Italian part songs, 20, 216, 217

WoO 109: *Trinklied*, 229

WoO 111: *Punschlied*, 184, 229

WoO 113: *Klage*, 220

WoO 117: *Der freie Mann*, 229

WoO 119: *O care selve*, 222

WoO 127: *Neue Liebe, neues Leben*, 133

WoO 130: *Gedenke mein*, 129

WoO 133: *In questa tomba oscura*, 218, 219

WoO 134: *Sehnsucht* (four versions), 133

WoO 136: *Andenken*, 129, 140

WoO 137: *Lied aus der Ferne*, 99, 129, 229

WoO 138: *Der Jüngling in der Fremde*, 99, 129, 229

WoO 139: *Der Liebende*, 99, 228

WoO 143: *Des Kriegers Abschied*, 99

WoO 144: *Merkenstein*, 220

WoO 145: *Das Geheimnis*, 114

WoO 146: *Sehnsucht*, 97–122, 149, 150, 157

WoO 147: *Ruf vom Berge*, 128, 129, 133
WoO 148: *So oder so*, 220
WoO 149: *Resignation*, 123, 157, 215
WoO 150: *Abendlied unterm gestirnten Himmel*, 100, 157, 235
WoO 153: Irish songs, 221
WoO 154: Irish songs, 221
WoO 158: folksongs, 221, 226
WoO 196: canon, *Es muss sein*, 197
Kinsky-Halm, *Anhang* 4: flute sonata in B♭, 184

UNFINISHED OR FRAGMENTARY WORKS

piano concerto in D, 1815 (Hess 15), 102, 192, 193, 207, 226
wind quintet in E♭ (Hess 19), 223
string quintet in D minor (Hess 40), 232
violin sonata in A (Hess 46), 228, 229
Vestas Feuer (Hess 115), 24
cantata, *Europens Befreyungsstunde* (Hess 317), 210
concertante in D, 1801, 190, 211, 212
arietta, "Grazie al'inganni," 24
music for *Macbeth*, 96
piano trio in F minor, 1816, 102

COPIES BY BEETHOVEN OF MUSIC BY OTHER COMPOSERS

J. S. BACH
two inventions, 185, 226
fugue in B♭ minor (WTC, I), 20, 236
fugue in B minor (WTC, I), 236
FUX
two fugues, 233
HANDEL
overture to *Esther*, 21
fugue from overture to *Solomon*, 205
HAYDN
string quartet in E♭, Op. 20, no. 1, 211, 228
KIRNBERGER
canon and chorale, 219
MOZART
excerpts from *Don Giovanni*, 221
fugue in C minor for two pianos, K. 426, 233
string quartet in G, K. 387, 185, 211
andante from string quartet in A, K. 464, 233

SKETCHES

Numbering of the sketches in accordance with Hans Schmidt's "Verzeichnis der Skizzen Beethovens" (SV).

BERLIN

SV 6: Artaria 183 (DStB), 190, 191
SV 10: Artaria 187 (DStB), 191, 192, 230
SV 11: Artaria 195 (StPK), 190, 191, 208
SV 12: Artaria 197 (StPK), 190, 191, 192, 208, 209
SV 13: Artaria 200 + 180 (DStB), 191, 192, 195, 196, 209, 212
SV 14: Artaria 201 (StPK), 190, 191, 192, 212

SV 17: Artaria 205 (DStB), 193, 194, 195, 196, 197, 215
SV 18: Artaria 206 (lost), 197, 198
SV 19: Artaria 209 (StPK), 197, 198
SV 20: Artaria 210 (StPK), 197, 198
SV 21: Artaria 211 (lost), 197, 198
SV 22: Artaria 213 (StPK), 197, 198
SV 23: Artaria 214 (lost), 197, 198
SV 24: Artaria 216 (StPK), 197, 198
SV 29: Aut. 19e (StPK), 189, 190, 214
SV 30: Aut. 24 (StPK), 190, 206, 207, 208

SV 31: Aut. 28, "Fischhof" (StPK), 21, 188
SV 45: Grasnick 1 (DStB), 87
SV 46: Grasnick 2 (StPK), 22, 87
SV 47: Grasnick 3 (DStB), 87
SV 49: Grasnick 5 (DStB), 215
SV 52: Grasnick 14 (DStB), 20, 236
SV 53: Grasnick 20a (DStB), 190, 191, 212, 213
SV 54: Grasnick 20b (DStB), 190, 191, 213
SV 56: Grasnick 24 (DStB), 189
SV 59: Landsberg 5 (DStB), 186, 190, 191
SV 60: Landsberg 6, "Eroica" (lost), 24, 69, 86, 87, 98, 186, 190, 192
SV 61: Landsberg 7 (StPK), 23, 186, 190, 191, 192
SV 62: Landsberg 8 (DStB), 186, 190, 191, 194
SV 63: Landsberg 9 (DStB), 186, 190, 191
SV 64: Landsberg 10 (StPK), 21, 69–96, 186, 190, 191
SV 65: Landsberg 11 (lost), 186, 190, 192
SV 66: Landsberg 12 (DStB), 186, 190, 191, 213
SV 67: Mendelssohn 15 (StPK), 188, 213, 235
SV 70 Mendelssohn 1 (lost), 193
SV 71 "Boldrini" (lost), 214, 215

BONN, BEETHOVENHAUS
SV 104: SBH 680, "de Roda," 190, 207
SV 107: SBH 664, "Engelmann," 209, 210
SV 116: SBH 635, 86, 210
SV 117: SBH 636, 86, 210
SV 118: SBH 637, 86, 190, 191, 210
SV 121: SBH 619, 71, 85
SV 135: SBH 638, 190, 191, 210, 211
SV 137: SBH 625, 190, 191, 210, 211
SV 138: SBH 655, 190, 191, 210
SV 140: SBH 648, 190, 191, 192, 207, 210

SV 164: SBH 706, 20, 21, 22, 43, 44
SV 178: SBH 712, 71, 85
SV 180: SBH 610, 189

LONDON, BRITISH MUSEUM
SV 184: Add. 29801, fols. 2–37, 188, 192, 222, 230
SV 185: Add. 29801, fols. 39–162, "Kafka," 21, 23, 98, 188, 191, 208, 222, 223, 229, 230
SV 186: Add. 29997, fols. 2–5, 188, 214
SV 187: Add. 29997, fols, 7–42, 136, 149, 188, 214
SV 188: Add. 31766, "Pastoral," 67–96, 98, 105

PARIS, BIBLIOTHÈQUE NATIONALE
SV 235: MS. 83, 188

VIENNA, GESELLSCHAFT DER MUSIKFREUNDE
SV 263: A 34, "Kessler," 23, 24, 34, 35, 36, 37, 42, 86, 98, 212

OTHER LOCATIONS
SV 308: Berkeley, Calif. (University of California Library), 189
SV 343: Moscow (Glinka Museum), "Wielhorsky," 24, 27, 86, 210
SV 357: New York (New York Public Library), 189
SV 359: New York (formerly in the possession of Arturo Toscanini), 189
SV 364: Princeton, N.J. (Library of William Scheide), 102–122, 136, 137, 142, 143, 144, 149–153, 190, 207
SV 371: Stanford, Calif. (University Library), 21
SV 378: Stockholm (Stiftelsen Musikkulturens främjande), 189
SV 393: Vienna (Stadtbibliothek), 87, 93, 96
Modena (Biblioteca Estense) (not in Schmidt), 86

LETTERS

Numbering and dates of the letters in accordance with Anderson.

1: Sept. 15, 1787, 11
23: 1797, 11
49: 1801, 11
51: June 29, 1801, 14, 15
54: Nov. 16, 1801, 12
59: July 13, 1802, 166
87a: Jan. 4, 1804, 24
110: spring, 1805, 14
143: May 11, 1807, 15
178: Nov. 1, 1808, 15
199: March 4, 1809, 200
373: July 6–7, 1812, 12, 131
479: April, 1814, 163
632: May 8, 1816, 130

740: Jan. 30, 1817, 16
764: Feb. 23, 1817, 15
801: shortly after Aug. 14, 1817, 159, 163
935: Jan. 30, 1819, 171
938: March 8, 1819, 171
1040: Dec. 20, 1820, 215
1100: Sept. 13, 1822, 225
Anderson Appendix A: Oct. 6–10, 1802 (the "Heiligenstadt Testament"), 14, 131
"January 23, 1782" [1802?] (not in Anderson), 1–17

General Index

Citations of the standard works by Thayer, Nottebohm, and Kinsky-Halm are not indexed.

Adams, F. J., 55
Adler, Guido, xiii, 176, 177
Agricola, Johann Friedrich, 31, 33, 34
Albrechtsberger, Johann Georg, 19, 23
Alekseeva, Mme. E. N., 86
Arnold, Denis, 101, 156
Artaria, August, xiii, 91, 176–236
Artaria, Carl August, 203
Artaria, Domenico, III, 91, 174–236
Artaria & Co., 68, 88–91, 114, 171, 172, 174–236
Artot, A.-J., 188, 209

Bach, Johann Sebastian, 20, 21, 185, 226, 236
Bartlitz, Eveline, 120, 174
Beer, Heinrich, 188, 200, 235, 236
Beethoven, Karl van (nephew), 131, 178
Beethoven, Ludwig van
    biography, 10–17, 129–135
    slips of the pen, 15, 17, 123, 126, 147, 169, 171
    transcriptions by, 158–173
    working methods, 97–99, 103, 120–122
Bekker, Paul, 13, 92, 93, 129, 132
Beta radiographs, 76–79
Bindtner, Josef, 126
Blume, Friedrich, 132
Bodmer, H. C., 19, 203, 209, 210, 219, 226, 228

Boettcher, Hans, 99–101, 126, 155, 156
Boldrini, Carlo, 214
Bory, Robert, 90, 177
Bouilly, Jean-Nicolas, 24
Brahms, Johannes, 68
Braunstein, Josef, 70
Breitkopf & Härtel, 166, 200, 218, 228
Brunsvik, Count Anatol, 11
Brunsvik, Charlotte, 12
Brunsvik, Franz, 12
Brunsvik, Count Joseph, 13
Brunsvik, Josephine, *see* Deym, Countess Josephine
Brunsvik, Therese, 12–14, 129
Bureau des Arts et d'Industrie, 134

Carpani, Giuseppe, 218
Castelli, Ignaz, 123, 126
Cone, Edward T., 45, 52–54
Cooper, Grosvenor W., 51, 52
Cooper, Martin, 129, 130
Copyist B, 161, 162, 166
Cornet, Alexander, 23, 217
Czeke, Marianne, 12, 14
Czerny, Carl, 38, 177, 219

Davy, G. B., 203, 207
Dean, Winton, 221
Dehn, S. W., 159
Derckum, Franz, 18, 19
Deym, Countess Josephine (*née* Brunsvik), 12–15, 129

243

Diabelli & Co., 175, 176
Dietrichstein, Count Moritz, 235
Dittersdorf, Carl Ditters von, 25
Doblhoff-Dier, Carl, 23, 217
Dumba, Nikolaus, 93

Einstein, Alfred, 145
Elvers, Rudolf, 174
Engelmann, W., 209

Fischenich, Bartolomäus, 99
Fischhof, Joseph, 179, 188, 203, 227
Fishman, N. L., 86
Floersheim, Georg, 178
Folksong (Volkslied), 132–135, 154
Forbes, Elliot, 55, 57, 59
Fortune, Nigel, 101, 156
Frederick II (the Great), 31, 32
Friedlaender, Max, 145, 201, 219, 221
Frimmel, Theodor von, 177, 180
Fuchs, Aloys, 22, 68, 88, 90, 177, 178, 180, 202, 236
Fux, Johann Joseph, 233

Gallenberg, Count Wenzel Robert, 13–15
Gallenberg, Countess, see Guicciardi, Giulietta
Gassner, Ferdinand Simon, 68, 69, 89
Gebrüder Kiesling, 161
Gellert, Christian Fürchtegott, 133
Genast, Eduard, 134
Ghiselin, Brewster, 97
Goethe, Johann Wolfgang von, 100, 132–135
Gounod, Charles, 221
Gräffer, Anton, 68, 87–91, 175, 177–236
Grasberger, Franz, 203, 235
Grasnick, F. A., 205, 213, 215, 236
Graun, Carl Heinrich, 18–44, 219
Gudewill, Kurt, 132
Guicciardi, Count Franz Joseph, 12
Guicciardi, Giulietta (Julia, Julie, later Countess Gallenberg), 12–17, 129
Guicciardi, Countess Susanna, 1–17

Handel, George Frideric, 21, 205, 219

Harris, Angela, 10
Haslinger, Carl, 19, 205, 206
Haslinger, Tobias, 18, 19, 175–177, 184, 206, 236
Hasse, Johann Adolph, 31–34
Haugwitz, Count Paul von, 123
Haydn, Franz Joseph, 19, 99, 139, 174, 176, 186, 211, 228, 235
Hecker, Joachim von, 156
Herre, Grita, 174
Hertzmann, Erich, 98, 212
Herzog, Johannes, 171
Hess, Willy, xiii, 20, 22, 24, 34, 39–41, 139, 158, 161, 223, 225, 229, 232
Heyer, Wilhelm, 227
Holz, Karl, 202
Horchler, Adolf, 68
Hotschevar, Jacob, 177–179, 199, 202, 220, 236
Huber, Franz Xaver, 38
Huijssen, J. M., 90, 235

"Immortal Beloved, The," 12, 129–131

Jahn, Otto, 13, 16, 17, 38, 184, 202
Jeitteles, Alois Isidor, 123–28, 131, 132, 134, 136, 145–47, 155, 157
Joachim, Joseph, 199
Johnson, Douglas, 72, 87

Kafka, Johann, 188, 189, 208, 214, 228, 230
Kastner, Emerich, 180
Kaufmann, Herr, 159, 161, 163, 166–69
Kerman, Joseph, 23, 67, 74, 98, 100, 102, 135, 223, 230
Kerst, Friedrich, 219
Kiesling brothers, 161
Kinsky, Georg, xiii, 18, 88, 102, 175, 177, 178, 221, 227
Kirnberger, Johann Philipp, 24–26, 31, 32, 219
Kleinheinz, Franx Xaver, 13
Koch, Louis, 102, 207, 221
Köchel, Ludwig von, 233
Köhler, Karl-Heinz, 174

Kramer, Richard A., 212
Kullak, Franz, 207

La Mara (Marie Lipsius), 12–15
Landon, Christa, 10
Landon, H. C. Robbins, 13
Landsberg, Ludwig, 70, 71, 89, 91, 186, 188, 189, 194, 236
Landshoff, Ludwig, 134
Lang, Paul Henry, 98, 102
Lavenu, Elizabeth, 172
Lehman, R. O., 218, 233
Levinsohn, A., 114
Lhuillier, Esmond, 188, 209
Lichnowsky, Countess Henriette, 14
Lichnowsky, Prince Karl, 16
Lichtenberger, Julius, 218
Lipsius, Marie (La Mara), 12–15
Lobkowitz, Prince, 131
Lockwood, Lewis, 67, 98, 102, 103, 105, 136, 149, 150, 200, 226

MacArdle, Donald W., 175
Malherbe, Charles, 218
Mandyczewski, Eusebius, 69, 103, 222
Mann, Alfred, 19, 23
Marshall, Julian, 68, 69
Matthisson, Friedrich von, 123
Mendelssohn, Paul, 199, 200, 235
Mendelssohn-Bartholdy, Ernst von, 199, 232
Metastasio, 24, 31, 35, 216
Meter, 45–66
Meyer, Leonard B., 52
Meyerbeer, Giacomo, 200
Miller, Eugen von, 102, 207
Moldenhauer, Hans, 221
Mollo, Tranquillo, 174, 175, 218, 219, 233
Mortier de Fontaine, L., 229
Moscheles, Ignaz, 175
Moser, Hans Joachim, 140, 145
Mozart, Constanze, 98
Mozart, Wolfgang Amadeus, 97, 98, 139, 174, 185, 211, 221, 233
Müller-Reuter, T., 57
Munter, Friedrich, 158, 162, 167

Nachlass, 174–236
Nohl, Ludwig, 126

Nottebohm, Gustav, xiii, 67–70, 88, 92, 98, 103, 136, 176, 178

Orrey, Leslie, 101

Peters, Carl Friedrich, 225
Petrarch, Francesco, 128
Petter, Gustav, 188, 214
Pölchau, Georg, 90, 204
Prieger, Erich, 176, 177
Puttick & Simpson, 68, 70

Racek, Fritz, 93
Ramler, Karl Wilhelm, 38
Rastrology, 21, 22, 71, 82, 83, 93
Rayneval, M. and Mme. de, 71
Recitative, 18–44
Reichardt, Johann Friedrich, 31, 32, 133, 134
Reissig, Christian Ludwig, 99, 100, 228
Rhythm, 45–66, 115–117, 126–128, 137
Riemann, Hugo, 59, 115
Ries, Ferdinand, 17, 130, 171, 172
Rio, Fanny del, 130, 131
Rio, Giannatasio del, 130, 131
Rochlitz, Johann Friedrich, 24
Roda, Cecile de, 207, 208
Rolland, Romain, 145
Rosenthal, Albi, 10
Rudolph, Archduke, 19, 222

Salieri, Antonio, 19, 22–24, 34, 35, 37, 217, 221
Salzer, Felix, 200
Sandberger, Adolf, 13
Sauer, Ignaz, 89, 177
Schannetzsky, Johann A., 174
Scheibe, Johann Adolf, 28, 44
Scheide, William, 102, 207
Schenk, Johann Baptist, 19
Schenker, Heinrich, 51, 55–63
Schering, Arnold, 115
Schiedermair, Ludwig, 99
Schikaneder, Emanuel, 24
Schiller, Charlotte von, 99
Schiller, Friedrich von, 99, 134
Schindler, Anton, xiv, 12, 13, 18, 90, 123, 204, 236

Schlemmer, Wenzel, 161, 162, 166, 169
Schlesinger, Adolph Martin, 134
Schmidt, Hans, xiv, 18, 90, 192, 203, 221, 233
Schmidt-Görg, Joseph, 11–13, 90, 203, 219
Schnaus, Peter, 19
Schubert, Franz, 100, 101, 155
Schulz, J. A. P., 24–35, 37, 38, 40, 42, 43
Schumann, Robert, 155
Schünemann, Georg, 13, 161
Schuppanzigh, Ignaz, 16
Sessions, Roger, 52
Seyfried, Ignaz von, 18–22, 26
Simpson, Robert, 156
Sketchbooks, make-up of, 72, 75–76, 82–87
Spender, Stephen, 97, 98
Spina, Anton, 175
Steger, Heinrich, 200
Steiner, Sigmund Anton, 131, 159, 163, 171
Sterba, Editha and Richard, 129
Sternfeld, Frederick W., 132
Strunk, Oliver, 31
Sullivan, J. W. N., 157
Sulzer, Johann Georg, 19, 23–31, 37–39, 43, 44
Supplemente zur Gesamtausgabe (ed. Willy Hess), 22, 24, 34, 40, 139, 223, 225, 229, 232

Thayer, Alexander Wheelock, xiv, 12, 176, 178, 189
Thomas, A., 188

Thomas, John, 10
Thomson, George, 133
Tiedge, Christoph August, 123, 133
Tovey, Donald Francis, 45–47, 49–51, 59
Treitschke, Georg Friedrich, 163
Tyson, Alan, 21, 22, 24, 38, 71, 72, 86, 87, 96, 124, 131, 155, 161, 172, 210, 221

Unger, Max, 15, 22, 71, 221
Unverricht, Hubert, 153, 203

Van Patten, Nathan, 218
Virneisel, Wilhelm, 20, 21

Wagener, R., 214
Watermarks, 10, 11, 20, 21, 75–86, 93, 161, 201
    and make-up, 75, 76, 81–86, 93
    molds and quadrants, 21, 76–86, 93
Wegeler, Franz Gerhard, 12, 14–17, 172
Weinmann, Alexander, 175
Weise, Dagmar, 67–71, 90, 91, 93, 98
Weitz, Hans-J., 135
Werner, A. E., 76
Willemer, Marianne von, 135
Wittgenstein family, 200
Wittmann, Gertraud, 134
Wolfmayer, Johann, 229

Zelter, Carl Friedrich, 133, 134
Zmeskall von Domanovecz, Nikolaus, 16